MW01118837

Spiritual Maturity

With skill and clarity, Bruce Baker takes the biblical principles of growing toward spiritual maturity and casts them in language that is both relevant and engaging. There is comforting truth to be found in *Spiritual Maturity: The Road to Wonderland,* but there is also much to challenge and even convict you. As well, the words found in *Alice's Adventures in Wonderland* never before enjoyed such eternal impact as they do in the pages of this book. Don't hesitate to read it all the way to the end.

Dr. Woodrow Kroll
President
Back to the Bible International

This book clearly presents the biblical evidence for how to mature in Christ, in an arresting and interesting way. Divine enablement and human responsibility are stressed. This is a layman's map providing directions for growing up in Christ. You will be blessed by reading and following the directions.

Dr. Robert Lightner
*Professor of Systematic Theology
(retired)*
Dallas Theological Seminary

Bruce Baker has provided a great help for our spiritual lives in *Spiritual Maturity: The Road to Wonderland*. The biblical and theological content is combined with great illustrations from a classic piece of literature and a modern-day narrative applying the truths about the Christian life to the realities of earth-side living. It maps the journey to spiritual maturity in a way that will be a guide to believers, offering fresh help and hope in their pilgrimage.

JAMES E. JEFFERY
President
Baptist Bible College & Seminary

Spiritual growth and maturity come only through the work of the Spirit of God in one's life. Pastor Bruce explains this with such clarity—and stresses that it is not an optional journey for a believer! His writing is easy to understand and enjoyable to read. I look forward to using it in our Women's Ministries! This book will challenge and bless each one who will take its message to heart!

LISA GEMMELL
Director of Women's Ministries
Mesa Hills Bible Church
Colorado Springs, Colorado

Spiritual Maturity

The Road to Wonderland

Bruce Baker

CULTIVATING JOY

LARKSPUR, COLORADO

Published by Grace Acres Press, P.O. Box 22, Larkspur, CO 80018.

Copyright © 2009 by Grace Acres Press.

The epigraph quotations are from Lewis Carroll, *Alice's Adventures in Wonderland* (1865) (cited as *Wonderland*) and *Through the Looking-Glass: And What Alice Found There* (1871) (cited as *Looking-Glass*).

John Tenniel's illustrations for *Alice in Wonderland* and *Through the Looking-Glass* are in the public domain. They were accessed at http://www.alice-in-wonderland.net on November 18, 2008.

Henry Holliday's illustration of the Ocean Map from Lewis Carroll's "The Hunting of the Snark: An Agony in Eight Fits," Fit the Second, used by permission of University of Virginia Library electronic collection; accessible at http://etext.virginia.edu/ebooks/

Scripture taken from the HOLY BIBLE, NEW INTERNATIONAL VERSION.® Copyright © 1973, 1978, 1984 International Bible Society. Used by permission of Zondervan. All rights reserved. [Identified in text as NIV.]

Scripture taken from the NEW AMERICAN STANDARD BIBLE.® Copyright © 1960, 1962, 1963, 1968, 1971, 1972, 1973, 1975, 1977, 1995 by The Lockman Foundation. Used by permission. [Identified in text as NASB.]

Library of Congress Cataloging-in-Publication Data:
Baker, Bruce, 1958–
Spiritual maturity : the road to wonderland / by Bruce Baker.
p. cm.
Includes bibliographical references (p.) and index.
ISBN: 978-1-60265-025-1 (cloth)
ISBN: 978-1-60265-024-4 (paper)
1. Spiritual formation. 2. Maturation (Psychology)—Religious aspects—Christianity. 3. Spiritual formation—Biblical teaching. 4. Maturation (Psychology)—Religious aspects—Christianity—Biblical teaching. I. Title.
BV4501.3.B352 2009
248.4—dc22   2009004875

Printed in Canada
12 11 10 09   01 02 03 04 05 06 07 08 09 10

THIS BOOK IS AFFECTIONATELY AND

GRATEFULLY DEDICATED TO MY MENTOR,

DR. JAMES RAIFORD,

WHO FIRST INSTRUCTED ME

ACADEMICALLY AND PRACTICALLY IN THE

PRINCIPLES OF SPIRITUAL GROWTH.

Contents

About the Author

Bruce Baker is Senior Pastor of Jenison Bible Church, Hudsonville, Michigan. Before he entered the ministry, he served in the Navy for more than eleven years as an electronics technician. He then left the service to work as an engineer at a Christian television station; it was during this time that he felt the call of God to enter the ministry full time. He enrolled at Calvary Bible College, graduating with a BS in Christian Ministries. He then continued his education at Calvary Theological Seminary, where he graduated with a Master's of Divinity (Pastoral Studies) degree with highest honors. He is currently pursuing his PhD at Baptist Bible Seminary.

Before accepting the call to his current church, he was Senior Pastor of Open Door Bible Church in Belton, Missouri, and Adjunct Professor of Bible and Theology at Calvary Bible College. It was during his tenure in Missouri that his passion for teaching Bible and theology to pastors who had no access to any formal education was kindled. To date, he has taught in more than six different countries on four separate continents.

The predominant emphasis of the ministry of Bruce Baker has been the forthright presentation of the Bible as God's Word. Like Ezra of old, his life is built around the study, practice, and teaching of Scripture.

In his teaching, he conveys the quality of steadfastness that emanates from one whose life is anchored in the authority of God's Word. You're encouraged to read his blog at www.BecomingMature.org.

He is a contributing author to the book *Progressive Dispensationalism,* as well as the author of numerous journal and magazine articles. *Spiritual Maturity* is his first full-length book.

Pastor Baker and his wife, Bonnie, have been married 27 years and have three grown children. He enjoys singing and has been a soloist in such works as Haydn's *Creation* and Handel's *Messiah.*

The good hand of his God was upon him. For [he] had set his heart to study the law of the LORD, and to practice it, and to teach His statutes and ordinances (EZRA 7:9B–10).

THREE QUEENS

You ought to return thanks in a neat speech," the Red Queen said, frowning at Alice as she spoke.

"We must support you, you know," the White Queen whispered, as Alice got up to do it, very obediently, but a little frightened.

"Thank you very much," she whispered in reply, "but I can do quite well without."

"That wouldn't be at all the thing," the Red Queen said very decidedly; so Alice tried to submit to it with a good grace.

("And they DID push so!" she said afterwards, when she was telling her sister the history of the feast. "You would have thought they wanted to squeeze me flat!")

In fact it was rather difficult for her to keep in her place while she made her speech: the two Queens pushed her so, one on each side, that they nearly lifted her up into the air: "I rise to return thanks—" Alice began and she really DID rise as she spoke, several inches; but she got hold of the edge of the table, and managed to pull herself down again.

—*Looking-Glass*, ch. IX, "Queen Alice"

Preface
Returning Thanks
in a Neat Speech

No work of God is ever accomplished by a sole individual. I'm convinced that the Holy Spirit brings together members of the body of Christ to assist one another in any work he ordains. This work is no different. Since thankfulness is a virtue which God wishes his people to possess in abundance, it is only appropriate to express my genuine, heartfelt thanks to those who have assisted me in so many ways during the composition of this volume.

First and foremost, of course, all praise, honor, and glory go to God alone for any good that is brought to pass from this book. Without the enabling of God the Holy Spirit, this volume would merely be words on a page. It is only because He blesses His word and enables His servant that any spiritual benefit will be gained from reading what is written here.

Nevertheless, God in his mercy allows His people the honor of participating in the work He could so easily accomplish without us. Those who have been willing instruments of His grace to me also deserve recognition. Though it may sound clichéd, it is nevertheless true that this book would not have been completed were it not for the assistance of those listed here.

There is no way to adequately thank Dr. James Raiford, my mentor through Bible College and Seminary, to whom this book is dedicated. A man of extreme intelligence, whose rigorous passion for God's truth didn't allow him to "suffer fools gladly" (2 COR 11:19, KJV), he nevertheless wore his learning lightly, laughing easily, loudly, and often. Dr. Raiford imparted his life to ours, encouraging us to follow him as he followed Christ (1 COR 11:1). His sense of duty toward us never waned and is most famously illustrated by what occurred when I attempted to make a pastoral call upon him while he was on a gurney awaiting serious surgery. I asked him if he would like me to read some Scripture to him and he replied, "Oh yes, you always read Scripture on a hospital call. PSALM 34 is usually the best one before surgery." The irony of having my attempt to minister to him end in his teaching me was not lost upon me.

He laid on us the heavy burden of being "God's man delivering God's Word to God's people," and warned us severely that ministry performed without prayer and an active dependence upon God the Holy Spirit was nothing short of practical atheism. He also lightened that load by his exacting yet gentle tutelage and his insistence that God the Holy Spirit would give us power from above to accomplish all that He has called us to do. Thank you, Dr. Raiford, for instructing and guiding me in the past and during the writing of this book.

Thanks also go to Dr. Ken Gardoski of Baptist Bible Seminary, in Clarks Summit, Pennsylvania, for allowing me to begin this project as part of my PhD studies. His patience and understanding for the many delays in producing a finished product give evidence of what a loving and gentle man of God should be.

Thanks also go to Anne Fenske, publisher of Grace Acres Press, for her constant encouragement, instruction, and eagerness to see this book go forward. Without our providential meeting and her wise counsel as a result, this book would most likely never have seen the light of day.

Trinka Jeffery, secretary of Jenison Bible Church, has spent innumerable hours reading and re-reading this manuscript. The value of her keen eye for style and helpful suggestions regarding content cannot be overstated. She is also the one who prepared the study questions, for which I am exceedingly grateful. Gale Anderson, who has faithfully edited my previous scholastic work, also consented to edit. As always, her keen attention to detail has been an enormous help.

Julie Scudder Dearyan is another whom God providentially brought into my life at just the right time. Her help (and loving but brutal honesty) has been invaluable in improving my first few feeble attempts at fiction. Thank you, Julie, for taking the time from your busy schedule to assist a fellow author.

God has blessed me with the opportunity to shepherd a wonderful congregation, many of whom eagerly reviewed my manuscript in various stages of completion. Thanks go to Carlyne Brinks, Sue DeGraw, Kim Dryer, Nikki Gott, Karen Johnson, Wannie Lowing, Marzena Roskiewicz, Virgie Olson, Wendy Schultz, Mike Vander Band, and Amy White for their encouraging words and constructive criticism. I would also like to thank my son Jacob for reviewing parts of this manuscript with a student's eye. His helpful criticism enabled me to make this book more suitable for the classroom. Alison Baustian and Lisa Gemmell, both pastor's wives whom I respect, also provided invaluable assistance, insight, and encouragement.

Thanks also go to Pastor Lee Buer, our visitation pastor and my senior in the ministry, for reviewing the content. His keen insight and understanding of the ways of God were invaluable in making sure that I remained theologically sound. Thanks also go to his wife, Joan (a spiritually mature woman), for her additional review of my doctrine and for making sure I said exactly what I wanted to say—no more and no less.

Likewise, thanks go to Drs. Dan Fabricatore, J. B. Hixon, and Richard McCarroll for their invaluable help in thinking through the implications of saving faith. Precision on such an important topic is vital, and they helped me to achieve some small measure of it. Thanks also to Rev. Gary Gilley for his valuable insights and criticism in the area of proper exegesis.

Saving the best for last, I'd like to thank my wife, Bonnie, the one love of my entire life, who has shared with me good times and bad, riches and poverty, sickness and health, who has forsaken all others for me. Her understanding of her "difficult"* husband and his calling enabled her to graciously bear the many nights I holed up in my study, leaving her with only the dogs and cats as companions. Without her gracious tolerance, gentle (and sometimes not-so-gentle, yet necessary) prodding, and loving endurance, I would never have been able to finish this book. I love you, sweetheart, for encouraging and putting up with me at the same time. "A wife of noble character is her husband's crown" (PROV 12:4, NIV), just as you are mine.

---

*This title was lovingly bestowed on me by my wife after she read Elisabeth D. Dodds, *Marriage to a Difficult Man: The Uncommon Union of Jonathan & Sarah Edwards* (Audubon Press, 2005). I'm sure she meant the comparison of me to Jonathan Edwards as a compliment.

Living in Canaan Part One

Christine Terril simply sat there.* For the moment at least, she seemed incapable of the slightest movement. All she could do was stare at the memo in her hands. The rest of her energy was focused on the cramping hollowness inside. She was familiar with that sensation. She had felt that wretchedness before . . . an aching so common it even had a name. It was called *betrayal.*

Christine had been fresh out of college when she married Tim. God blessed them with a child quicker than they had planned. A month to the day after their anniversary, she was holding their first child. After much discussion and prayer, they decided it would be best for Christine to be a stay-at-home mom. Two more children followed, and Christine's life became a whirlwind of changing diapers,

---

*This short story is added to help illustrate in real life what the spiritual person looks like. It is dedicated to the memory of Alice Liddell, the main character in and inspiration for Lewis Carroll's most famous works. It is upon her advice that I added this story—for "what is the use of a book, . . . without pictures or conversation?" (Carroll, *Wonderland,* ch. 1).

nursing colds, settling petty disputes, attending and arranging school functions, and of course, actively participating in church.

Both Tim and she had been raised in the church and had made public professions of trust in Christ in their junior-high years. When she met him in college, it seemed to everyone like a match made in heaven. When they married, included in their vows was a commitment to preserve a Christian home.

That had been twenty-six years ago. At that time she could never have imagined the horrible day when Tim announced he'd found someone else. "I just don't love you anymore," was the only reason he gave. She had known her marriage was in trouble. Still, she had never dreamed it would end like this.

The problems started when he accepted a new position that offered more money, more incentives, and of course, more hours. She was friends with the people he had worked with before, but his new working environment was unlike the family atmosphere that existed at his old job. His new co-workers' priorities were vastly different. They craved status and money and prestige and saw nothing wrong with those desires. Slowly, their worldview began to seep into Tim, and it changed him.

She noticed, for example, that he began to be less active in church; coincidentally, this was about the time when he stopped praying with the children in the evening. Near the end, only her promptings had kept him going to church at all. Then there were the silent rides home on Sundays. Oh, the kids would chatter animatedly about youth group and Sunday school, but not a word from Tim. Christine blamed it on his job. He was working longer and longer hours, taking more frequent trips, becoming more and more distant. Somehow, though, she was blind to what was actually going on. It wasn't just his changed priorities; his newly adopted value system brought about a change in behavior as well. He stopped fighting the constant flirting that was part of the office politics and actually began to enjoy it. And that's when he met her.

The rest followed as one might expect. There were no custody issues, because the children, thank God, were old enough to avoid that trauma at least. Still, they felt a rejection similar to what Christine experienced. And there still was child support, the division of property, and that last court date when it all became official . . . and final. Of all she endured, though, the accusations were the worst.

Incredibly, Tim blamed everything on her. She wasn't perfect, she knew that, but she had been a faithful and supportive wife—at least she thought she had. But none of that seemed to matter. The hurt, the financial ruin, the emotional damage: it was "her fault." She could still recall the hate in his eyes as he sneered, "You've been worthless since the day I met you!" She knew it was a lie, but evidently it was a lie that he now believed. Still worse, it was a lie he communicated to the kids.

Tim quickly married his new love and continued in his career. Christine, for the first time in more than twenty years, stepped gingerly into the work force, praying that someone would still value her now-ancient degree. She was elated when she was hired as an account representative by Miller & Johnson Industrial Mouldings, because without Tim to support her, she desperately needed the money.

The past three years had been a struggle, particularly at first. She relied heavily on the encouragement and prayers of her church. She had been taught that trials developed Christian character as nothing else could, but now she experienced this truth firsthand. In the midst of the worst three years of her life, her faith grew deeper, her time with God more precious, her love for the Savior more intense.

When her supervisor, Ed Mercer, informed her that he was recommending her for a promotion, it seemed to be the tonic her battered self-esteem had longed for. This promotion proved that she could do it. That she still had skills people valued. That despite what her husb— . . . her ex-husband had said about her, she still had worth, and there were people outside of church who recognized it. It was to be the defining moment of her recovery.

And now it had been taken from her. She couldn't—she wouldn't—believe it. She forced herself to read the memo again. The promotion she'd been promised, the one she worked so hard for, had, at the last minute, been given to Ben Ackerman.

It would have been easier to accept if the person being advanced had been one of the competent people in her department. She was realistic enough to know that there were other qualified candidates. At least then it wouldn't have been so personal. But it had been promised to her, and now . . . Ben Ackerman of all people! . . . the Ben Ackerman few liked and no one trusted had his name in the subject line of this memo.

Ben was coarse and vulgar. When Ed was around, he was the textbook example of a "yes man," but he talked plenty big when Ed was away. Most people in the department had been publicly speared by one of his snide comments. If gossip was spreading, you could be certain that somewhere at its root was Ben. And now he was being promoted to "her" position.

The deep ache grew close to nausea. It was then that another memory crowded aside the pain. It was a verse from the Bible her pastor had shared with her during the darkest days of Christine's divorce. She had clung to it before and it seemed so appropriate now:

The LORD is good, a refuge in times of trouble. He cares for those who trust in him" (NAHUM 1:7, NIV).

So she carefully centered the memo on the desk in front of her. She placed both hands on top of it, palms down, fingers spread. Then she bowed her head and prayed . . . and wept.

ALICE IN SHEEP'S SHOP

What is it you want to buy?" the Sheep said at last, looking up for a moment from her knitting.

"I don't QUITE *know yet," Alice said very gently. "I should like to look all round me first, if I might."*

"You may look in front of you, and on both sides, if you like," said the Sheep: "but you can't look ALL *round you—unless you've got eyes at the back of your head."*

But these, as it happened, Alice had NOT *got; so she contented herself with turning round, looking at the shelves as she came to them.*

The shop seemed to be full of all manner of curious things—but the oddest part of it all was, that whenever she looked hard at any shelf, to make out exactly what it had on it, that particular shelf was always quite empty; though the others round it were crowded as full as they could hold.

—*Looking-Glass*, ch. V, "Wool and Water"

Chapter 1
Empty Shelves Full of Books

Every Christian should lead a life of self-examination. By this I mean that anyone who has been born again by the Spirit of God should recognize that life is not the result of the random collision of atoms, nor is it reducible to political or sociological trends. Instead, a man who is born into the family of God—given new life as a gift from God, not by works, so that no one can boast (EPH 2:9)—should realize that God has claimed him for His own and, as a result, exercises special control over his life, working all things together for his good (ROM 8:28). Thus, any event that takes place in the believer's life should be scrutinized on several levels. For example, he should ask, "What is God's purpose for me?" or "How should I best respond in order to bring God glory?" (1 COR 10:31).

As a pastor, I am occasionally asked to recommend resources on particular subjects. The books I recommend are usually quite old, and their grammar and sentence structure sound odd to modern ears. My search for more recent resources, however, has proven frustrating, to say the least.

Recently I walked into a local "Christian" bookstore (the names are withheld to protect the guilty) and asked one of the staff—the manager, actually—to recommend a good book on Christian growth. He said, "Well, we used to have a whole section on that, but now anything we have is just sort of mixed in the 'Christian Living' section in the back of the store. You probably should just go back there and look around."

So advised, I went to the back of the store and started working my way through the shelves of books, which were ordered by author, not subject. After about an hour, I came to the conclusion that there wasn't a single book in that section, written within the past twenty years, that had anything truly meaningful to say regarding Christian growth. I walked away empty-handed.

A few weeks later, I went to another "Christian" bookstore (yes, the quotes are on purpose). The only person I saw in the store was the young girl (I'm guessing eighteen to twenty years old) behind the register. So I asked to speak with someone who was well acquainted with the store's inventory. She answered in a perky little voice, "I can help you."

I smiled back at her and said, "No, I really need someone who knows the books in the store well."

"I can help you," she insisted.

I sighed heavily and said, "Okay, I'm looking for a book that will help me become a mature believer. I want to know how to grow in Christ."

Her forehead wrinkled as she pulled her eyebrows together and frowned. "Let's see," she said, as she typed into her computer. "Hmmm . . . no . . . no . . . no . . . Ah, here's one. It's called *Be*—" and she stopped suddenly.

"Is there a problem?" I asked.

"Well, we have one called *Be Mature*, but it's in our commentary section."

"So why is that a problem?"

I received a patronizing smile as she patiently explained, "That means that you'd actually be delving into the Bible."

I stood there speechless. When I was finally able to squeak out, "May I see it?," she led me to the commentary section and handed me *Be Mature: A Commentary on James,* by Warren W. Wiersbe, written in 1978 (that's more than 30 years ago for those who, like me, are math-challenged). Even though it is an excellent book, I already had it, so again I left empty-handed.

I made one more attempt at yet another "Christian" bookstore. This time I found someone with more years (he was maybe 25) whose main job evidently wasn't to work the register. I asked him the same question as before. What I received was a blank stare. "Christian growth?" he asked as if he'd never heard the term.

"Yeah, you know, growing in Christ, Christian maturity, becoming spiritually mature?" I prodded, trying to jog his memory of the concept. When I said the words "spiritually mature," he looked at the ceiling thoughtfully and then his face brightened.

"Oh, you mean 'spiritual formation,'" he said with a smile, and started walking toward the appropriate aisle near the front of the store.

"Whatever," I said.

The first title that jumped off the shelf at me was a book whose concept of spiritual growth involved praying with beads. The rest of the books were pretty much of the same stripe. All of them (that I noticed, at any rate) were directing the believer to practice the disciplines of the Roman Catholic mystics. Not one that I saw pointed to the Bible as the sole authority for rule and life.

I felt like Alice in the Sheep's shop: the shelves were full until you looked at them. Then you realized they were empty.

Normally I'm irritated when I walk out of a "Christian" bookstore because I find so little that is actually Christian and so much that is merely a religious knock-off of what the world has to offer. But that day, instead of the normal—and by now expected—irritation, I experienced an overwhelming sadness. "Is there no one who is interested in what the Bible has to say about becoming mature?" I kept asking myself. "I just can't believe that no one is interested in becoming mature or what the Bible has to say about it."

The sorrow engendered in that last bookstore has since been transformed into a fixed determination to provide, to those who will hear, what the Bible has to say about becoming mature. This book was written for the sole purpose of getting out the word that maturity is demanded by God and that He has given clear instructions regarding how to move in that direction.

I am all too painfully aware of my inadequacy for this endeavor. Nevertheless, for many years this task has been restless within me. As I have prayed about this, God the Holy Spirit has impressed upon me to undertake with His power what I clearly could not do on my own.

It's been said, "If it's new, it isn't true, and if it's true, it isn't new." While that statement is applicable to knowledge generally, it is especially correct when speaking of biblical instruction. Therefore, although the illustrations and the explanations are mine, I make no claim to originality in the spiritual principles taught in these pages. I merely stand on the shoulders of countless thousands in the church who have come before me, who have taken their stand on God's Word and believed His promises to be true.

I have been particularly influenced by Lewis Sperry Chafer's view of sanctification in general and have largely recreated his argument here. I also owe a debt to Dwight Pentecost in my understanding of the Sabbath-rest. Charles Ryrie's understanding of salvation is also evident in this book. As you can see, I have taken my stand firmly within the traditional dispensational system of theology. That being said, I have used Scripture extensively to show that the truths presented here are not the result of man's reasoning, but are indeed the revelation of God.

One final note on the issue of style: I have made no attempt to be gender-neutral. I have decided to use the masculine gender to speak for all people, male and female. There are three reasons for this:

- First, this is biblically accurate; the original languages use the masculine exclusively unless specifically referring to a female. This, by the way, has been universally true of all languages until the recent onset of political correctness.

- Second, writing to be purposely gender-neutral is cumbersome (for one of my limited abilities, at least). Whatever is gained in political correctness is nullified by the awkward language and almost complete loss of style.

- Third, I suspect that only the most ardent feminists will find the use of the gender-neutral masculine pronoun intellectually taxing.

It is my prayer that God the Holy Spirit use this (very imperfect) book to bring glory to Christ and maturity to His church. *Soli Deo Gloria.*

Discussion Questions

1. Do you think it is true that there has been a lack of interest in spiritual growth in the past twenty years?

2. What topics are currently most emphasized in contemporary North American Christianity?

3. Why do you think there has been a resurgence of Roman Catholic mysticism?

4. Why do you think the store clerk was wary of recommending something that "delved into the Bible"?

5. Has this chapter brought any questions to mind, or any thoughts you would like to discuss with the group?

6. Is there any issue you would like prayed for, or accountability in, over the course of this week?

7. Please note any other group members' answers that you would like to follow up on this week, either by praying for them or by making an encouraging contact.

Living in Canaan Part Two

Later that afternoon, Christine stood in front of her supervisor's door. She paused just long enough to pray: "Lord, this really hurts. And I confess that I'm really angry right now. I want to tell Ed all the things I never said to my husband! But I ask that You would control my temper for me, let me speak only words that You would speak, and use my response to this situation be a good testimony for You. I can't do that . . . but I know that You can. So please be with me so that I would live these next few minutes well." With that, she sucked in a deep breath, wiped away a lone tear, squared her shoulders, knocked gently on the door, and waited.

"Come in," called Ed Mercer's voice. She opened the door. "Oh, Christine," he said as he rose to greet her. "I . . . uh . . . was hoping to see you today. Sit down, sit down," he said quickly. "Let's talk."

"I suppose you know why I'm here," Christine said, hating the slight quiver that had suddenly crept into her voice. Sitting up straighter, hoping that would help somehow, she continued, "I'd like to know what happened."

"Well, so would I!" Ed said. "I thought this was a done deal. I went to the departmental managers' meeting to finalize the promotion. All the names that were brought forward were approved with little discussion. But the minute I mentioned your name, the mood suddenly changed. There were lots of questions, mostly from Frank Seaton."

"Frank Seaton! Why would the head of shipping care about me?" Christine took off her bracelet, a gift from her pastor's wife, and held it in her hand. "I've only sent memos to him about packages. I don't think I've even met the guy face to face!" She stared down at the bracelet as though hoping for answers from it.

"Well, that may be," Ed continued, "but he's heard of you and has a pretty negative opinion. He brought up stuff . . . well, it doesn't matter what . . . but accusations, mostly about your work . . . but there were other things—"

At these words, Christine's bowed head shot up. She stared at Ed and her formerly slumped back slowly straightened. "*What* other things?"

"Anyway, I told him they just weren't true," Ed continued. "I really went to bat for you, honest. But he had his mind dead set against you. And then out of nowhere he started talking up Ben to get the job."

"Why would the head of shipping start singing Ben's praises?" Christine asked. She narrowed her gaze.

"Well . . . you know . . . Ben's job does require him to make frequent trips to shipping . . . ," Ed said as his voice trailed off. He frowned as he looked away.

"But . . . but . . . what about the others in the meeting? Didn't they have anything to say?"

"Frankly, no," Ed sighed. "It was getting late, and I think most of them just wanted the meeting over with. Someone mentioned the time and another said something about traffic, so they just gave the job to Ben. I don't think anyone else had anything against you, but . . . well, you know . . . it was a Friday before a long weekend and people wanted to get out of what had turned into—" here Ed cleared his throat, "an uncomfortable situation." Once again he frowned and stared out the window.

Christine let out a long, slow breath. She was angry, but not at Ed, so she made a conscious choice to be kind. "Thanks for trying anyway,

Ed. I really appreciate the trust you've shown in me since I've worked here," she said. Not knowing what else to say, Christine started to get up, but Ed wasn't finished.

"Um . . . Christine . . . uh, there's one more thing." Ed again cleared his throat.

Now what? Christine lowered herself back into the chair.

Ed sighed heavily. "There's no easy way to say this, so I'll just say it. These promotions are part of a bigger reorganization, which includes this department."

Oh, no. The dread rose from her stomach to her throat.

Ed's voice changed to a more businesslike tone. "You'll still work for me, but you'll have a new direct supervisor, who will report to me." He paused. "You'll be reporting to Ben Ackerman."

THE KING IN COURT

*The White Rabbit put on his spectacles. "Where
shall I begin, please your Majesty?" he asked.*

*"Begin at the beginning," the King said gravely,
"and go on till you come to the end; then stop."*

—*Wonderland,* ch. XII, "Alice's Evidence"

Chapter 2
Considering the Journey

When I was about 11 years old, I learned how to read a map. My father was interested in moving closer to his extended family members, so the two of us took a a road trip from Illinois to Alabama to explore the possibilities.

I still remember that expedition as a great adventure: going to a far-away place, looking at houses that could become ours, visiting relatives I only rarely got to see. I remember how Dad, at my request, left the interstate and endured heavy traffic on local roads just so I could see a gen-u-wine Army fort. I also remember how my preadolescent imaginings were dashed by the plain buildings and chain-link fence that we drove by.

It was on that trip when Dad and I had "the talk" that fathers have with boys that age.

Of all my memories, though, it is the hours we spent in the car, with Dad as the pilot and me as the navigator, that I remember most. Before we left, Dad provided a quick education on how to read a map. I remember his instruction on the importance of knowing where we were, where we were going, and how we were going to get there. "If we keep our eye on those three things on the map," Dad explained, "we won't get lost."

It felt very grown-up to be entrusted with such an important responsibility. As we clicked off the miles, I kept my finger on that maze of colored lines, solemnly announcing the next town we should see or how far it was to the next rest area.

It sounds so simple now, but knowing where we are, where we want to be, and how to get there is still essential for any journey. Yet, it is this basic information, particularly in the realm of a spiritual journey (a journey that seeks and requires spiritual truth), that sometimes seems the hardest to find. It is clear (or at least it should be to anyone who has even a casual understanding of the Bible) that God wants us to grow spiritually—but how is that accomplished? What is the goal? How do we determine how far along we are now? How do we know when we have arrived? This assumes, of course, that one can arrive (and by the way, what exactly does "arriving" mean?). Why is it that some people seem to intuitively understand God's will when others of us seem to struggle so much?

This book isn't intended to be our map. Only God's inspired Word can fulfill that function. Instead, this book is meant to help us discover, by reading the map, where we are now, where God wants us to go, and how we get there.

I am convinced that every person who is born again needs to understand the basic principles of moving toward spiritual maturity. Therefore, this publication isn't designed to be a scholarly treatise that only seminary graduates can understand. There are countless multitudes of such books, and the church doesn't need another. Nor is this study intended to be a dumbed-down, pop-psychology, self-help book that merely parodies what the Bible has to say. If you are looking for that, you would be better served looking elsewhere and, may I say, you will not have to look very far. For, if I may borrow (with many apologies) the song of the dancing women who met Saul and David after David killed Goliath and Israel routed the Philistines (1 Sam 18:6–7), "The seminary has its thousands and the popular Christian press its tens of thousands." This, of course, is not a new problem. The great Swiss theologian Friedrich Böringer (1812–1879) put it better than I ever could:

> We have enough and to spare of light-weight, entertaining goods on the one hand and ponderous works serviceable to comparatively few readers on the other; and the cream of the educated Christian public goes away empty.[1]

Believing this to be true, my goal is to be as clear and understandable to as many people as possible, without watering down the deep truths God has revealed in His Word. This work is intended to be a serious Bible study for the believer who genuinely desires to live for Christ more completely and more consistently (and therefore more joyously!). My prayer is that it will be used by all who seek to grow spiritually and by those in the body who desire to help them. Nonetheless, I have endeavored to keep the tone light so that this book will be a joy, rather than a burden, to read.

That's why I've begun every chapter with what I hope will be an illustrative quotation from Lewis Carroll. Not only do these quotes bring a smile to my face (and I hope to yours as well), they also emphasize some aspect of the topic discussed in the chapter. After all, in one respect at least, spiritual maturity really can be described as Wonderland.

It is my prayer that we will be able to study the map together, as fellow travelers, "so that the body of Christ may be built up until we all reach unity in the faith and in the knowledge of the Son of God and become mature" (Eph 4:12–13, niv).

Discussion Questions

The author says that his father's instruction regarding map reading consisted of three things that had to be remembered. Briefly discuss why each of these three points must be considered if one is to accurately plan a journey, whether it is a physical one or a spiritual one.

1. Where are you?

2. Where do you want to go?

3. How do you want to get there?

4. Has this chapter brought any questions to mind, or any thoughts you would like to discuss with the group?

5. Is there any issue you would like prayed for, or accountability in, over the course of this week?

6. Please note any other group members' answers that you would like to follow up on this week, either by praying for them or by making an encouraging contact.

THE CHESHIRE CAT

Would you tell me, please, which way I ought to walk from here?"

"That depends a good deal on where you want to get to," said the Cat.

"I don't much care where," said Alice.

"Then it doesn't matter which way you walk," said the Cat.

—*Wonderland,* ch. VI, "Pig & Pepper"

Chapter 3
Going the Right Direction

There are two reasons I'm using the idea of a road trip to explain what the Bible says about our journey to maturity:

- First, the picture of a road trip fits well with the biblical words used to describe this life and the activities in it.

- Second, our use of maps shows acceptance, at least at some level, of the concept of absolute truth. However, the topic of absolute truth requires a lengthier discussion, so it is considered in the next chapter.

Following the road to maturity is not optional for the believer. It is not a destination we are free to visit if we so choose. Paul commands: "Brethren, do not be children in your thinking; yet in evil be babes, but in your thinking be mature" (1 COR 14:20, NASB). Because maturity is a command, striving for anything less is simple disobedience. That means, of course, that not moving toward maturity is sin. It's really as simple as that. We will also see, as we discuss this subject further, that the Bible has a great deal to say about maturity.

We should note from the outset that *maturity* is not sinless perfection. Although it isn't possible to become sinless in this life (I for one consider that an unfortunate, though biblical, truth), it is possible to become mature! Listen to what the Apostle Paul says:

> *Not that I have already obtained all this, or have already been made perfect, but I press on to take hold of that for which Christ*

*Jesus took hold of me. Brothers, I do not consider myself yet to have taken hold of it. But one thing I do: Forgetting what is behind and straining toward what is ahead, I press on toward the goal to win the prize for which God has called me heavenward in Christ Jesus. **All of us who are mature should take such a view of things*** (PHIL 3:12–15, NIV, emphasis mine).

Here we see that straining toward the goal of being like Christ (PHIL 3:10–11) is something that mature believers do. Again, it is possible to reach maturity! Notice, too, the imagery Paul uses for his pursuit. He describes it as a race, something that involves moving from one point to another. There is a goal to be reached—which assumes, of course, that we know in which direction that goal lies. Paul's analogy of a foot race presupposes the existence of clearly defined boundaries. Paul explicitly states that he does not run "like a man running aimlessly" (1 COR 9:26). To get the prize, he must stay on the course that has been laid out ahead of time. Running a cross-country race requires a map, so you will know where you are to run.

When we review the New Testament commands about how we are to move toward maturity, we discover that we are commanded not only to run, but also (among other things) to walk, to pursue, to fight, to not be led astray. Although some more modern translations replace the original word "walk" with some other word, such as *live,* for the sake of more understandable English, the metaphor of walking through life seems to be a main image (if not *the* main image) God uses to describe the actual activities in which we are to engage. For example, we are to:

- Walk in newness of life (ROM 6:4)
- Walk not after the flesh, but after the Spirit (ROM 8:4)
- Walk honestly (ROM 13:13)
- Walk by faith, not by sight (2 COR 5:7)

- Walk by the Spirit (GAL 5:16, 25)

- Walk in good works (EPH 2:10)

- Walk worthy of the vocation with which we are called (EPH 4:1)

- Walk in love (EPH 5:2)

- Walk as children of the light (EPH 5:8)

- Walk worthy of the Lord (COL 1:10)

- Walk in Christ Jesus the Lord (COL 2:6)

- Walk in wisdom (COL 4:5)

- Walk worthy of God (1 THESS 2:12)

- Walk to please God (1 THESS 4:12)

- Walk in the light (1 JOHN 1:7)

- Walk as Christ walked (1 JOHN 2:6)

- Walk after the Father's commands (2 JOHN 6)

In fact, God not only uses the image of walking to describe living obedient lives in this age (the church), but also used the same picture when He spoke to His chosen nation living under the covenant of the Law (Israel). In fact, walking with the LORD was considered a requirement for every individual: "He has showed you, O man, what is good. *And what does the Lord require of you?* To act justly and to love mercy and to *walk humbly with your God*" (MICAH 6:8, emphasis mine).

Walking implies a journey, a moving from one point to another. As we walk through our lives, we are constantly moving in some direction. We need to be sure we are walking in the direction and in the manner God would choose. As on any journey, a map—correctly understood—can be enormously helpful. We can give thanks that God has provided us with one.

Discussion Questions

1. PSALM 84:5–7 (NIV) says "Blessed are those whose strength is in you, who have set their hearts on pilgrimage. As they pass through the Valley of Baca, they make it a place of springs; the autumn rains also cover it with pools. They go from strength to strength, till each appears before God in Zion." As we begin this study on spiritual growth, are you prepared to "set your heart" on the "pilgrimage" to maturity? Please take a minute to write about your commitment to this journey here, or to write a prayer asking God to give you a desire to commit to this journey.

2. In the next chapter, we discuss the concept of absolute truth. Do you believe in absolutes? Let's get beyond the theoretical: Are you able to declare an activity to be either right or wrong independent of its emotional implications?

3. Choose one of the verses from pages 29–30 that stands out to you. Look it up, write it out in its entirety, and memorize it prior to the next meeting. Write a short (one- or two-paragraph) devotional about this verse and how it applies to our growth toward maturity.

4. Has this chapter brought any questions to mind, or any thoughts you would like to discuss with the group?

5. Is there any issue you would like prayed for, or accountability in, over the course of this week?

6. Please note any other group members' answers that you would like to follow up on this week, either by praying for them or by making an encouraging contact.

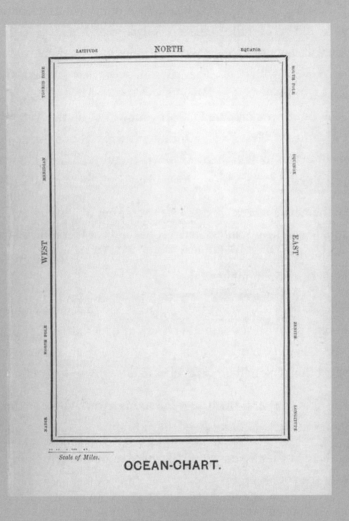

OCEAN-CHART.

He had brought a large map representing the sea,
    Without the least vestige of land:
And the crew were much pleased when they found it to be
    A map they could all understand.
"What's the good of Mercator's North Poles and Equators,
    Tropics, Zones, and Meridian Lines?"
So the Bellman would cry: and the crew would reply
    "They are merely conventional signs!
Other maps are such shapes, with their islands and capes!
    But we've got our brave Captain to thank"
(So the crew would protest) "that he's bought us the best—
    A perfect and absolute blank!"
This was charming, no doubt; but they shortly found out
    That the Captain they trusted so well
Had only one notion for crossing the ocean,
    And that was to tingle his bell.

—Carroll, *The Hunting of the Snark: An Agony
in Eight Fits*, "Fit the Second"

Chapter 4
Some Thoughts about Maps

To say that the concept of absolute truth (a statement that is true in any circumstance) is under attack is somewhat akin to saying "water is wet." Depending on the survey you read, somewhere between one-third and one-half of all North Americans reject the idea that there could be a statement that is true in every conceivable situation. Of course, the statement, "There is no such thing as an absolute truth," is, in and of itself, a claim of absolute truth. Therefore, the proposition is self-negating. Still, it seems that this rather obvious (dare I say the word) "truth" is lost on those who argue against the existence of absolute truth.

One of the most curious inconsistencies of those who hold this position (which in fact overflows with inconsistencies) is that they use maps. You see, a map shows landmarks and roads that are fixed at a certain location. Thus, a map, by its very nature, makes an implicit claim to absolute truth. The vast majority of people (there are always exceptions, I suppose, but I can honestly say I have never met any) assume that an up-to-date map is a correct representation of what actually exists.

For those who believe that truth is relative (what is true for you might not be true for me, and what was true for me five minutes ago might not be true for me now), one might expect that the best map* would be the one described by our snark-hunting sailors above: a blank sheet of paper. That way, each individual map reader/maker would be empowered to change and create his own personal, fluid, truth-of-the-moment. The inscriptions would have to be in pencil, of course, since it would be necessary to erase and rewrite as the "truth" changed. Now, using a map like this would be as ridiculous as stocking up on powdered water, but this position is demanded by logical consistency if a man rejects absolute truth. If absolute truth is a socially designated or agreed-upon fiction, then maps are a useless impossibility—yet the existence and reliability of maps is as widely accepted as is the reality of electricity.

This topic must be discussed for three reasons:

1. I have written with professing Christians as the target audience.

2. Even many professing Christians no longer consider the existence of absolute truth to be an accepted fact.

---

*Technically, sailors use a *chart,* not a *map.* This was vividly burned into my memory one night as our ship transited the Atlantic. Bored and unable to sleep, I went to visit my shipmate standing watch on the bridge. It was his job to determine the ship's exact location at any moment. Walking up to him, I asked, "So, where are we on the map?" He slowly and deliberately put down his instruments, turned to me with a look of disdain mixed with contempt, and replied, "A map takes you to Philadelphia. *This* is a *chart.*" He then slowly turned back to his table and resumed his work as if I had just disappeared. As I sheepishly retreated from the bridge, let's just say I committed the difference between a map and a chart to memory. Nevertheless, since Lewis Carroll uses the word "map," albeit incorrectly, I will follow his example, even though the memory of those few moments still makes me wince.

3. The idea that there is such a thing as absolute truth is assumed in these pages, and the (rude and unpopular) idea that the Bible contains such truth is also presupposed.

Therefore, before we can proceed, a defense of the concept of absolute truth appears to be necessary.

It is impossible to walk through this life and behave consistently if one accepts no absolute truths. No one doubts the reality of gravity when standing on the edge of a cliff, especially when he is looking down. No one says, "Well, that bottle marked 'poison' may be harmful to you, but my truth is different than yours." At least, they don't say it very often if they act on that belief. The absolute nature of truth is so often assumed in so many different circumstances that one wonders how people can deny it.

Because it is so obvious, some are forced to admit the existence of absolute truth in regard to the material world. However, when they deal with the nonmaterial, their worldview changes radically. They may say, "Your ideas about what lies beyond this material universe might be helpful to you, but they aren't helpful to me. I have my own ideas. And since both you and I are helped by our ideas, and they lie outside the realm of verification, what is true for you might not be true for me."

The problem with separating the material from the immaterial, when it comes to the nature of truth, is that the very act of making this distinction implies that the immaterial is less real than the material. Whereas the material world can be examined, weighed, measured, quantified, and categorized, these activities are impossible with the immaterial world. Therefore, some claim, we can't truly know the reality of the immaterial realm. It is the possibility of such knowledge, and the means by which such knowledge may be obtained, that is at the heart of this study.

Consider two people—let's name them "Tom" and "Bob"—who have spent their whole lives in a room with no windows and only one door. Outside the door they hear noises, faint and muffled, but loud enough to let them know that something lies beyond. Tom and Bob each hear those noises a little differently, so each comes to different conclusions about what is behind the door. Knowing that he must pass through that door at some undefined point in the future, each lives his life according to his idea about what is back there. Nevertheless, the fact that they can't know what is behind the door does not change the reality of what really is behind the door. The fact is that something exists that they can't experience directly, but it is still just as real as they are.

Now consider what would happen if someone on the other side of the door provided a television that Tom could access and Bob couldn't. The person behind the door chooses images to inform Tom how he should live in preparation to pass through the door. Tom could, therefore, make a claim to absolute (but incomplete) truth based upon the revelation supplied from behind the door. If Bob were to say, "Well, that's your truth. I have my own," his claim would seem absurd to Tom, who has actually experienced the reality, even though indirectly.

It is the same in the spiritual world. God the Holy Spirit has revealed spiritual truths to those who trust in Christ that He has not revealed to the world (because these truths are beyond their understanding). Those who are born again know that the spiritual world is just as real as the material one in which we currently live. And, just as there is absolute truth in the material world, so there is absolute truth in the immaterial world.

Those who insist that "what might be true for you is not necessarily true for me" are trying to portray spiritual concepts as a matter of preference rather than truth, thereby relegating such concepts to the realm of nonreality. The basic question is changed from "What is true?" to "What is most helpful to me?" In changing the question, they deny the very existence of truth in the spiritual world, because truth cannot be altered by our preferences about it. A person in prison would undoubtedly prefer to be someplace else, but his preference doesn't remove the locks from the door. His desire has no bearing on what actually *is*.

Therefore, if a person really believes that something lies beyond this life, then he must hold that there can be correct and incorrect information about that "something," if he is to be consistent. Absolute truth must be assumed in the spiritual world if we hold that such a world actually exists. I should add that the evidence for such a world is so overwhelming that all cultures have assumed the existence of some sort of spiritual world.

Those who deny absolute truth cannot live a life consistent with their belief. The fact that people use maps, for example, illustrates how absolute truth is assumed as we walk through life. Below, in no particular order, are some basic assumptions that all people make about maps. I assume these truths apply to the Bible as well.

1. **A map is a correct representation of what actually is, and therefore is true for everyone.**

My wife and I recently visited the Columbus zoo. At the entrance, we were handed a map of the zoo. After strolling around aimlessly for a bit, we decided we wanted to see the gorillas. But how to get there, that was the question! We unfolded the map given to us and found it to be remarkably unhelpful. We studied it and turned it around various ways trying to figure out which way to go. Eventually, we just guessed and meandered in what we thought was the general direction of the great apes. Finally, we spied signs that pointed us down the correct path.

What is interesting about this incident (at least for the purpose of this chapter) is that it never occurred to us that the map was wrong. We just assumed that the zookeepers wouldn't be in the business of handing out maps designed to mislead. We trusted that they distributed maps in order to show people where the exhibits were and to guide the crowds to them. Rather than doubting the accuracy of the map, we automatically concluded that either (a) we were reading it wrong, (b) the map was confusing and poorly written, or (c) all of the above. What we didn't do was try to trade someone else for their map. We assumed that everyone had the same map because its truths (confusing as they were) were universal.

In the same way, the truths expressed in the Bible are universal. There isn't one set of truths for you and another for me. The ultimate author of the Bible (God) intended to communicate universal truths in a way we can understand.

2. Maps must be interpreted before they can be applied to life.

What the Columbus zoo map didn't do was tell us where we were. We were compelled to look around us for the various landmarks indicated on the map to determine our current location. And there was the root of our problem: We couldn't agree on our location, so we couldn't decide which way we ought to go. The landmarks listed didn't appear to correspond with our surroundings. Simply put, we had an interpretation problem! We couldn't answer the questions required to properly use the map. What does this symbol mean? Is that hot-dog stand shown on the map? We know we're at an intersection of three roads, but there are several places like that on the map. Which one is ours?

In the same way, the Bible doesn't tell you your spiritual condition. What it does is give you landmarks and signs so you can view the landscape of your personal life and determine your location.

Fortunately for us, God is the perfect communicator. After all, language was His idea in the first place! Therefore, we can count on the clarity and accuracy of Scripture. When we speak of the clarity of Scripture, we don't mean that all Scripture is equally straightforward, for that obviously isn't the case. Instead, we are asserting that the main idea the Bible is trying to express in any given passage is clear enough that we can understand and, more importantly, act upon it. Even though we may not be able to answer every question, the information necessary for us to move on to maturity is clearly presented.

3. Maps don't take you anywhere. They just show you the way you should go.

As we stood at that crossroads in the zoo and stared at the map, we didn't move at all. The map didn't magically transport us to our desired destination. All it did was point the way. We had to actually *do* something! The reason we didn't move for a while was that we didn't know where we were going. However, even if we had understood the map— after staring at it, studying it, finding the intricate relationships between one exhibit and another, even memorizing it—none of this would have taken us one step closer to seeing the gorillas.

In JAMES 1:22 (NIV), the Bible warns against such inaction: "Do not merely listen to the word, and so deceive yourselves. Do what it says." So, merely learning facts from the Bible (or from this book) profits you not at all if you don't put what you learn into action. Maps don't move people. They merely point you in the proper direction.

4. Although there may be many roads that lead to the same place, the destination doesn't move.

We discovered that more than one road led to the gorillas. What we wanted to see on our way determined the road we took. Nevertheless, nothing represented on the map changed its location. The destination remained fixed. Only the route we took to get there was (somewhat) optional.

When God begins to work in His servants, He doesn't always take us down the same road. We don't all pass the same points. He determines the route for us depending on what is necessary to change us. Some of us need one thing and others another. Some might need to be freed from greed or lust or anger. Others might need to add humility or patience or endurance. What's more, God's ways of suppressing those vices and producing those virtues are as varied as the individuals God calls to serve Him.

What is crucially important to realize is there is no mystical prayer to pray, any more than there is magical fairy dust to sprinkle, to move a person toward maturity. There are general principles and even specific commands to be followed, to be sure. But God works in us individually, according to our individual needs.

Next time you go to church, ask someone you consider to be mature to tell you a little about his life. Ask what God did in him to bring him to maturity. Then ask that same question of several others. You will undoubtedly find similarities in their stories, but each story will be unique, because each person is unique. God works in a multitude of ways to bring us to maturity. That being said, the goal of maturity remains fixed; the way of moving down the road remains the same, even if the road down which God leads us varies from person to person.

5. Not all roads take you where you want to go.

Although many roads led to the gorillas, not all the roads did. It was possible to head in the wrong direction and miss the goal entirely. I say this not to take away from the preceding point, but merely to restrict it somewhat. While it remains true that God deals differently with His servants according to their needs and His designs, not all roads lead to the top of the mountain, as the saying goes. It is possible to misinterpret a map and thus end up where you don't want to be.

Some would say that the journey is the important thing, not the destination. But if your journey leads you to the middle of a desert where you are dying from thirst, chances are you would reconsider that opinion. The journey is certainly important (see above), and it isn't the same for everyone, but the destination (and the representations of it on the map) remain fixed, and not every road takes you there.

That's why asking for help in reading the map is a good idea—as long as the person giving the directions knows how to read the map himself and knows the lay of the land.

That's what this book hopes to be: a friendly guide that is willing (even eager) to help you read the map so you can travel to that wonderful place called maturity.

Discussion Questions

As we approach chapter 5 where we think about "Where Are You?," it's important that we look at how we're going to interpret our map—the Bible. This chapter listed five foundational truths about maps that also apply to our interpretation of the Scriptures.

Here, under each of these truths, note how this applies to how we read the Bible, and the consequences of accepting (or of not accepting) it as we read.

1. *A map/the Bible is a correct representation of what actually is, and therefore is true for everyone.*

2. *A map/the Bible must be interpreted before it can be applied to life.*

3. *A map/the Bible doesn't take you anywhere. It just shows you the way you should go.*

4. *Although there may be many roads that lead to the same place, the destination doesn't move.*

5. *Not all roads take you where you want to go.*

6. Has this chapter brought any questions to mind, or any thoughts you would like to discuss with the group?

7. Is there any issue you would like prayed for, or accountability in, over the course of this week?

8. Please note any other group members' answers that you would like to follow up on this week, either by praying for them or by making an encouraging contact.

Christine did her best to avoid her co-workers during the two weeks prior to the official reorganization. Lots of talk was going around the office, and she wanted nothing to do with it, but try as she might, there was no way to avoid it. People would stop talking when she entered the break room, or would rapidly change the subject when she approached. It didn't take a genius to figure out the topic of their conversation. She wasn't sure if their little chats were filled with pity or ridicule, but she was sure that she didn't want to know.

She did see one positive result from the reorganization, however. It would mean she would soon be working with Steve Carnes. They had formerly worked in different departments, but now the reorganization would put them not just in the same department, but in the same workgroup. "This at least," mused Christine, "is a bit of good news."

Unlike the rest of the staff, Steve was a believer, just like her. In fact, Steve credited her with his conversion.

Christine had bumped into Steve only occasionally when she started working at Miller & Johnson. She didn't get to know him well at first, but most people liked him. He was a happy-go-lucky, slap-you-on-the-back kind of guy. Most of the time, he acted like he didn't have a care in the world. He was married with children, but that's all she had really known about him.

It was about a year ago on a Friday afternoon that Christine had stayed late for some reason—for what, she no longer remembered. That's when Steve had walked slowly to her desk.

"Hey, Christine, working late?" he asked as he scanned the room, looking to see if they were alone. Not waiting for her to answer, he continued, "Um . . . got a moment for a question?

"If you're too busy, I'll understand," he added, speaking quickly.

Christine lifted her eyebrows as she turned from her desk and leaned back in her chair. She smiled and said, "I always take questions. It's getting me to answer that's more difficult." She began chewing on the end of her pen as she waited.

"Look, I know that you're a . . . religious person." He took another quick survey of the room and found that the coast was still clear. "I've got a friend whose . . . uh . . . marriage is . . . uh—well, going through some tough times. And I thought maybe you could . . . ah . . . give me some advice so I could, you know, help him out a little bit."

Christine smiled slightly and looked Steve straight in the eye. "I'm not sure I could give you any advice until you tell me what's wrong with your marriage."

"Wow, am I that transparent?" He leaned against the edge of her cubicle and gazed at the floor.

"Only when you're so obviously uncomfortable." This time her smile was broad and reassuring.

The conversation stopped until the security guard, who had just entered, finished patrolling the area. When the door closed behind him, Steve was the first to speak.

"I don't know what's wrong." He lifted his gaze from the floor and directed it toward the ceiling. "It's like we try and try, but nothing ever works. We fight about stupid stuff: what to watch on TV, her leaving toothpaste on the sink, me forgetting to take out the garbage. I mean, it's not like there's been an affair or anything! We just . . . "

An awkward silence followed. Despite Christine's best efforts, the smile slowly faded from her face.

"Sorry," Steve said with genuine remorse. "That was stupid. It seems like everything I do is stupid these days. I'm sorry I bothered you." He was turning to leave when Christine finally spoke.

"Steve, I can't help your marriage, but I know someone who can." He turned back to her as she swallowed the lump in her throat. "Why don't you and—what's her name?"

"Nancy."

"Why don't you and Nancy come to church with me this Sunday?" Steve was noncommittal, but she gave him directions to the church anyway, along with service times and her phone number.

Christine looked for them on Sunday, and was disappointed when she couldn't find them. But they had come, she found out later. They had slipped in late, sat in the back row, and left before the service was done—but they had come. To her surprise, they came the next week—on time—and they stayed until the end of the service. They were there the following week as well. The week after that, they put their kids in Sunday school and gingerly tiptoed into one of the adult classes themselves.

Christine and Steve talked a lot during those four months, mostly over lunch. She shared the gospel with him as plain as she knew how, as often as possible, but he never quite got it. It seemed as though every time she thought she was beginning to get through to him, it was time to go back to work. It was as if some sort of mental block stopped him from grasping all that Christ had done for him. Nevertheless, Christine prayed for Steve and Nancy every day. She even enlisted some close friends at church to do the same.

Then came the surprise. One Monday morning, Steve approached her desk with long, purposeful strides. "I got it, Christine. I got it yesterday." Steve had a look of utter seriousness on his face. "So did Nancy."

"Got what?" Christine was going to make him spell it out for her. He had missed the simple message so many times before that she wanted him to tell it to her plain and simple.

"The gift of eternal life," he said, pinching his eyebrows together. "What pastor said Sunday just made it so clear."

"What did pastor say?"

"What's up with you, weren't you there?"

"Yes, Steve, I was there!" Christine sighed heavily, closed her eyes, and held her forehead in her fingertips. "I just want to know what you heard."

"I wrote it down so I could keep it with me. So did Nancy. We did it together." His complete seriousness made him look like a different person. He unfolded a piece of paper from his pocket and cleared his throat.

When you were slaves to sin, you were free from the control of righteousness. What benefit did you reap at that time from the things you are now ashamed of? Those things result in death! But now that you have been set free from sin and have become slaves to God, the benefit you reap leads to holiness, and the result is eternal life. For the wages of sin is death, but the gift of God is eternal life in Christ Jesus our LORD (ROM 6:20–23, NIV).

Christine wasn't satisfied. Anyone can write some verses on a piece of paper. "So what does it mean?" she asked.

"Don't you get it? This was the problem. Nancy and I were slaves to sin. We couldn't stop hurting one another, no matter how hard we tried, because we were in slavery to all the stupid stuff we fought about. But the Bible says Jesus Christ set us free from sin so we could serve Him instead of sin."

"So how did He do that, Steve?"

"Okay, grill me all you want." A grin was beginning to creep across his face. "But I get it!

"Just like I get a wage by working here, so sin produces a wage. That wage is death. And just like these clowns have to give me my paycheck because I've earned it, so death has to come to me for the same reason—I've earned it. Spiritual death in this life is being a slave to sin. Death in the next is eternity in hell. God had to pay out my wage or it wouldn't be fair. But instead of giving it to me, He gave it to Jesus Christ when He died on the cross."

At this point Steve made a huge sweep with his hand, hitting the edge of her cubicle wall and knocking her vase with its few daisies to the floor, spilling water on her desk in the process. Christine quickly began to mop up the water and move her paperwork away from the spreading tide, but Steve didn't seem to notice. He kept on as if nothing had happened.

"He got what was coming to me and He gave me what I couldn't get: eternal life. He gives it as a gift, see . . . " he pointed to a line on his paper, "and a gift by definition is something you don't earn. So I can stop being a slave to sin in this life and have eternal life in the next. There's nothing for me to do except trust in what He did for me. I mean, is this cool or what?"

Christine sat there with her mouth dropped open in a half-grin. When she started to laugh, Steve's grin broadened. "Okay, what?"

"Steve, that certainly wasn't the most eloquent presentation of the gospel I've ever heard, but it's still a good one!"

"Well, I got help," Steve admitted, still grinning. "Nancy and I met with the pastor after church Sunday. I want you to know that he didn't say anything that you haven't been saying, but it was like . . . like someone turned on a switch or something. Suddenly, it made sense. It made sense to Nancy, too. We both confessed our sins and trusted Christ right there, when we prayed with pastor."

The twelve months since that day had been good for both Christine and Steve. A bond had developed between them that their co-workers couldn't understand—but the two of them understood. It was the bond that only members of a family can share. And now they would work together.

Christine took down her calendar and circled the dreadful day in red. As she stared at the number in the little square, she took solace in the fact that God had given her an ally for what she expected to be a difficult time.

ALICE SPEAKS WITH THE CATERPILLAR

What do you mean by that?" said the Caterpillar sternly. "Explain yourself!"

"I can't explain MYSELF, I'm afraid, sir" said Alice, "because I'm not myself, you see."

"I don't see," said the Caterpillar.

"I'm afraid I can't put it more clearly," Alice replied very politely, "for I can't understand it myself to begin with; and being so many different sizes in a day is very confusing."

"It isn't," said the Caterpillar.

"Well, perhaps you haven't found it so yet," said Alice; "but when you have to turn into a chrysalis—you will some day, you know—and then after that into a butterfly, I should think you'll feel it a little queer, won't you?"

"Not a bit," said the Caterpillar.

—*Wonderland*, ch. V, "Advice from a Caterpillar"

Chapter 5
Where Are You?

After someone is truly born again, certain differences between types of people become obvious. First, there is a difference between those who are born again and those who are not. This difference is due, at least externally, to the differences in the value systems between the lost and the saved. The saved person will more highly regard the things of God and place a higher value on them than the lost person finds reasonable. Often the contrast is striking, but in fairness it isn't always so. Sometimes the lost person is a very nice, sociable, generous, even religious person. Eventually, though, there will come a time when the differing worldviews of the lost and the saved come into stark relief. One acknowledges God the Creator as He has revealed Himself in the Bible, and thus recognizes the obedience the Almighty is due; the other does not.

However, this isn't the only difference that becomes clear. One begins to notice that there are also differences in the character and quality of the daily lives of believers. Some believers always seem to be in the midst of some crisis or quarrel. They jolt through life, bouncing from one predicament to the next. Their lives are constantly in tatters. Other believers might have the externals of their lives under control, but the peace that God provides, the gentleness and patience, the joy that one would expect of a believer, all seem to be strangely absent or, at the very least, sporadic. Other believers, in contrast, seem to naturally exhibit the fruit of the Spirit: "love, joy, peace, patience, kindness, goodness, faithfulness, gentleness, and self-control" (GAL 5:22–23, NIV).

What causes such differences? Observant folk will note that although believers who exhibit Christ-likeness have often walked with God a long time, the amount of time a person has been saved is a poor predictor of his character. In fact, you will discover among these more mature believers no commonality that can be measured, weighed, examined, or catalogued. It is simply impossible to predict a person's character merely by knowing the circumstances of his life. Trials, for example, make some people bitter, some people better.

One obvious conclusion is that a person's relationship with God is what determines the content of his character. Just as the difference between the believer and the unbeliever is grounded in their differing relationships with God, so it is with believers as well. It is simply a fact that some believers have a closer, more intimate relationship with God their Savior than others.

Various theories have been put forward to explain the differences in believers' relationships to God. Some have suggested that we simply need to make Christ Lord of our lives—and this is correct, as far as it goes. After all, we as the created owe our Creator allegiance and service. He is the Master; we are the servant. He is the one who has the sole right to order our lives. Any attempt on our part to direct our own steps is treasonous rebellion. Therefore, to live righteously, we need to submit to Christ's lordship.

The problem with this suggestion is that, while it correctly states what we must do, it doesn't tell us how to do it! Anyone who has ever tried to live righteously can testify that saying is much easier than doing. It isn't as easy as just making up your mind to begin living righteously. Sin dogs our steps—it goads us, it nags us, it is relentless in its pursuit of us, it speaks in an ominous voice, "Resistance is futile!"

(to borrow a phrase). If all we had to do to make sin go away was make our decision, snap our fingers, and click our heels three times, the majority of the church would be set free! (I sadly say "the majority" because, alas, some would still prefer sin.) Of course, it's just not that easy. Anyone who has ever made a serious attempt at righteousness could provide first-person testimony to that terrible truth.

So: What, then, is the difference among the three types of people described here (the person without Christ, the immature, and the mature)? Is it how much time they spend reading their Bibles? How consistent they are in their devotions? How much they pray? How much money they give? How many works of service they do, either inside the church or outside? None of these answers satisfies, for it is possible to find bitter, angry believers who do all these things regularly.

Ultimately, the Bible teaches that the differences among these three types of people are a result of their relationship, not just with the Godhead generally, but more specifically with the third person of the Holy Trinity: God the Holy Spirit.

The Apostle Paul discusses this topic in detail in 1 Corinthians 2:8–3:5. In this passage he divides the entire human race into three categories. The first is the "natural" man (1 Cor 2:14). Everyone who has ever been born (excepting Jesus Christ) has belonged to this group at one time, for it describes (as you might expect) the "natural" condition of a person from the moment of birth. This is the man who has not been changed spiritually, who has not been born again, and therefore has no relationship with the Holy Spirit.

The second category is the "carnal" man (literally, "men of flesh" [1 Cor 3:1, NASB]). These people have been born again, but are still "mere infants in Christ," and thus "act like mere men" (1 Cor 3:1, 3, NIV). This brief description may seem a bit confusing, but don't panic! A whole chapter is devoted to explaining this concept.

The third category is the "spiritual" man. The people in this group are able to "make judgments about all things" (1 Cor 2:15, niv). Again, this is explained in detail later on.

What separates these three types of people is their ability to understand and put into practice those truths that have been "revealed" by the Holy Spirit. First Corinthians 2:9, 10 (niv) describes the means available to humanity to receive knowledge:

> However, as it is written: "No eye has seen, no ear has heard, no mind has conceived what God has prepared for those who love him"—but God has revealed it to us by his Spirit.
>
> The Spirit searches all things, even the deep things of God.

Notice that Paul lists three avenues of receiving knowledge:

1. Physical investigation—the eye, the ear
2. Human reason—the mind
3. What is revealed by the Spirit

Thus, all humans are classified according to their ability to receive what God has revealed by His Spirit: those truths that are the "deep things of God."

At this point a vital definition is in order. It would be easy to confuse the "deep things of God" with difficult theological problems such as the relationship between election and free will, the internal workings of the Trinity, or how Christ is a priest after the order of Melchizedek. It is true that our understanding of knotty doctrinal issues becomes greater or lesser depending on our maturity level (more on this in chapter 8, "Standing on Your Old White Head"). But Paul doesn't speak of difficult theological issues in this passage. Instead, throughout the passage, his emphasis is upon how a person behaves.

This could be thought of as the difference between knowledge and wisdom. *Knowledge* is a theoretical understanding of something, whereas *wisdom* is the (correct) application of knowledge and experience to a specific situation. Since wisdom is the application of knowledge, it becomes obvious that what you think has a profound impact upon what you do. What you believe strongly influences how you behave. In the same way, a person's lack of knowledge—in this case spiritual knowledge—will affect his behavior as well. It is this interrelationship between belief and behavior that Paul is discussing in this passage. The "deep things of God," therefore, are those truths that are directly related to our behavior: those spiritually discerned truths that make us act differently from the world.

For example, if the rulers of this world had understood the wisdom of God, "they would not have crucified the Lord of glory" (1 COR 2:8). Their lack of wisdom prompted an action. In contrast, the spiritual man is able to "make judgments about all things" because he has "the mind of Christ" (1 COR 2:15–16). He is able to evaluate how to behave in all situations because of his maturity. The carnal man is involved in "jealousy and quarreling" because he is still "fleshy" (1 COR 3:1, 3). He doesn't behave correctly because he is relying on the knowledge available to the flesh instead of knowledge attainable only through the Spirit.

These deep truths can only be understood through the power and enabling of the Holy Spirit. Paul describes it this way:

For who among men knows the thoughts of a man except the man's spirit within him? In the same way no one knows the thoughts of God except the Spirit of God. We have not received the spirit of the world but the Spirit who is from God, that we may understand what God has freely given us. This is what we speak, not in words taught us by human wisdom but in words taught by the Spirit, expressing spiritual truths in spiritual words. The man without the Spirit does not accept the things that come from the Spirit of God, for they are foolishness to him, and he cannot understand them, because they are spiritually discerned (1 COR 2:11–14, NIV).

Just as one person can't read the mind of another person (since they don't share the same spirit, each being an individual), so a person can't know the mind of God unless he is able to share the same Spirit with God. Thus, only the person who has been born again can truly understand the things of God. Of course, this makes complete sense when you consider the plight of the unsaved. If they really understood their condition before God—if they really knew that there was a heaven to gain and a hell to shun—wouldn't they turn to Christ for salvation? Only through the enabling power of God the Holy Spirit can a human truly understand what God has revealed.

Now it is important to note just what it is that God has revealed. When we speak of God's revelation of deep truths, we are not speaking of mystical visions or hearing voices. Instead, we see that God has revealed these truths in "words taught by the Spirit, expressing spiritual truths in spiritual words." Because this wisdom is taught in "words," we must conclude that the Spirit reveals truth through language. In fact, this is exactly what God has done.

The Bible is a book filled with words. Because these words are the same words that are used to express human wisdom, everyone can understand them, in one sense at least. We are not claiming that the unsaved person suddenly loses the ability to read when picking up a Bible! Instead, we are stating that the only truths a person will be able to understand are those available through physical perception (his five senses) or through reason (his mind). The truths that can be accessed and verified only by divine revelation will be completely beyond the scope of the normal individual.

Thus, to summarize, the difference between the natural man, the carnal (or fleshy) man, and the spiritual man is the ability to receive and put into practice those things the Bible teaches that can be known only through the Holy Spirit. Spiritual truths must be communicated by spiritual means. Without enablement by the Spirit, a person can have no understanding of the deep things of God.

Discussion Questions

In each of chapters 5–9, we will be revisiting your answer to the question "Where are you?" Please go back to your answer to that question, and examine it in light of this chapter.

1. List the three types of people mentioned in 1 CORINTHIANS 2:8–3:5. What is the crucial element in determining into which category a person falls?

2. This chapter talks about the "deep things of God" being those things in Scripture that have affected our behavior. Can you recall a situation in which the Holy Spirit has used the Scripture to modify your behavior?

3. Has this chapter brought any questions to mind, or any thoughts you would like to discuss with the group?

4. Is there any issue you would like prayed for, or accountability in, over the course of this week?

5. Please note any other group members' answers that you would like to follow up on this week, either by praying for them or by making an encouraging contact.

BEWARE THE JABBERWOCK

JABBERWOCKY

'Twas brillig, and the slithy toves
    Did gyre and gimble in the wabe;
All mimsy were the borogoves,
    And the mome raths outgrabe.

'Beware the Jabberwock, my son!
    The jaws that bite, the claws that catch!
Beware the Jubjub bird, and shun
    The frumious Bandersnatch!'

He took his vorpal sword in hand:
    Long time the manxome foe he sought—
So rested he by the Tumtum tree,
    And stood awhile in thought.

—*Looking-Glass*, ch. 1, "Looking-Glass House"

Chapter 6
Spiritual Jabberwocky

aul describes the natural man with these words:

> However, as it is written: "No eye has seen, no ear has heard, no mind has conceived what God has prepared for those who love him"—but God has revealed it to us by his Spirit. . . .

> The man without the Spirit does not accept the things that come from the Spirit of God, for they are foolishness to him, and he cannot understand them, because they are spiritually discerned (1 COR 2:9, 10, 14, NIV).

What the New International Version calls "the man without the Spirit," the New American Standard calls "the natural man" (as does the King James). Both phrases are accurate, but each in a different way.

If you look up the word Paul uses in the original Greek, you find that it means "natural" or "unspiritual." It refers to "one who lives on the purely material plane, without being touched by the Spirit of God."[1] Therefore, the word *natural* is a good translation because it accurately describes everyone in their, well, natural condition. From the moment a person is born, he lives merely on the material plane. The "natural" or "unspiritual" man has not experienced the "new birth" (JOHN 3:3, 7; 1 PET 1:23) and therefore remains unchanged. Hence, the "natural" man is indeed the "man without the Spirit."

Have you ever watched a monster movie? One thing all movie monsters have in common is that they are just a collage of bits and pieces we've seen before. The monster-makers take the claws of one animal and make them bigger, some slime from another creature and make it slimier, and the fangs of a third critter and make lots more of them, only longer and sharper. They give their beast the power to become invisible (we witness invisible things all the time—think of wind), or vanish in a wisp of smoke (but we already know what smoke looks like, don't we?). So there really isn't a truly "original" monster. There might be original or clever or novel combinations, but no one has been able to come up with anything really new, because our minds cannot conceive of what we haven't experienced.

Don't believe this? How would you describe the color red to a person born blind? What frame of reference would the blind person have to imagine what he has never experienced—color? Now do you grasp the problem?

In the same way, the natural man can't conceive of what is spiritually true. It is outside his ability to conceive, because he has never experienced it. Again, any truth that is not available on the material plane is outside the natural man's ability to grasp. Only what is perceived by the senses ("no eye has seen, no ear has heard") or available to human reason ("no mind has conceived") is recognizable as truth. Because the natural man has no awakened spiritual consciousness, spiritual truths are beyond his ability even to experience, let alone to understand.

At this point, it might be helpful to state what I'm *not* saying, to avoid any confusion or misunderstanding. I'm *not* saying that the natural man is unable to understand the content of a spiritual argument, or that suddenly everyday language becomes unintelligible when the discussion turns to the things of God. Instead, this person will understand as best he is able, but because the real substance of the matter lies outside his experience, he just can't believe it's true. That's what the word *accept* means in this context. The man without the Spirit is unable to receive the information and "regard it as true."[2] In fact, Jesus said of the Spirit, "The world cannot accept him (the Spirit of Truth), because it neither sees him nor knows him" (JOHN 14:17).

Likewise, I'm not stating that the man without the Spirit cannot think about spiritual things. The world is full of religion. Every brand and stripe of "spirituality" that can possibly be cobbled together is being taught all around the world. The problem is that, just like the monsters in the movies, the natural man will only be able to glue together those things that are available to his senses and reason. The interesting paradox of all these religions is that, while they claim to speak of spiritual truths that lie outside this world, these "spiritual" truths are really bound to *this* world, because of their origin. They begin and end with humanity's limited experience and knowledge.

Therefore, the results of natural humanity's best attempts to think spiritually end up being Jabberwocky. Did you notice that in Carroll's famous poem (excerpted at the beginning of this chapter), there is the appearance of wisdom in the midst of all the nonsense? The "wise" father is warning his son about the dangers of the Jabberwock (with the jaws that bite, the claws that catch!), the Jubjub bird, and especially the frumious Bandersnatch! The poem purports to recount the son's bravery (he took his vorpal sword in hand), his perseverance in the face of imminent death (long time the manxome foe he sought), and the wisdom that he learned from this harrowing experience (so rested he by the Tumtum tree, and stood awhile in thought). But it's all gibberish! In the same way, the natural person may spout lots of spiritual-sounding mumbo-jumbo, but in the end it's all gobbledygook. True spirituality remains outside his grasp.

In the interest of fairness, we must acknowledge that although the natural man doesn't need any help to dream up spiritual Jabberwocky, he nevertheless receives help in doing so. Satan has "deep things" of his own to reveal (Rev 2:24), so people are deluded into believing "deceiving spirits and things taught by demons" (1 Tim 4:1). Because Satan does not "have in mind the things of God, but the things of men" (Matt 16:23), his teaching is predictably tantalizing to the person who lives merely on the material plane. Satan knows what fallen humanity wants to hear, and provides it with relish.

A case in point is man's ability to produce religious systems that, though false, nevertheless contain moral principles pleasing to God. This is because Satan knows that people inwardly long to establish some type of righteous order, because God has written His law on their hearts (Rom 2:15). Therefore, Satan "assists" the natural man to teach, preach, fight, and even die for things that are universally regarded as good. Nevertheless, these good teachings are intertwined with elements designed specifically to appeal to an individual's pride, lust, and greed, so that the false system will be received as true by the natural man and the truth will be regarded as foolishness.

We should also be quick to notice that Paul is not blaming this "natural" man for his failure to understand the things of God. Paul is merely giving an accurate account of the limitations of the man without the Spirit. The man without the Spirit will find the deep things of God "foolishness." In fact, Paul is quite specific in defining what part of God's revelation the natural person will consider foolish:

For the message of the cross is foolishness to those who are perishing, but to us who are being saved it is the power of God. For it is written: "I will destroy the wisdom of the wise; the intelligence of the intelligent I will frustrate."

Where is the wise man? Where is the scholar? Where is the philosopher of this age? Has not God made foolish the wisdom of the world? For since in the wisdom of God the world through its wisdom did not know Him, God was pleased through the foolishness of what was preached to save those who believe. Jews demand miraculous signs and Greeks look for wisdom, **but we preach Christ crucified: a stumbling block to Jews and foolishness to Gentiles,** *but to those whom God has called, both Jews and Greeks, Christ the power of God and the wisdom of God* (1 COR 1:18–24, NIV, emphasis mine).

It is specifically the message of the cross—our need of it, God's justice in demanding it, God's grace in providing it—that is "foolishness to those who are perishing." The natural man can understand the historical fact of the cross, because that is available to human experience. But God's gracious plan of redemption made possible by the cross is beyond his intellectual reach and spiritual comprehension.

In fact, regardless of how much religious education a person may receive—no matter the honors or number of diplomas—if a man doesn't have the Spirit of God to lead him into truth, he will not recognize the cross for what it is. When he attempts to think theologically, he will inevitably reformulate or restate the "faith that was once for all entrusted to the saints" (JUDE 3) so that it is better suited to his own sinful nature. This new theology will inevitably twist the real meaning of the cross or the nature of the Savior Who died upon it. The new doctrine will either misrepresent the nature of Jesus Christ (either denying His humanity, or more often denying His deity), or will fail to properly present the purpose of Christ's death, revising and recasting it to be nearly anything except a sacrifice for sin that satisfied the wrath of God on our behalf. The fact that God would become man in the person of Jesus Christ and pay the sin debt of the entire world is "foolishness" to the natural person because of his limitations in spiritual understanding. That's why "the world through its wisdom did not know Him [God]."

The bottom line for the natural man is this: The only means he has of verifying truth are natural/physical—those things that are tied to this world. Thus, because spiritual truth lies above the material plane (just as God Himself is above the material plane), the natural man will never accept the spiritual reality that God reveals because he has no capability to validate those claims to his satisfaction. He makes himself the final judge of truth rather than submitting to God's wisdom and authority.

Knowing this to be so, what inferences follow?

1. Not all opinions on spiritual matters are of equal worth.

Regardless of how much training a person may have (even in the field of religion), if the person speaking does not have the Spirit of God, he will never come to correct conclusions concerning the things of God. I use the word *never* on purpose. The lost will *never* come to correct conclusions about "deep things" of God because these truths are beyond their capacity to understand.

This is not to say that they will not accomplish good or even noble acts. However, they will always do so for the wrong reasons. Let me give you an example. Suppose two people, one without the Spirit and one with the Spirit, are standing outside an apartment building when a fire breaks out. People begin pouring out of the building as the smoke billows after them. Then a woman screams: "My baby is still in there! Oh, someone please save my baby!" These two strangers glance toward each other and, knowing what they must do, run into the building together, braving the flames. Through their combined efforts, they rescue the baby unharmed.

Afterward, the media arrive on the scene, interview each man, and ask, "Why did you risk your life like that?"

The man without the Spirit responds, "Well, I believe children are our future. There is no sacrifice too great to save a child. So my risk was a small price to pay if I could help just one child grow up and help build a better world. Besides, when I heard that woman scream I remembered the Golden Rule: 'Love your neighbor as yourself.' So I had to act." Now, this may sound wonderful, and there is even a little bit of truth in it, but, in reality, most of it is Jabberwocky.

To this man's credit, he does mention a spiritual truth. We are commanded to love our neighbors as ourselves (although the standard has been made even more exacting; see JOHN 15:12). Nevertheless, this commandment is one that is available to the human senses. We can see people love one another. This command still lies on the material plane, even if the power to obey it must come from outside that plane. The rest of his statement, however, is false. First of all, children are not our future, God is our future. "He does as He pleases with the powers of heaven and the peoples of the earth" (DAN 4:35). Second, when this child grows up, unless he comes to Christ, he will join with the rest of the world that does not know God. He won't help build a better world; he will assist in its active rebellion against God. Third, there *are* some sacrifices too great to save a child. If some crazed man broke into my house, held a gun to my child's head, and ordered me to deny Christ or he'd pull the trigger, I'd be forced to choke out the words, "Pull the trigger." Denying Christ would be too great a sacrifice for the life of a child, even my own!

Then the microphone moves to the man with the Spirit, who responds, "Well, I know God loved me so much that he sent his one and only Son to save my soul. And I want to be just like him. So I figured if Christ loved me enough to die for me, even when I was his enemy, then I should love others the same way. Sure, I could've died, but I would've died acting in love for the helpless, just like Christ. And that's why I did it."

Did you notice the difference? Although each man performed the exact same act of bravery, their motivations came from different spheres. The man without the Spirit gave answers tied to this material world, ignored his Creator, and placed his hope in other people (in this case, children in general). The man with the Spirit tied his motivation to God's love as expressed on the cross, because he has access to such deep truths due to the Spirit's residing within him.

2. **Although people without the Spirit may make valuable insights into the things of this world, they cannot be trusted to accurately describe the things of God.**

Physical observation, the determination of cause and effect, and investigation of the natural laws that exist are clearly within the grasp of the natural man. For example, if I were to be diagnosed with some deadly disease, I would go to the best specialist I could find. In the case of medicine, I would trust the doctor, as both the problem (physical illness) and the solution (medical treatment) involve the material principles of this world. I would trust the doctor's judgment regarding the choice of a treatment regimen. Still, if my physician was not a Christian, when the discussion moved to the spiritual plane, I should recognize that he will never be able to know the truth, because it is beyond him. He may say good things about prayer and knowing God, but he will never accurately attain the specifics of a true relationship with God, because he is unable to comprehend them.

3. **Spiritual growth does not come from hard work, personal study, or professional education.**

If it were possible to grow spiritually that way, then the natural man would be able to attain spiritual maturity. Although God may, and often does, use these things to accomplish His purposes, they are no guarantee of spiritual growth. One can grow only through the work of the Spirit of God in one's life. Spiritual truth is revealed to every person, saved or unsaved, the same way: through the revelation of God the Holy Spirit. Simply put, "these things are spiritually discerned."

Thus, one of the most important lessons to be learned from the inability of the natural man to discern spiritual truth is that, just as the man without the Spirit will not learn God's wisdom by going to school, neither will the man with the Spirit. The "deep things" of God are spiritually discerned, whether we are speaking of the natural man or the believer. You will not learn God's wisdom by going to school, reading your Bible, going to church, or any other natural activity by itself! If you could, all believers would be mature and all unbelievers would have access to this wisdom. No, just like the natural man, spiritual maturity resides in the spiritual realm and must be revealed to us from that realm by God the Holy Spirit. He may do this in a number of natural ways—such as reading your Bible, going to church, becoming educated—but these things, in and of themselves, do not make someone mature. That is a work reserved for God the Holy Spirit alone.

Discussion Questions

In each of chapters 5–9, we will be revisiting your answer to the question "Where are you?" Please go back to your answer to that question, and examine it in light of this chapter.

1. In your own words, describe the "natural man," with particular emphasis on his ability to comprehend spiritual truth.

2. This chapter examined how the natural and spiritual man could both perform what appeared to be a good deed, but from radically different motivations. Think of another example to illustrate this truth.

3. This chapter identified one commonality regarding truth available to the natural and spiritual man. Can you recall it and state it in your own words?

4. Has this chapter brought any questions to mind, or any thoughts you would like to discuss with the group?

5. Is there any issue you would like prayed for, or accountability in, over the course of this week?

6. Please note any other group members' answers that you would like to follow up on this week, either by praying for them or by making an encouraging contact.

TWEEDLEDEE AND TWEEDLEDUM
PREPARING FOR BATTLE

Tweedledum and Tweedledee
Agreed to have a battle;
For Tweedledum said Tweedledee
Had spoiled his nice new rattle.

Just then flew down a monstrous crow,
As black as a tar-barrel;
Which frightened both the heroes so,
They quite forgot their quarrel.

—*Looking-Glass,* ch. IV,
"Tweedledum and Tweedledee"

Chapter 7
Arguing Over a Rattle

While there is only one classification for the person without the Spirit, there are two for those who have the Spirit: the carnal man and the spiritual man. The Apostle Paul describes the carnal man in 1 CORINTHIANS 3:1–4 (NASB):

And I, brethren, could not speak to you as to spiritual men, but as to men of flesh, as to babes in Christ. I gave you milk to drink, not solid food; for you were not yet able to receive it. Indeed, even now you are not yet able, for you are still fleshly. For since there is jealousy and strife among you, are you not fleshly, and are you not walking like mere men? For when one says, "I am of Paul," and another, "I am of Apollos," are you not mere men?

Depending on which translation you read, you will see such persons described as either "worldly" (NIV), "men of flesh" (NASB), or "carnal" (KJV). I have chosen the word *carnal* for two reasons:

- First, it is a very accurate translation (though not as clear as it might be). The word *carnal* means "fleshy" or "meaty." We see the root when ordering chili con **carn**e (literally, "chili with meat"). At the in**carn**ation, God took on flesh. So, the **carn**al man is the "fleshy" man.

- Second (and this is really the main reason), it seems foolish to try to change terminology that has so worked its way into the common Christian vocabulary. Even though people might not fully understand what they mean when they say someone is "carnal," they know the word and they know it isn't good.

The distinguishing feature of the carnal man is his limited ability to receive (and subsequently put into practice) God's revealed truth. He is able to drink milk, but not to eat solid food. This, of course, is an analogy to the difficulty of receiving God's revelation. The ability to eat solid food develops only after a period of growth. Even then, there are different levels of solid food.

I remember when I was a child, there were two categories of meat at our house: hard meat and soft meat. Soft meat, like hamburgers and hot dogs, I could chew and swallow without problem. But if the family was having a roast, for example, it didn't matter how long I chewed that piece of meat, it just seemed to get bigger and bigger in my mouth. I would sit there with tears in my eyes until my parents showed me mercy and let me spit it out. I tried to eat it, but was unable because of my age. I was just too young to eat the "hard" meat.

Because the carnal man cannot receive solid food—that is, the more difficult spiritual truths—he is, to follow the analogy, a baby in Christ. To state it more plainly, he is spiritually immature. Nevertheless, despite the fact that the babe in Christ has a severely limited ability to know the things of God, he still possesses more depth of insight than the natural man, and occupies a spiritual position that is far and away superior to that of the natural man.

At this point I should mention that some object to my equating carnality with spiritual immaturity. This objection becomes more intense when I state that every believer begins his new life in Christ as carnal. This objection isn't totally without merit. After all, the carnal man in 1 CORINTHIANS 3 is clearly in a state of sin, being chided for his fleshly behavior. So how can it be correct to place in this category one whose state isn't the result of sin, but rather of obedience to the Gospel?

There are at least three answers to this objection:

- First, and most important, Paul equates "men of flesh" with "babes in Christ" (1 COR 3:1). These two phrases are used back to back so that each phrase explains and expounds on the other. Both receive milk instead of solid food. Both must undergo the process of spiritual growth, for they are "not yet able to receive" Paul's teaching.

- Second, the underlying problem of the spiritual infant, which necessitates spiritual growth, is his need to move beyond the elementary truths of God's Word (described as milk in HEB 5:12) to solid food (defined as teaching about righteousness in HEB 5:13). This is the same problem of those who are rebuked for being carnal.

- Third, Peter admonishes his readers to "rid yourselves of all malice and all deceit, hypocrisy, envy, and slander of every kind. Like newborn babies, crave pure spiritual milk, so that by it you may grow up in your salvation" (1 PET 2:1–2). In other words, they are to rid themselves of attributes that belong to the flesh (see GAL 5:19–21) and crave milk so that they can "grow up"— that is, move on toward maturity.

Therefore, although the circumstances causing the condition might be different (in one case being newborn in Christ, in the other being in rebellion toward Him), the situation of both men remains the same. They need milk to grow up so that they may leave behind the works of the flesh and become practically acquainted with teaching about righteousness.

With this explanation in mind, we should make several observations about children, both physical and spiritual.

- *Being carnal is not the same as being sinful.* To become a child of God, one must be "born again" (JOHN 3:3, 7; 1 PET 1:23). Just as in the physical realm, so in the spiritual: one is not born an adult. Each of us begins as an infant. Therefore, everyone begins their spiritual life as carnal, because everyone begins as a baby. It is possible to have your sins confessed and be filled with the Spirit at any time after the new birth, even when you are just a newborn, and thus be pleasing to God. Just as growth takes place in the physical world, so it takes place in the spiritual world as well. In fact, such growth is commanded: "Like newborn babies, crave pure spiritual milk, so that by it you may grow up in your salvation" (1 PET 2:2, NIV). Additionally, we must remember that the process of growth takes time. As a result, we need to recognize the limitations of babies, whether physical babies or spiritual ones.

- *Carnal Christians can please God, just as babies can please parents.* I remember when my child took his first few faltering steps before falling on his diapered behind. Did I run over to him and spank him for failing? (After all, he didn't do it right!) What a silly question. Of course not! My wife and I got on the phone and called the grandparents and bragged about their above-average grandson! You see, it wasn't the doing that was as important as the attempt. We were pleased merely because our (above-average) child had moved to a new stage in his development. Now, it goes without saying that we weren't satisfied with those few steps. We weren't satisfied until he was walking in maturity as an adult—but we were very pleased! In the same way, God is easy to please even if He remains impossible to satisfy. We won't satisfy God until our glorification comes when we are given new bodies and are walking in sinless perfection. Nevertheless, God can still be very pleased as we grow up and take steps toward maturity.

- **Even though they are still children, they can still be useful.** One of the common questions parents hear from their children (until the children become teenagers, at least) is, "Can I help?" It is the wise parent who says yes. "Here, sweetheart, you can mix the eggs and flour for mommy." "Sure, son, you hold the flashlight right on this spot." Of course, as any parent knows, a measurable portion of the flour and eggs will probably end up somewhere other than the bowl. The light will wander as if hung from a string. Nevertheless, there are tasks that children can perform. As they grow and mature, so does their ability. It was a great comfort to me when I realized that you can still drink tea out of a cracked cup! In other words, I don't have to be perfect to be used. And neither do you. Isn't that a blessing?

- **When a baby doesn't grow, there is a problem.** When I was around seven or eight, my Uncle Teddy was my favorite uncle. I didn't get to see him very much, because he lived so far away, but when I did, it was great. Uncle Teddy played with me like no other adult. He had an imagination just like mine. At first I was frightened by Uncle Teddy. He looked different from all the other adults, and when they saw him around me, they always watched with (what looked like to me) worried expressions. When I realized how gentle he was, though, my fear went away. I loved my Uncle Teddy in spite of—or maybe because of—the fact that he was so very different. He had Down syndrome. He was an adult physically, but a child mentally.

  This, unfortunately, describes many believers. In fact, it is this aspect—the lack of growth—that comes to mind when most believers hear the word "carnal." This is why it has such a negative connotation. Also, the Bible speaks the most about carnality in this context.

- *Some knowledge is beyond the grasp of children.* There's a reason the origin of children is described to them with cabbage-patch and stork stories over and over again. Until children reach a certain age, human reproduction is simply beyond their grasp. Likewise, correct behavior does not come naturally either. It must be learned. Little girls must be taught not to lift their dresses above their heads when company comes. Little boys must be tutored not to relieve themselves in the driveway when the urge comes upon them. It is this aspect of being a child—the ability or inability to grasp certain truths—that defines whether or not a person is carnal.

Two Aspects of Carnality

Paul mentions two aspects of carnality in the passage quoted earlier. First, there is the lack of ability to eat solid food, so that he couldn't teach what he desired to teach. Second, there are the behavioral issues that naturally result from a lack of spiritual understanding. His listeners and readers were filled with jealousy and strife, which means they were acting like "mere men"—men without the Spirit. These two aspects of carnality—the inability to receive some spiritual truth, and ungodly behavior—are linked together as cause and effect. Their behavior was a result of what they believed. Because they had limited abilities to access spiritual truth, their belief system (and thus their behavior) was similar to the beliefs of those who had no access at all.

We should remember at this point that the elementary truths of the faith, those things dismissed as foolishness by the natural man, have already been accepted as true by the carnal man. He has access to these truths because he has been born again and is indwelt by the

Spirit of God. Rather, it is the more difficult truths that he fails to receive and comprehend.

Difficulty, in this case, doesn't refer to complex subjects learned in theology classes. We have already discovered that spiritual truths are spiritually discerned. Therefore, education through the material world, by itself, is insufficient to instruct with regard to spiritual truth. Instead, the doctrines that are beyond the carnal man are those truths that run the most contrary to his fleshy nature. He will tend to rely on those truths verifiable by his physical senses and reason before he will rely on those truths unavailable except by the Spirit. In a given situation, his flesh will demand one course of action, and God will demand another. The further these two actions diverge from one another, the more difficult the doctrine is to receive.

One illustration that has been used many times to describe this situation (translation: this isn't original with me) is that of a factory coming under new ownership. Suppose that a factory originally built to produce industrial acids is bought by a company that produces purified water. Obviously, some changes will have to be made! New equipment will have to be installed and the old removed. A purification process will have to be set up to ensure that all the acids are purged from the pipes and valves, so as to not contaminate the water. This whole process will take some time. Similarly, learning to rely on the Spirit for guidance is a process that requires growth. Growth, by definition, is a gradual process. It takes place in some quicker than in others, but it isn't instantaneous in anyone.

It is important to notice that Paul links the carnal believers' behavior to their reliance upon the flesh. Remember, this is exactly what the term *carnal* means: fleshy.

Indeed, even now you are not yet able, for you are still fleshly.
For since there is jealousy and strife among you, are you not

fleshly, and are you not walking like mere men? For when one says, "I am of Paul," and another, "I am of Apollos," are you not mere men? (1 Cor 3:3–4, nasb).

Carnal believers are very similar to Tweedledee and Tweedledum. These two "agreed to have a battle;/For Tweedledum said Tweedledee had spoiled his nice new rattle." Adults acting like children arguing over a broken rattle is an excellent picture of carnal men. Giving in to envy, greed, argument, and division is the telltale sign of carnality, because this is when we are acting the most like "mere men."

The flesh tells us that we must fight to place ourselves—and, by extension, our ideas—first. What we think is what matters most. Our position, our rights must be protected at all costs. So, there are some slights that we just won't take, some positions that are beneath us. Consequently, we become jealous of those who receive more attention or make decisions with which we disagree. Who do they think they are, anyway? Then we fight, because such "injustices" must be opposed. Our way is correct and others must see (or be made to see) that. After all, you can't just lie there and be a doormat, or people will walk all over you. Or we fall under the influence of an eloquent leader, adopt his agenda as our own, and label "outsiders" as "not in our camp." Division and controversy break out among the believers. If we are fortunate, in the end we see that we are acting no differently than "mere men."

I remember the first funeral where I was the presiding minister. Thankfully, there was an older and more experienced pastor at my side to walk me through what I should do. I presided because I was the new pastor of the church and doing so was in keeping with my position, but he was with me because he was the beloved pastor from years before. Being new, I didn't know the man we were burying; he had never darkened the door of the church while I had been there. I just knew his family. The other pastor, however, knew him well. After being walked through the service, I asked this pastor about the deceased. I knew the family's views of the departed, but I was interested in the viewpoint of his long-time pastor. "Oh," the pastor said with a shrug, "he was a church fighter from way back." That was his entire assessment of the deceased. What a terrible summation for a believer's life!

This is the wisdom of the world. It places self first. When the prophet Isaiah spoke of sin, he described us as sheep having gone astray, "each of us has turned to his own way" (Isa 53:6). This is the essence of sin: placing your will first, doing your own thing, engaging in the "evolutionary" struggle for supremacy. This is why there is so much fighting, warring, bitterness, and prejudice in the world. There are too many wills fighting to be supreme. This is also why, if we really want peace, we must pray the way our Lord taught his disciples to pray: "Our Father in heaven, . . . Your will be done on earth as it is in heaven." Only when the one will of God is done will the conflict cease.

In contrast, when we "walk by the Spirit" (Gal 5:16, nasb), we will "walk in love, just as Christ also loved you" (Eph 5:2, nasb), so we will be "diligent to preserve the unity of the Spirit in the bond of peace" (Eph 4:3, nasb). Unfortunately, this is so contrary to what we see around us. Oh, in principle we agree with all these ideals, but when we need to exercise them in a specific circumstance, we always seem to find a reason why they don't apply in that instance. In other words, the carnal believer will be unconvinced of the "rightness" of these truths when the situation calls for them to actually be applied. It is the application of these truths that the fleshly man is "not able to receive," because he relies on the flesh for his wisdom—and the flesh only verifies as true what can be received by the physical senses or reason.

The Necessity of Faith

Put another way, the carnal man tends to walk by sight and not by faith. *Faith* is defined as being sure of what we hope for and certain of what we do not see (HEB 11:1). Therefore, if you can see it, it isn't of faith. Faith, by definition, exists only in the realm that can't be apprehended by the senses. So if it adds up on a calculator, if the result is assured, if it appeals to our reason, if we see everybody else doing it, then it isn't of faith. The carnal man is so accustomed to living only by what he can see, or understand with his mind, that the truths of God that run contrary to his senses or reason are beyond his reach. Thus, he acts like the natural man who has no access at all to spiritual truth, because each acts solely on what he can see or conclude intellectually.

In contrast, the believer must be taught not to regard what he can see as his primary source of information. He must develop a virtue that is often discussed but seldom demonstrated: faith!

According to the author of HEBREWS, there are three things a person cannot do without:

1. Without the shedding of blood there is no forgiveness (HEB 9:22).

2. Without holiness no one will see the Lord (HEB 12:14).

3. Without faith it is impossible to please God, because anyone who comes to him must believe that he exists and that he rewards those who earnestly seek him (HEB 11:6, NIV).

These "withouts" signal a total inability. It isn't just more difficult to get forgiveness without the shedding of blood, it is impossible. It's not unlikely that someone will see the Lord without holiness, it is impossible. In the same way, without faith it is impossible to please God.

According to HEBREWS 11:6, there are two requirements for pleasing God. First, you must believe that He exists. The carnal man meets this requirement, since he has already accepted that fact as evidenced by the new birth. With the next requirement, though, things get sticky. If you are going to please God, you must believe that "he rewards those who earnestly seek him." This runs contrary to everything we see around us. Our old nature doesn't trust what it cannot see. But if we are to please God, we must have faith, that is, a reliance upon God that goes beyond what we can investigate. Thus, the more faith required to obey an action commanded by God, the more difficult that command will be to receive.

Consider, for example, the increased difficulty of obedience in the following statements:

- I shouldn't say something spiteful or untrue about someone else.

- I shouldn't say anything spiteful in response to someone's malicious comment about or to me.

- I shouldn't rejoice when the person spreading malicious gossip about me falls.

- I should pray for those who mistreat me.

- I should be actively doing good for those who hate me.

- I should love my enemies just as God has loved me.

As you move down the list, obedience becomes more difficult because the command requires more faith. We are tempted to believe that, unless we act in a certain way, evil will go unchecked and unpunished. So, it's up to us to make things right.

The commands listed here are based on the facts (1) that God is actively involved in the life of the believer, and (2) that He will protect

His children. Therefore, trusting in His faithfulness and justice, we are to act like God, who "is kind to the ungrateful and wicked" (LUKE 16:25, NIV). Sometimes this truth, particularly in the area of interpersonal relationships, can be so difficult that the believer rebels against God. This is the subject of the next chapter.

Discussion Questions

In each of chapters 5–9, we will be revisiting your answer to the question "Where are you?" Please go back to your answer to that question, and examine it in light of this chapter.

1. Discuss how it is possible that a person could be carnal and yet please God.

2. This chapter says that one quality of growing spiritual maturity is the ability to handle "difficult" teaching. What does *difficult* mean in this context?

3. How are our relationships affected by whether we are walking in the flesh or in the Spirit?

4. Hebrews lists three things that a person can't do without. How do these relate to your answer to "Where are you?"

5. Has this chapter brought any questions to mind, or any thoughts you would like to discuss with the group?

6. Is there any issue you would like prayed for, or accountability in, over the course of this week?

7. Please note any other group members' answers that you would like to follow up on this week, either by praying for them or by making an encouraging contact.

FATHER WILLIAM STANDING ON HIS HEAD

"You are old, Father William,"
the young man said,
"And your hair has become very white;
And yet you incessantly stand on your head—
Do you think, at your age, it is right?'

"In my youth," Father William replied to his son,
"I feared it might injure the brain;
"But, now that I'm perfectly sure I have none,
Why, I do it again and again."

—*Wonderland*, ch. V, "Advice from a Caterpillar"

Chapter 8
Standing on Your Old White Head

ld salts like to tell the story of the young sailor learning to become a navigator. While at sea, the captain turned to him and said, "Please tell us where we are."

So the sailor picked up his instruments, made a complicated set of calculations, and studied the charts. After a while, he wrote down the coordinates of longitude and latitude and handed it to the captain. The captain studied it for a while, checked his charts, and said to the young sailor, "Are you completely certain that these are the right coordinates?"

"Yes, sir, I'm completely certain."

"There could be no conceivable mistake in your calculations?"

"Absolutely not, sir. I've done my very best."

"You know exactly where we are?"

"Yes, sir."

The captain said, "Well, then, I would suggest you put on your cold-weather gear, because according to your calculations, we are planted squarely atop Mount Rainier."

Have you ever met people like that: absolutely convinced they are right when you know they're wrong? I've found that no age group is completely free from such thinking, but those most often guilty of stubbornly misplaced conviction are children. The real problem arises when the adult body grows and the childish mind doesn't. In the physical world, this indicates a larger problem, such as with my Uncle

Teddy. What is truly sad is when those formerly on the path to maturity revert to being childish. In the physical world, this phenomenon is usually associated with advanced age. Unfortunately, in the spiritual realm, any person, at any time, can revert to childhood.

The author of Hebrews expresses frustration with his readers for this very reason:

> We have much to say about this, but it is hard to explain because you are slow to learn. In fact, though by this time you ought to be teachers, you need someone to teach you the elementary truths of God's word all over again. You need milk, not solid food! Anyone who lives on milk, being still an infant, is not acquainted with the teaching about righteousness. But solid food is for the mature, who by constant use have trained themselves to distinguish good from evil (HEB 5:11–14, NIV).

The author of Hebrews wants to go into a detailed explanation of a difficult subject: a comparison of Melchizedek and Christ (which he does in the following chapters). First, though, he warns his readers about the difficulty they will have in understanding this subject.

Now, there are many reasons why a topic could be difficult to understand. The difficulty could lie in the complexity of the subject, for example. Some things are just naturally complicated. Another difficulty could be that the instructor doesn't have an adequate grasp of the subject himself. I've found that if the professor doesn't thoroughly understand the subject, he will inevitably make up for his lack by making the topic more complicated than it needs to be. However, these aren't the reasons given in Hebrews.

Instead, these believers have become "slow to learn." This word in the original language means "sluggish" or "dull." It's used to describe a lazy and careless worker.[1] So, two ideas are expressed with this one word. First, it describes one who is careless because he doesn't put great importance upon the task, due either to a lack of energy or interest, or (more likely) both. Second, it describes someone who cannot learn because of his mental condition. A third idea is also expressed by the tense of the verb, which is translated well in the New American Standard Version. It isn't just that they were slow to learn, but "you have become dull of hearing" (Heb 5:11, NASB). They had entered into a state that didn't previously describe them.

As we've seen earlier, the ability to receive spiritual truth is directly related to one's reliance upon the Holy Spirit for discernment. The fact that the intended audience of Hebrews would find this teaching difficult indicates that they had moved backward in their spiritual walk so that they were again carnal.

This passage alone doesn't tell us why they moved backward. The larger context of Hebrews, however, does provide the answer. The author of this letter (I keep saying "the author" because we don't know his—or her—identity) is writing to believers who were undergoing tremendous persecution. At first they performed admirably:

> *Remember those earlier days after you had received the light, when you stood your ground in a great contest in the face of suffering. Sometimes you were publicly exposed to insult and persecution; at other times you stood side by side with those who were so treated. You sympathized with those in prison and joyfully accepted the confiscation of your property, because you knew that you yourselves had better and lasting possessions* (Heb 10:32–34, NIV).

Because the persecution had gone on for so long, though, some were being tempted to deny Christ and return to Judaism. Hence, this author spends the entire book of Hebrews presenting a tightly argued defense of the superiority of Christ over anything that Judaism had to offer with its Old Testament practices and rituals. However, that argument is interrupted from time to time with passages warning about the dangers of falling away. After those passages, the author picks up the argument again and continues teaching until he abruptly stops and gives another warning about falling away. This pattern continues throughout the book. For example, after spending the entire first chapter showing the superiority of Christ over the angels, he stops the argument and says:

> We must pay more careful attention, therefore, to what we have heard, so that we do not drift away. For if the message spoken by angels was binding, and every violation and disobedience received its just punishment, how shall we escape if we ignore such a great salvation? (HEB 2:1–3, NIV).

Drifting away is exactly the danger they were facing. In fact, the author uses more direct language just a page later: "See to it, brothers, that none of you has a sinful, unbelieving heart that turns away from the living God" (HEB 3:12, NIV). And therein lies the problem: Some of them had a "sinful, unbelieving heart"! They had become slow to learn because they had entered into a prolonged state of sin. As a result, they no longer had the spiritual maturity necessary to understand any truths of the Word except the most elementary. That's why the comparison of Melchizedek to Christ would be difficult for them to understand.

We might not realize it, but the longer we stay in a state of rebellion (for that's what sin really is), the more "dull of hearing" we become. Even those who have studied the Scriptures for years can become "slow to learn" if they don't move forward spiritually.

There are many ways to enter into a state of rebellion, but one common path opens when a believer is suddenly faced with a difficult—what he might consider impossible—choice and chooses to react in an ungodly manner. This usually happens when believers are convinced they've been wronged:

- "The Bible teaches that I should forgive, but how can I forgive that? You obviously don't understand what she did to me."

- "How can God command me to submit to him? You don't know what he's like!"

- "Okay, sure, I know that we're supposed to consider others better than ourselves, but c'mon, you can't just let people walk all over you."

- "How in the world am I to honor my father when all he's ever done is make my life difficult?"

Questions like these soon turn into willful rejection (that is, a refusal of the will to obey):

- "No, I don't believe it! God can't expect me to just forgive her and pretend nothing happened!"

- "I hear what you're saying, Pastor, but there isn't a woman alive who would put up with this!"

- "I refuse to believe that God would have me just be a doormat. There are limits to what a person can stand!"

- "If God had given me a father worthy of honor, I'd be pleased to oblige. But he didn't!"

The sad reality is that these people are actually able to discern good from evil. This is clear from the questions they ask. But because the commands of God feel so contrary to what their flesh desires, they actively choose against what they know to be right, justifying their decisions with their minds, all the while turning against God in open rebellion. When this takes place, spiritual growth stops. Our reliance upon the flesh, instead of the revealed will of God, in one area soon begins to spread to the rest of our lives. If we reject the truth God's Spirit has revealed, our ability to discern begins to vanish, because we no longer desire to listen to the Spirit. Every time we listen to the Spirit, we are reminded of our sin and are convicted to repent.

This is the spiritual principle at work: When we cease moving forward, we start moving backward. There is no such thing as standing still. Once we begin to drift backward, our sensitivity to the Holy Spirit begins to lessen, understanding the Bible becomes more difficult, and we slowly lose our discernment about right and wrong as we become increasingly like the world. This is just one more reason we should commit ourselves to a steady, consistent walk toward maturity.

We must remember that although we are like God in many ways (because we were created in His image and likeness), we can't reverse that idea and say that God is like us. He is completely above and beyond what we can know with our senses—so much so that if He hadn't chosen to reveal Himself to us, we would have no way of knowing that He even exists! That's why we shouldn't be surprised when He says, "'For my thoughts are not your thoughts, neither are your ways my ways,' declares the LORD. 'As the heavens are higher than the earth, so are my ways higher than your ways and my thoughts than your thoughts'" (Isa 55:8–9, NIV).

The believers addressed in Hebrews had previously been aware of this. Evidently, they had been born again for an extended time, and they had been taught sound doctrine, because "by this time" they ought to have been teachers (Heb 5:12). Thus, we know that these were long-standing, educated members of the church. At some point, though, they allowed sin to take hold of them.

We can't be certain, but it appears that their sin was entirely internal rather than external. In other words, it wasn't a sin that others could see right away, because it took place in the heart. It was the sin of not having faith, which led them to fear. Always remember, *without faith it is impossible to please God,* and the opposite of faith is fear. These believers had given way to a totally internal sin. Whether others can see it or not, sin is still sin, and like fire it destroys all it touches. This is the reason the author of Hebrews continually calls his readers back to faith.

The problem with these believers is that they didn't retain or use the truth they had been taught. As a result, they needed to be taught the "elementary truths of God's word all over again" (HEB 5:12, NIV). We might say that, even though they had once passed courses in advanced English literature and composition, they needed to go back and learn their ABCs again! They had moved backward from maturity to immaturity.

They had become like Old Father William, incessantly standing on his white head. At one point he was rightfully afraid of such a practice: "'In my youth,' Father William replied to his son,/'I feared it might injure the brain.'" Nevertheless, because he'd been at it so long, he was sure that it must be a harmless activity: "'But, now that I'm perfectly sure I have none,/Why, I do it again and again.'" After all, he no longer had a brain!

Some believers are like that. They've been in sin for so long that they are sure it's harmless. It could be some habitual sin, or it could be just a general laziness about the things of God. Whatever the reason or the rationale, they have settled into a lifestyle that relies on the flesh for their judgments about right and wrong. Hence, they, like the infants they have become, need "milk, not solid food."

I have often wondered what it would be like if God suddenly dressed us according to our spiritual maturity. How many of us would be in diapers? How many in toddler's clothes? How many old faces in the church would be sucking on a pacifier? How many of us would be dressed according to the age we should be by this time? That's a difficult question, isn't it?—and one that should make us all uneasy. Nevertheless, it is an important question that must be asked if we are to be honest with ourselves so we can walk toward maturity.

As discussed when we were formulating our definition of maturity, these elderly infants were "not acquainted with the teaching about righteousness." The original language uses a word meaning "unskilled" or "without experience."[2] Just as a child is without experience in so many things, so these children were without experience in what it means to be righteous. What a terrible indictment!

In contrast to the children without experience, there are the mature, "who because of practice have their senses trained to discern good and evil" (HEB 5:14, NASB).

When I first enlisted in the Navy, like all recruits, I enjoyed that wonderfully relaxing vacation they call "boot camp." Then, upon graduation, we were sent to various schools to learn skills necessary to do the jobs for which we enlisted. During this schooling, I and several others picked up the game of racquetball. We played nearly every day. At first, I was terrible, but through hard work and determination, and hours and hours in the gym, I worked my way up to almost mediocre. The hours spent in the gym trained my hand-eye coordination. I trained my muscles to move in a certain way. I practiced my serve repeatedly. I practiced to train my muscles so they would perform in the way I desired when called upon.

I still remember how to play. I remember some of the strategy. However, my years away from the gym were painfully evident the last time the music director of our church asked me if I wanted to play a game. I wasn't quite terrible, but I was close.

I mention this because it is exactly what the author of Hebrews is talking about in verse 14. The mature have reached that level because of "practice." They practiced choosing righteousness. The hours spent in practice "trained" their senses. The word translated "train" is actually the word from which we get our English word "gymnasium."[3] We have to practice in the gym of righteousness, so to speak, if we want to be able to distinguish good and evil.

It should be clear from this illustration that the training process occurs over time. Neither training nor maturity nor righteousness comes naturally or instantly; rather, these things must be diligently pursued. We need to undertake regular workouts to make progress, not make just a sporadic attempt now and then. We must constantly strive after righteousness if we are to train our senses—with the help of the Holy Spirit—to discern. It is this continued training in righteousness that moves the believer from infancy to maturity.

In the same way, if we stop going to the gym, we lose what abilities we previously possessed. When we become lax in our lives, when we believe the lie that this particular sin is really no big deal, when we think that we've trained enough, we walk away from the gym and back toward the diapers.

The one who can distinguish good from evil is the one who will not, in an unwary moment, follow his natural attraction toward doing the wrong thing. The one who lacks perception and discernment will find that his Christian service will always be partial and incomplete. He will find that petty bickering, laziness, or temptations of another sort will always get in the way.

Which direction are you headed? Are you moving toward maturity? Then don't give up! There is danger in giving up, because slowly, almost imperceptibly, you will begin to move backward in your spiritual life. Instead, stay in the gym! Keep at it! Give your training in spiritual maturity the same priority that an Olympic athlete gives to his daily workout. Continue practicing righteousness! Move on toward maturity!

Discussion Questions

In each of chapters 5–9, we will be revisiting your answer to the question "Where are you?" Please go back to your answer to that question, and examine it in light of this chapter.

1. Give instances that could cause a believer to go backward in spiritual growth. What reasons might he use to justify this to himself?

2. Are you facing any situations in your life where God's instructions in Scripture are contrary to what seems to be a reasonable response? Or have you in the past? Write about how you will or did handle this.

3. Our training in righteousness is likened to the training our bodies receive when practicing for a specific sport. How do we "build up our muscles" in righteousness? Do you have something in mind that might build these muscles in your life this week?

4. What is the result if we allow our growth to come to a standstill?

5. Has this chapter brought any questions to mind, or any thoughts you would like to discuss with the group?

6. Is there any issue you would like prayed for, or accountability in, over the course of this week?

7. Please note any other group members' answers that you would like to follow up on this week, either by praying for them or by making an encouraging contact.

ALICE AND THE WHITE QUEEN

*You needn't say 'exactly,'" the Queen remarked;
"I can believe it without that. Now I'll give* YOU
*something to believe. I'm just one hundred and one,
five months and a day."*

"I can't believe THAT!" *said Alice.*

*"Can't you?" the Queen said in a pitying tone. "Try
again: draw a long breath, and shut your eyes."*

*Alice laughed. "There's no use trying," she said:
"one* CAN'T *believe impossible things."*

*"I daresay you haven't had much practice," said the
Queen. "When I was your age, I always did it for
half-an-hour a day. Why, sometimes I've believed
as many as six impossible things before breakfast."*

—*Looking-Glass*, ch. V, "Wool and Water"

Chapter 9
Believing the Impossible

There are two great spiritual transformations that may occur in a person's life. The first is the change from the natural man to the carnal man. The second is the change from the carnal man to the spiritual man. The first change is instantaneous when a sinner places his faith in Jesus Christ and His finished work on the cross. The second is gradual and occurs as the believer becomes rightly oriented toward the Spirit.

The title of this chapter, "Believing the Impossible," is only a partially accurate description of the spiritual man. This is because the first transformation, moving from the natural man to the carnal man, requires a person to believe the impossible, or, at the very least, the unseen. Simply put, it requires faith.

Only by faith can a person trust that God became man in the person of Jesus Christ; that somehow, through a miraculous birth, He was like us in His humanity, but unlike us in that He had no sin. How can that be possible?

Even more incredibly, though He was without sin, the Lord Jesus was able, in some mysterious fashion, to take on the sins of the whole world and pay the penalty we owe, satisfying God's wrath completely. How can one man take another's guilt? Not only that, but He also gave us His righteousness, so that nothing else had to be done for sinful man to have eternal fellowship with God.

Only by faith can a believer profess, with complete earnestness, the truthfulness of such an incredible story. Believing that God is present everywhere at once, and yet in some special way His Spirit takes up residence within us and gives us new spiritual life that we didn't possess previously—this is unfeasible to us. We have no prior example of such spiritual wonders upon which to draw. These things must be impossible, because we can't imagine what we haven't already experienced.

The Christian faith is filled with "impossibilities" that are nevertheless real and true. There are realities that suspend or transcend the laws of nature as we understand them through physical investigation (the eye, the ear, the mind), but have been revealed to us by supernatural means. Thus, believing the impossible is part and parcel of the Christian faith.

What separates the carnal man from the spiritual man is his level of ability (which is related to his willingness) to receive what the Spirit reveals. This revelation goes beyond the initial leading to salvation and reaches into every area of our lives. The spiritual man will act in faith while the carnal man relies heavily on the flesh.

Review of 1 Corinthians 2:9–3:4

Perhaps the best way to illustrate this is to go back through the passage we have been studying and see the progression of events listed there. The following quotation is taken from the New American Standard Version.

> [B]ut just as it is written, "Things which eye has not seen and ear has not heard, And which have not entered the heart of man, All that God has prepared for those who love Him." For to us God revealed them through the Spirit; for the Spirit searches all things, even the depths of God. For who among men knows

the thoughts of a man except the spirit of the man, which is in him? Even so the thoughts of God no one knows except the Spirit of God. Now we have received, not the spirit of the world, but the Spirit who is from God, that we might know the things freely given to us by God, which things we also speak, not in words taught by human wisdom, but in those taught by the Spirit, combining spiritual thoughts with spiritual words. But a natural man does not accept the things of the Spirit of God; for they are foolishness to him, and he cannot understand them, because they are spiritually appraised. But he who is spiritual appraises all things, yet he himself is appraised by no man. For who has known the mind of the Lord, that he should instruct Him? But we have the mind of Christ.

And I, brethren, could not speak to you as to spiritual men, but as to men of flesh, as to babes in Christ. I gave you milk to drink, not solid food; for you were not yet able to receive it. Indeed, even now you are not yet able, for you are still fleshly. For since there is jealousy and strife among you, are you not fleshly, and are you not walking like mere men? For when one says, "I am of Paul," and another, "I am of Apollos," are you not mere men?

We can draw several truths from this:

- God has given us revelation that surpasses what we obtain through our senses and reason. This revelation comes from the Spirit of God and is available only through Him (1 COR 2:9–10).

- This revelation concerns all things, even those things so remote that they reach the depths of who God is. Yet this revelation can be known through the Spirit because the Spirit is God and has revealed it to us (1 COR 2:10).

- Believers have received the Spirit so that they may access this knowledge—"[t]hat we might know" (1 Cor 2:12). This knowledge, of course, is not the final word on all that the Spirit accomplishes in the life of the believer. It is listed as a reason here, however, because it helps Paul explain the relationship between the Spirit and the Spirit's revelation in the believer's life.

- This revelation is communicated, not through visions or voices, but through words. These words accurately communicate the thoughts of the Spirit (1 Cor 2:13). Though this is not expressly stated in the text, these words are found in the Bible. The Bible is "God-breathed" and "is useful for teaching, rebuking, correcting and training in righteousness, so that the man of God may be thoroughly equipped for every good work" (2 Tim 3:16–17, NIV). This indicates that becoming mature (having the ability to discern good from evil) is directly related to one's ability to understand the Bible, as it is useful for training the believer in righteousness.

- The natural man will not accept God's revelation in the Bible as true, because he lacks the capacity to verify its truthfulness. He depends on his senses (eye has not seen, ear has not heard) and reason (has not entered into the heart of man) to determine what he will accept as true. Even though spiritual truths are available as words on a page to which he has access, these truths can be verified only by the Spirit of God, to Whom the natural man does not have access (1 Cor 2:14). Therefore, he will never accept God's revelation in the Bible as truth. The further God's revelation is removed from his natural abilities, the more strenuously he will reject it.

- The carnal man is born again and, therefore, has access to the truths that God's Spirit reveals. His tendency to rely on the flesh, however, hinders his ability to accept as true those things that stray too far from what he can verify through his senses and reason. His reliance upon fleshly wisdom affects his behavior in a negative way, so he is prone to jealousy and strife, just like the natural man (1 Cor 3:1–4). In fact, he is prone to all the behaviors that originate in the flesh: "Now the deeds of the flesh are evident, which are: immorality, impurity, sensuality, idolatry, sorcery, enmities, strife, jealousy, outbursts of anger, disputes, dissensions, factions, envying, drunkenness, carousing, and things like these" (Gal 5:19–21, nasb). He is described as a baby in Christ, which indicates that all believers begin as carnal. The problem arises when the believer refuses to grow and remains in that carnal state long after he should have begun to move on to maturity (you are still fleshly) (1 Cor 3:3).

- The spiritual man appraises or makes judgments about all things. Just like the natural man, he has access to that limited body of knowledge that is available to the senses and reason. Yet, because of his relationship with the Spirit, there is no limit on his ability to receive divine revelation. He is able to distinguish good from evil because he possesses the mind of Christ (1 Cor 2:15–16).

The spiritual man is also a mystery to those who aren't spiritual. When others view the life of the spiritual man, it will make no sense to them (1 Cor 2:15). This is perfectly in keeping with what we have seen so far. The natural man judges all things by his senses and reason, so he is unable to understand any motivation that originates from the spiritual realm. The carnal man still largely depends on the flesh for his understanding. Thus, when the spiritual man strays too far, in action and motivation, from what the flesh finds reasonable, the carnal man shakes his head in bewilderment or worse. He dismisses his mature brother's faith by responding with, "Well, yeah, but you've got to be practical."

I have never seen it fail to happen. When a spiritual believer takes a step of faith to accomplish something that God has laid upon his heart, he will receive opposition, both from within the church and from without. Criticism from those outside the faith is often easier to take, because we really don't expect them to understand. When the resistance comes from what should be the "household of faith," however, it can be demoralizing beyond description. I've witnessed this time and time again in other believers and have experienced it personally.

When I got out of the Navy, I began working as a television engineer at a small station in Kansas City. At first, I thought the job would work out, because I was promised training on the various pieces of equipment that were assigned to me, even though I had never worked in this area of electronics before. The promised training, however, never materialized. I struggled to make sense of the manuals and worked as best I could, but I never could seem to do enough.

It didn't take long before I loathed my job. I didn't just dislike it, I *hated* it. I despised getting up every morning and going to work. When I came home at night, I was irritable and short-tempered from the day's frustrations. When I laid my head on the pillow, all I could think of was that I had to do it all over again the next day. Even on Friday nights, with a weekend ahead of me, I couldn't escape the dread of my employment, because I knew what awaited me Monday morning. I was miserable, and that of course made me miserable to live with.

One day, when I was expressing my frustration to a friend in another department, he asked me a question. He said, "Bruce, if you could do whatever you wanted for the rest of your life, what would you do?"

"That's easy," I replied, "I'd preach the Gospel!"

Then came the life-changing question: "Then why aren't you doing that?"

I was speechless. I had no answer. A few days later, I twisted my knee and was laid up for several days. All I could do was sit and think. That question kept running through my mind. As I thought and prayed for those few days, I finally came to a conclusion. "Lord," I prayed, "if you provide the money, I'll go back to school and go into the ministry."

God provided a grant to pay for my schooling, so I made plans to make good on my promise. Those plans included quitting my job and going to work part-time for less than half per hour of what I was currently making. I still had the same mortgage, the same bills, and the same obligations, but I decided that God was true to His word when He said, "And my God will meet all your needs according to his glorious riches in Christ Jesus" (PHIL 4:19, NIV). This, of course, is when the trouble began.

People who genuinely cared about my wife and me began asking questions. "How will you support your family?" "Work and school? What about time with your children?" "How do you really know this is God's will? How do you know it's not just you trying to escape a job you hate?"

All my answers to these questions assumed four fundamental truths:

1. God communicates with His people in a way they can understand.

2. God has a will for the individual and disobedience to that will is sin.

3. When God calls us to do something, He gives us the abilities and resources to accomplish His will. This is true whether or not we can see how He will provide.

4. Everything that God calls us to do requires faith. God requires us to act upon what is not seen, because "without faith it is impossible to please God."

Because those asking such questions of my wife and me were believers, I assumed that they would understand when I said, "Well, I don't know all the answers, but I believe this is what God is calling me to do. As for providing for our needs, I trust that God will do as He promised when I'm being obedient to Him."

I assumed wrong.

The questions about my decision soon turned into accusations concerning my judgment. "You're being irresponsible." "You can't just hope that everything will work out somehow." "Don't you realize that you're putting your family at risk?" And then there was the memorable encounter that began with, "What are you going to do when all this blows up in your face?"

You see, the problem revolved around the fact that I was willing to act on what was not seen, and no one else—*no one* else, except my wife—could understand that. She stood by my side and understood. To everyone else, however, I was a mystery. The guy who had been so responsible in the past had just lost it, as far as they were concerned.

I should quickly add that the following year, all the bills were paid, although to this day I still don't know how. People would anonymously leave bags of groceries in the back of our car. Checks came in the mail from unexpected sources. Another time there was a substantial bank error in our favor. When my wife called the bank to correct the error, they insisted that their records were correct. They had made a mistake and owed us money! (How often does that happen?) Once we received a sizable check from a utility cooperative that we had belonged to years before. Evidently, their records showed that we had been substantially overcharged, and they returned the money.

We never saw any of these provisions coming. They just appeared. Nevertheless, even remembering all these details, I haven't any idea how the bills were paid and the family was fed. You can't add it up on a calculator—but it happened just the same. God provided for all our needs, not according to the finite resources of our household, but according to His glorious riches in Christ Jesus, just as He said He would.

Eventually, I obtained a schedule that allowed me to go to school at night and work during the day. So great was His goodness to me, God provided me with a job that was interesting, sometimes fun, and that allowed me to shine. And just as when the children of Israel crossed into the promised land and ate of its food (JOSH 5:12), when I received employment that enabled me to pay my own way, the manna no longer came.

Now, why have I given this testimony? It is meant to illustrate the truth of 1 CORINTHIANS 2:15. The man who acts in faith (which by definition means acting in a way that assumes God's promises are true, even when the means are unseen) will inevitably face opposition, even from those in the family of God. Those who walk by what is unseen will never be understood by those who walk primarily by what is seen.

May I urge you to take God at His word? I admit it's scary if you've never done it before. Few will understand and many will accuse. However, if you are convinced, by providence, by confirmation from the Word, by the prompting of the Spirit in your life that God would have you step out in faith, you will find, in the end, that you will sing with the prophet Isaiah:

> O LORD, *you are my God; I will exalt you and praise your name, for in perfect faithfulness you have done marvelous things, things planned long ago* (ISA 25:1, NIV).

Discussion Questions

1. In each of chapters 5–9, we revisited your answer to the question "Where are you?" Now that we've completed this section of the book, please rewrite your answer to that question, and compare it to your original answer.

2. This chapter begins by discussing the two great transformations that may occur in a person's life: from natural to carnal man, and from carnal to spiritual. Has your life been transformed in either, or both, of these two ways? Please share your experiences.

3. Why is it that the carnal man is so often baffled by the choices made by the spiritual man?

4. Four points were made regarding fundamental truths about God's will for our lives. Copy them onto a 3 × 5 card that you can tuck into your Bible and reference as needed.

5. Has this chapter brought any questions to mind, or any thoughts you would like to discuss with the group?

6. Is there any issue you would like prayed for, or accountability in, over the course of this week?

7. Please note any other group members' answers that you would like to follow up on this week, either by praying for them or by making an encouraging contact.

Living in Canaan Part Four

On the day of the reorganization, work was nearly impossible amid the chaos of maintenance workers taking and moving desks, dismantling some cubicles and erecting others, phone and data technicians crawling under the desks lucky enough to be untouched, and staff bustling about with cardboard boxes. In the midst of the confusion, Steve strode up to Christine's desk and announced, "You need to hear this."

Christine looked up and flashed him a smile that was not returned.

"I've found out what happened," he whispered through clenched teeth. "It's unbelievable. I'm so mad I could just spit."

"Okay, simmer down, big guy," she said, still forcing a smile. What she wanted most at that moment was a friend, not more drama. "Getting mad doesn't help. You know that."

"You say that now, but wait till you hear what I've got to tell you."

"Do I have to?" sighed Christine as she turned back to her desk and rested her forehead in her hands. Just then a large crash came from the other end of the office. Steve jerked his head in that direction, but Christine didn't move. "Don't tell me you've been a party to all these rumors."

Turning back to her, he repeated, "Christine, you need to hear this." The story spilled out, rapidly and forcefully.

Just as she suspected, her failure to receive the promotion had been engineered by Ben. He had made excuses to go more often to shipping when he found he could get Frank's ear. He had planted lies and half-truths about her with Frank, and had told bawdy stories with plenty of innuendo to the guys on the loading dock. He knew Frank couldn't help but overhear the way they talked about Christine. Anything Ben could do to undermine her work and her character, he did.

Throughout this recitation, Christine glanced about the room, as if suddenly interested in what was going on around her. She knew it was a futile attempt to escape the horrid details, but she couldn't help it. Steve's intense face was the one place she couldn't look. So, like a hunted animal, anything that moved caught her attention as her eyes darted around.

"Oh, sure, he made the pretense of sticking up for you," Steve said, finally winding down, "but always in such a way as to make you look as bad as possible."

"You shouldn't be listening to all these rumors, Steve, you know that!" Christine suddenly turned back to her desk and began thumbing through her paperwork, making a pretense of working, hoping he would take the hint and leave. But Steve wouldn't let it go.

"Rumors! Christine, I heard some of it with my own ears! Just this morning, I was on my way to the break room. Just before I reached the door, I heard his voice," he said, jerking his thumb in the direction of their new supervisor's office. "So I stopped just short of the door and listened. You know what he said? He—"

"No, I don't know what he said, and I don't *want* to know what he said!" Christine snapped.

Steve leaned in with his eyes narrowed and his teeth clenched. "He said that the reason you never date anyone was probably because of your 'sexual orientation,'" he hissed, using his fingers to make quote marks in the air, "and that this was probably the reason your husband dumped you!"

Steve fixed an angry stare on Ben, who happened by just then, making no effort to conceal his hostility. Ben caught the glance and then quickened his pace to escape the withering glare.

"What a gutless, cowardly thing to do." Steve spat out the words, "That sonofa . . . " Steve stopped himself and looked at the floor, his fists clenched. Glaring holes in the floor, he growled through still-clenched teeth, "I'd love to catch that guy outside and show him what being a man is really about!"

By this time, Christine's eyes were brimming with tears. She was glad that her desk was relatively secluded and that most of her co-workers were currently involved in a project setting up the other side of the office. She picked at some imaginary lint on her sleeve. Taking off her glasses and making a half-hearted attempt to clean them with the tissue she had been shredding, her words came out uneven and broken.

"Be still before the LORD and wait patiently for him," she recited slowly, her breathing labored. "Steve," she said, looking up, tears now streaming down her face. Steve was still staring at the floor, but his hands unclenched. "Steve," she whispered again, waiting until his eyes met hers, "do not fret when men succeed in their ways, when they carry out their . . . " here she swallowed hard, "wicked schemes."

"What?" Steve murmured. The flare of his nostrils and the creases around his eyes disappeared. They were replaced by a furrow between his eyebrows.

Her tears continued to flow, but she refused to divert her gaze. Unlike before, now she could look nowhere else. "Refrain from anger and turn from wrath; do not fret, it leads only to evil. For evil men—" Steve tried softly to interrupt, but Christine shot up her hand, stopping him. "For evil men will be cut off," she said, her voice still shaky but now more resolute, "but those who hope in the LORD will inherit the land." She picked up her purse and stood up. Her self-control nearly exhausted, she pushed past Steve, now speechless, and fled to her car. She locked the doors, put her head on the steering wheel, and sobbed, all the while crying out to the Lord in utter desperation.

BE STILL BEFORE THE LORD AND

WAIT PATIENTLY FOR HIM; DO NOT

FRET WHEN MEN SUCCEED IN

THEIR WAYS, WHEN THEY CARRY

OUT THEIR WICKED SCHEMES.

REFRAIN FROM ANGER AND TURN

FROM WRATH; DO NOT FRET—IT

LEADS ONLY TO EVIL.

FOR EVIL MEN WILL BE CUT OFF,

BUT THOSE WHO HOPE IN THE LORD

WILL INHERIT THE LAND.

PSALM 37:7–9, NIV

A GRIN WITHOUT A CAT

*Would you tell me, please, which way I ought
to walk from here?"*

*"That depends a good deal on where you want
to get to," said the Cat.*

"I don't much care where" said Alice.

*"Then it doesn't matter which way you walk,"
said the Cat.*

"—so long as I get SOMEWHERE*," Alice added
as an explanation.*

*"Oh, you're sure to do that," said the Cat,
"if you only walk long enough."*

—*Wonderland*, ch. VI, "Pig and Pepper"

Chapter 10
Where Do You Want to Go?

As we've seen earlier, if you don't care about the destination, it doesn't matter which way you head. But, as the Cheshire Cat points out in an impeccable bit of logic, you're bound to get somewhere "if you only walk long enough." Alice's problem is that she doesn't know enough about the possible destinations to make an informed decision. In her case, it didn't really matter, as insanity awaited in either direction. Our lives, in contrast, are different.

In my years as a pastor, I've discovered that most counseling sessions fall into one of four categories:

1. Please explain this passage of Scripture.
2. I've already made up my mind about what I'm planning to do, but I want you to validate my decision. If you don't, I'll
   a. Ignore you
   b. Get mad at you
   c. Tell you why you don't really understand
   d. Accuse you of being uncaring
   e. Explain to you the obvious truth that a person needs to live in the "real world" (always undefined)
   f. All of the above

(For those who are interested, the answer most often is "all of the above." I can also state with certainty that many reading these words could give first-person testimony to this truth. Have you ever been asked for advice and then actually given some? Then you know what I'm talking about.)

3. I'm in deep trouble because of my own sinfulness, and I need you to bail me out. (That last phrase is usually metaphorical, but not always.)

4. I am in the midst of a difficult situation, and I need help in knowing the right thing to do.

This last scenario most closely resembles Alice's dilemma: several different paths are available, and we need help determining which one is best. By "best" I mean the one that is most pleasing to God, because all His ways are right and just and He always chooses what brings Him the most glory—which, simultaneously, brings the most benefit to His people.

Most of us face this sort of problem at one time or another: deciding what is the right thing to do in a particular situation. Recently I received an email that illustrates this frustration perfectly. A young married woman asked my counsel concerning her relationship with her father. Here are the facts as she related them to me:

> My dad became a believer when I was pregnant with my first child. We lived in the same area at the time and he would go to church with us on Sundays. He knows the spiritual basics. After we had to move away (due to a job transfer), my dad stopped going to church.
>
> Shortly after my mom passed away, my dad started dating a woman to whom he had been married before my mom. There were a lot of red flags right from the start, but my dad refused to acknowledge them. After a short period of dating, they moved in together.
>
> The hardest part is how much my dad has changed. My "old" dad was the most generous person I have ever met. He never

had much but what he had he would give to anyone who needed it. He was always very honest, and I knew I could trust him. He was very loving and always enjoyed being with his family (especially when his grandkids were born!). I was the biggest "daddy's girl" there ever was.

My "new" dad (since living with this other woman) is very different. Most of the time I talk to him, I can catch him in at least one lie. He has become very selfish, only doing what is best for him. Recently his sister lost her house in a natural disaster and instead of showing sympathy, all he could say was that "it was no loss because she only lived in a trailer, and it was an old one at that." The kids and I visited for a week, and he was "too busy" to see us until Thursday. And the list goes on.

When confronted with his sin, he tells me "It's OK, because I ask God every day to forgive me." He tells me he is completely at peace with God, which I know can't possibly be true. But he has convinced himself that God just wants him to be happy and that it doesn't matter what he does. He has told me that his new partner makes him grow as a Christian "because we pray together."

A few months ago, they broke up for a while. My dad worked himself into a frenzy and decided to blame their break-up on me. He told me that he was ashamed I was his daughter and that I was "wrapped up in the devil." He also told me that because I was such a horrible person, God was going to punish me in a severe way, and that God didn't live inside me. He also said he no longer wanted to have a relationship with me at all. Thankfully, and only by the Holy Spirit, I was able to just keep my mouth shut and not blow up in anger! I know that all these things aren't true, but at the same time it was (is) devastating to hear from someone you love. Several weeks later, they got back together, and he tried to talk his way out of all that he had said (without apologizing or admitting he was wrong).

After almost a year and a half of praying and searching the Scriptures, there are a lot of times when I just don't know what to do or how to feel. What does the Lord want me to do? Should I continue to keep reaching out to him, just so that he knows I love him no matter what? Do I take a stand for what is right, and not have anything to do with him? What do I tell my kids when they ask why Grandpa never wants to see them or spend time with them or talk to them? Or when they notice things that have changed with him? How do I help him see that he has changed and needs to get back on the right path? My brother is not a believer so while he agrees with me that this woman is not good for our Dad, he doesn't see the problem with their lifestyle. But I know that the way that I react could have an impact on my brother.

So I guess my question is this: what do you do when you are trying to grow in the day-to-day choices, but then you get sideswiped with something huge, and all of a sudden you don't know what is the right thing to do, when it's not just a week long trial, but an ongoing trial? Why don't I know the right thing to do? Is it because I have yet to learn it, or is it because of something I am doing wrong, or is the answer just having to go day by day on faith and trust that one day the Lord will make everything right?

That's what life is like: difficult situations, hurtful relationships, ongoing trials, unanswered questions. It's been said that every person is either entering into a trial, in the midst of a trial, or exiting a trial. It doesn't take long for something to pop into your mind when the word *trial* is mentioned, does it?

Job was right on the money when he said, "Yet man is born to trouble as surely as sparks fly upward" (JOB 5:7). Nevertheless, it's good to remember another "5:7" that acts as a companion verse to this one: "Cast all your anxiety on Him because He cares for you" (1 PET 5:7).

The question, "What is the right thing to do?" isn't limited, however, to times of trial. As we walk through life, we are constantly confronted with choices. Sometimes the correct course of action is obvious, such as not lying, not stealing, not committing adultery, and so on. But what of those other times? More often than not, the "right thing" isn't as obvious as we think. Choosing the right thing, or at least cultivating the ability to recognize the most God-honoring choice, is what we need to develop.

Definition of Spiritual Maturity

At this point, it might be a good idea for us to formally define *maturity,* as it is directly related to the topic at hand. We've been using the word, but what does it really mean? Fortunately, the Bible gives us the definition in HEBREWS 5:11–14 (NIV):

> *We have much to say about this, but it is hard to explain because you are slow to learn. In fact, though by this time you ought to be teachers, you need someone to teach you the elementary truths of God's word all over again. You need milk, not solid food! Anyone who lives on milk, being still an infant, is not acquainted with the teaching about righteousness. But solid food is for the mature, who by constant use have trained themselves to distinguish good from evil.*

This introduces several important contrasts:

- Between teachers and those who need to be taught.
- Between milk and meat.
- Between an infant and a mature adult.

To get a complete picture of what maturity really is, we must consider these contrasts and draw the appropriate conclusions.

Teachers and Those Needing to Be Taught

One of the primary characteristics of the mature believer is that he is able to teach and no longer needs to be taught. Now, we must understand exactly what that statement does and doesn't mean. It doesn't mean that the mature believer knows everything about the Bible, that he doesn't need to study, that he can't be stumped on "Jeopardy" in the Bible category. What it *does* mean is that he is able to read the Bible and understand the practical implications of Scripture without the help of others. We might say that the mature believer is able to feed himself. In contrast, the immature person cannot understand the practical ramifications of the Bible without the help of others.

Not only can the mature man feed himself, he can also feed others. In other words, he is able to accurately articulate what he knows so that others benefit. When I taught in Bible College, I used to drive my students crazy at this point. I would ask for a definition of a word or the meaning of a sentence, and inevitably someone, after flailing about for a minute or two, would answer in frustration, "I know what it means, I just can't put it into words." I would respond, "If you can't put it into words, you don't know what it means." (Insert heavy sighs and severe eye-rolling here.) Despite my students' frustrated assertions to the contrary, true understanding includes the ability to communicate to others.

Of course, the ability to teach others presupposes that you have attained a certain level of knowledge. The mature believer is not ignorant of the Bible. Quite the opposite: he is a student of the Word because this is the primary means by which God has chosen to reveal Himself to us. It is through "words taught by the Spirit, expressing spiritual truths in spiritual words" (1 COR 2:13, NIV) that God teaches us. These words are found in the Bible. Therefore, the mature believer knows the Bible well enough to apply it to his own life and teach its truths to others.

Milk and Meat

This distinction is commonly misunderstood. We tend to think of some doctrines, such as the Trinity, the relationship between the biblical covenants, or Bible prophecy, as "meat" doctrines. Other doctrines—the "milk" doctrines—are easier, such as salvation or prayer. Therefore, if you are only interested in the "simple" doctrines like salvation, you are living on milk. When you dig deep into the intricacies of biblical prophecy, you are eating meat.

This conception is completely false. The difference between "milk" and "meat" is not which doctrine is being discussed, but rather the depth to which a person can go within that doctrine. Sure, there are some "milk" elements to salvation. If that weren't so, there would be no nourishment for the newborn child of God. But there are "milk" elements to biblical prophecy as well. The fact that Jesus is coming again is within easy reach of every child of God. In the same way, there are "meat" elements to salvation, such as election or propitiation. The doctrine of future things contains "meat" as well, such as understanding Daniel's 70th week (DAN 9:24–27) or the meaning of the rituals and sacrifices in the Millennial Temple (EZEK 40–48).

We must get rid of the idea that some doctrines, by themselves, belong only to babies and others only to the mature. With regard to spiritual maturity, it is the depth that one may reach in these doctrines, not the doctrines themselves, that is at issue. The mature believer will venture beyond a mere surface understanding and delve deep into God's word, understanding those things that are more difficult to understand or accept.

Infant and Mature

The infant is described as one who is "not acquainted with the teaching about righteousness" (HEB 5:13, NIV). The original language uses a word meaning "unskilled" or "without experience."[1] Just as a child is without experience in so many things, so the spiritual infant is without experience in what it means to be righteous. In other words, the infant doesn't understand, in practical terms, what it means to live righteously on a day-to-day basis. This goes beyond the fact that none of us consistently live up to what we already know. Instead, this is speaking about a limitation in actually understanding, in real-life situations, what righteousness looks like.

In contrast, mature believers have " by constant use . . . trained themselves to distinguish good from evil" (HEB 5:14, NIV). Notice that the primary difference between the infant and the mature is the ability to distinguish, in practical terms, what is right and wrong in a given situation. The mature believer's ability, however, doesn't come automatically as he gets older. Instead, this skill is learned through practice. By habitually choosing the right instead of the wrong, one learns the difference between the two.

As we shall see, this crucially important ability is not something we can acquire on our own. We do not, on our own, have access to the information needed to distinguish between good and evil. The wisest man who ever lived understood this. When God offered to give King Solomon whatever he wanted, recognizing his own limitations, he made a wise request: "give your servant a discerning heart to govern your people and to distinguish between right and wrong" (1 KINGS 3:9, NIV). Solomon recognized that merely possessing the written Word of God wasn't enough. He needed divine help to understand it. In the same way, we require supernatural help to distinguish good from evil so we can apply God's Word accurately in everyday life.

With these distinctions in mind, we are ready to formulate a definition of spiritual maturity.

> **Definition:** The spiritually mature are those who, through the power of the Holy Spirit, both understand God's Word well enough and have consistently put its truths into practice long enough that they are capable of distinguishing good from evil in practical circumstances and are competent in teaching others to do the same.

Please notice that there is no promise of sinless perfection in this definition. The mature believer still sins—but he doesn't remain in his sin for an extended period of time. He is quick to confess his sins and be restored to fellowship. His life is characterized, for the most part, as being filled with the Spirit, not being controlled by the flesh.

Now the problem is that, while some people readily admit they don't know the right thing to do in a given situation, most people think they know the difference between good and evil. Regardless of a person's spiritual condition, each man takes the information he has and makes a judgment about right and wrong in a given situation. Of course, sometimes we choose to do what is wrong. Often we protest that, even though we may choose to do wrong, the fact that we *know* it's wrong shows our ability to distinguish between right and wrong. Yet this clearly isn't the case. As we will see, the source of the information on which a person relies, when making choices that require distinguishing good from evil, indicates the maturity level of that individual.

At this point, you might wonder what difference it would make if the young woman who wrote the email set out earlier didn't bother herself about what was right and wrong in this situation. After all, her father has misused her, betrayed her confidence, broken faith with her children, and verbally abused her, all without apology or any evidence of remorse. Why shouldn't she just give back to him what he's got coming? Okay, it would displease God, but this is just one area of her life. It's not like she's committing any big sin. Can't she be godly in the other areas of her life and just ask forgiveness when she treats her father like he deserves?

Are there any long-lasting consequences of sustained disobedience in a believer's life, even if that disobedience relates to just one area? In the same vein, are there any long-lasting benefits to enduring the struggles associated with doing the right thing? Forget about eternity for a moment. What about in the here-and-now, in the "real world"? That is the question addressed in the next chapter.

Discussion Questions

In each of chapters 10–13, we will be revisiting your answer to the question: "Where do you want to go?" Please look back at your answer to that question and examine it in light of this chapter.

1. One of the qualities of the spiritually mature person is that he is able to teach and no longer needs to be taught. Are you able to competently articulate what you believe? Please write out how you would explain the foundational truths of the Gospel to another who was unfamiliar with your faith.

2. How is spiritual maturity different from sinlessness?

3. Has this chapter brought any questions to mind, or any thoughts you would like to discuss with the group?

4. Is there any issue you would like prayed for, or accountability in, over the course of this week?

5. Please note any other group members' answers that you would like to follow up on this week, either by praying for them or by making an encouraging contact.

THE MARCH HARE AND THE MAD HATTER
DUNK THE DORMOUSE

Alice felt that this could not be denied, so she tried another question.

"What sort of people live about here?"

"In THAT *direction," the Cat said, waving its right paw round, "lives a Hatter; and in* THAT *direction," waving the other paw, "lives a March Hare. Visit either you like; they're both mad."*

—Wonderland, ch. VI, "Pig and Pepper"

Chapter 11
Identifying the Destinations

s the Cheshire Cat observed, you're sure to get *somewhere* if you walk long enough. If you view our journey toward maturity as a road upon which we walk, you may observe five truths about this road:

1. Because this is a spiritual road, only those who have been born again walk on it. Those who are still lost in their sins and in rebellion against God do not tread this path. This road is for believers only.

2. This spiritual road is contained entirely in time. The direction we walk on this road affects eternity, but the road itself, and the destinations on it, refer to this life, the here-and-now, our existence this side of the grave.

3. Like the road Alice was walking, this road has a destination at each end. At one end is immaturity, at the other is maturity. So, if you are heading in one direction, you must turn 180 degrees and start walking in the opposite direction if you want to change your destination. You can't be heading toward both destinations at the same time. To state it more bluntly, if you harbor unrepentant sin in just one area of your life, you cannot be walking toward maturity at the same time.

4. We begin our walk at one end of the road. It is God's desire that we walk to the other end in this life.

5. If we walk in one direction long enough, we will reach the end of the road and make it our home, either to our great good or to our pathetic distress.

Although these five truths can be found throughout the book of Hebrews, one passage in particular illustrates these truths clearly: HEBREWS 3:7–4:13. HEBREWS 3:7–19 teaches that sustained rebellion results in God's judgment upon the believer so that he is condemned to remain immature. HEBREWS 4:1–13 encourages us, in that obedience to God results in a "Sabbath-rest." We'll look at these two passages in detail in the next two chapters. In the meantime, the question that begs to be answered is, "What is that promised Sabbath-rest?"

> *There remains, then, a Sabbath-rest for the people of God; for anyone who enters God's rest also rests from his own work, just as God did from His. Let us, therefore, make every effort to enter that rest, so that no one will fall by following their example of disobedience* (HEB 4:9–11, NIV).

Some have suggested that this rest refers to eternal rest or salvation. Those who hold this position maintain that the author of Hebrews is writing to a group where all profess to be believers, but which actually contains a mixture of some who believe and some who do not. Therefore, the intent of the passage is to motivate those who belong to the visible local church to ensure that they are in fact saved. One way to do this is to see if they continue in belief.

Unfortunately for these interpreters, there is simply no evidence that the author of Hebrews ever addressed unbelievers. Quite the contrary: there is an abundance of evidence that he is addressing only those who are truly born again. A quick survey of the book makes this very plain.

2:1–3   The author warns about "ignoring," not rejecting, the salvation that was "confirmed to us."

3:1   The author calls his readers "holy brothers, who share in the heavenly calling." Only believers are "holy brothers."

4:14   The author includes himself with his readers by using the pronoun "we" and states that both he and his readers "have a great high priest who has gone through the heavens, Jesus the Son of God." Jesus is not the great high priest to any but the saved.

4:16   The recipients of this letter are urged to approach the throne of grace with confidence. How could a lost person do that?

5:12–13   Even though the readers of this letter are immature, they had been saved long enough to have been teachers. True, they still needed milk! They might have remained babies, but they had been born again.

6:4–5   Readers are described as "those who have once been enlightened, who have tasted the heavenly gift, who have shared in the Holy Spirit, who have tasted the goodness of the word of God and the powers of the coming age." Although it is possible to interpret some of these phrases as describing merely professing, but not real, believers, only those who have been born again have shared in the Holy Spirit and have tasted the heavenly gift. This could not be said of unbelievers.

6:9   Their works are described as "things that accompany salvation."

7:26–8:1 Again Jesus is described as the high priest who intercedes for the readers of this letter. This cannot be said of the lost.

10:10   The author speaks of their common experience: "we have been made holy through the sacrifice of the body of Jesus Christ." Again, we have a statement that is true only of believers.

10:15   "The Holy Spirit also testifies to us about this . . . ." As we shall see later in Hebrews, the Holy Spirit only speaks to those who are born again. The lost have no access to His wisdom.

10:19   "Therefore, brothers, since we have confidence to enter the Most Holy Place by the blood of Jesus . . . ." The readers, again called "brothers," have confidence by the blood of Jesus. There is no way to apply this to the lost.

10:21–25 Again there is mention of Christ as high priest, the fact that we can draw near to God with a sincere heart, and that our hearts have been sprinkled to cleanse us. This passage also shows that the author isn't speaking merely to some of his readers, because he speaks of the hope "we profess." If his readers were a mixture of genuine believers and those who had made merely an outward profession of faith without the required inward belief, this statement wouldn't be accurate.

10:36–39 Their need wasn't salvation, but endurance in the face of persecution.

12:2   Jesus Christ is called the "the author and perfecter of our faith." Notice that it is "our" faith, so readers were partaking of the same faith as the author. This faith is authored and perfected by Christ Himself.

12:7   "God is treating you as sons . . . ." God does not treat unbelievers as sons.

| 12:8 | They were receiving a kingdom. This promise is made only to believers. |
| 13:1–19 | All the commands in this section are applicable only to believers. |

When we view the evidence, it becomes clear that believers, not unbelievers, are the recipients of this letter.

That said, some still argue that the "Sabbath-rest" refers to the eternal rest of salvation. They wish to make the case that the warnings against falling away deal with the possibility of the believer losing his salvation because of unbelief. If all we had was the letter to the Hebrews, this might be a legitimate argument. However, when you examine the rest of the Bible—and if you assume, as I do, that the Bible doesn't contradict itself—then this option must also be discarded.

Let's review what the Bible says about the security of the believer. Because each person of the triune God is involved in our salvation, we will look at the work of each member of the Trinity—Father, Son, and Spirit—as it relates to our security.

God the Father

God the Father has a purpose in mind for those whom He has called. This purpose works all things in the believer's life for good (Rom 8:28).

There's a story about H. A. Ironside, the famous author and pastor of Moody Memorial Church, at breakfast with several other pastors. They were discussing Romans 8:28, all the while helping themselves to an abundance of delicious biscuits. The biscuits were so good, in fact, that they asked for the cook to come to their table so that they could thank her. She came to the table and humbly accepted their praise for the fabulous biscuits. As she was walking away, Ironside and the others returned to their discussion of Romans 8:28. When the cook heard this, she turned around and went back to the table. She explained that her biscuits were a tasty illustration of the truth that God works all things together for good. She said that lard, by itself, isn't good to eat. Neither is salt, flour, or any of the other ingredients she used. But when she worked them all together, in just the right amounts, and placed them in the right amount of heat for the right amount of time, all these things that weren't good by themselves turned into mouthwatering biscuits.

God does the same for us. Notice, though: Paul doesn't say that all things *are* good, for that clearly isn't the case. But God *is* working all things together for the good of believers, because He has a purpose for them. He takes just the right amount of what He allows into our lives, works those ingredients together, and puts them under just the right amount of heat for the exact amount of time, so that all things in our lives (not only some things) can bring about His good purpose.

What is this purpose? That each believer be conformed to the image of His Son. The believer has this destination set out ahead of time for him ("pre" as in before, "destined" as in destination—that's what *predestined* means. It's a word that's used only of believers!). Those whom God predestined, He called, justified, and glorified (Rom 8:30). This is an amazing statement! If any of those He predestined didn't arrive at their appointed destination, then there is no way this verse could be true.

Next, although nearly everyone agrees that God the Father has the ability to keep the believer secure (Jude 24), some insist that God only keeps secure those who continue in belief. They contend that since belief is the condition of our salvation, lack (or loss) of belief removes from us the one condition that is necessary to keep our salvation. However, Jesus argues against that notion:

> I give them eternal life, and they shall never perish; no one can snatch them out of my hand. My Father, who has given them to me, is greater than all; no one can snatch them out of my Father's hand (JOHN 10:28, NIV).

Call me simple, but I take "no one" to mean no one—not even the believer himself. Jesus didn't qualify "no one" in any way. He didn't say "no one but yourself," He said "no one." That includes you!

God the Son

God the Son paid for all our sins on the cross. As a result, no sin, even the sin of unbelief, can take away what God has given us. In ROMANS 8:33–34, Paul asks two questions: Who will bring a charge against those God has chosen, and who is he that condemns? These are rhetorical questions to which the answer is "no one can." This answer is based entirely on Christ's death, burial, resurrection, ascension, and active ministry of intercession on our behalf (ROM 8:34). His death, burial, and resurrection are what paid the penalty for our sins. His active intercession for us protects us from any who would bring an accusation. We know, for example, that Satan accuses believers before God day and night (REV 12:9–10). He stands before the throne and constantly brings to God's attention every sin and rebellion we commit. Fortunately, by God's grace, we have an Advocate, a person who speaks to the Father in our defense: Jesus Christ the righteous (1 JOHN 2:1). When Satan brings my sin before God as a charge against me, Jesus shouts, "I object! That evidence can't be admitted to this courtroom because my death paid all that was owed." The case is thrown out of court, because Jesus constantly stands ready to defend me against all charges based on what He accomplished on the cross.

Also, the prayers of Christ on our behalf keep us secure. JOHN 17 records Jesus' prayer for His disciples immediately prior to their leaving the Upper Room. In this prayer, He prays not only for those present, but "also for those who will believe in me through their message" (JOHN 17:20, NIV). As He prays for us, He prays that all whom the

Father has given Him would be with Him where He is to see His glory (v. 24). God the Son, who always prays according to the Father's will, makes a special request on our behalf that we join Him in the presence of God so that we might see His glory. This is a prayer God is certain to answer!

God the Spirit

God the Spirit is the seal that God the Father uses to mark us as His own (2 COR 1:21–22). This sealing is permanent, in that it lasts until "the day of redemption" (EPH 4:30). This sealing is tremendously important because it indicates a finished transaction. We have been purchased with Christ's blood (1 COR 6:20, 7:23; REV 5:9), so we now belong to Him. To show this change of ownership, so to speak, we are marked with a seal that is really a person, the Holy Spirit. This mark of ownership stays on us until that great day when our salvation is made complete and we are glorified in our bodies in the presence of Christ.

Similarly, God the Spirit is the "earnest money" that God deposits in us to guarantee our redemption. If you've ever purchased a home, you know that part of the contract usually consists of putting up earnest money, given as a guarantee that you won't back out of the contract. If you do renege on your promise to purchase, the seller gets to keep the money you've deposited. In the same way, God the Father gives us the indwelling Holy Spirit as earnest money (2 COR 1:21–22). He "is a deposit guaranteeing our inheritance until the redemption of those who are God's possession" (EPH 1:14, NIV). This means that if God does not provide those whom He purchased through the blood of Christ with the final redemption He promised, the Holy Spirit, the third person of the Trinity, would somehow have to leave the Godhead! Seriously now, can any notion be any more ridiculous?

Definition of "Sabbath-rest"

Given this evidence that our salvation is secure—that once we are born again, it is a permanent condition—we see that the "rest" that is promised simply can't be salvation, because it was possible for the readers of Hebrews to "fall short" of it. So, what other options are available?

It seems the only alternative is what might be termed a "life of rest" in the here-and-now. This raises yet another question: What is a "life of rest"? Is it a life without conflict? Is it a life where no labor is performed? Is it a life of self-actualization (whatever that means)? Is it a life of dreams fulfilled? I'm sure that for each of these options, you could find someone embracing it as the definition of a "life of rest." Nevertheless, although there is a morsel of truth in each option, none of them fits the biblical profile.

Several passages of Scripture speak of the rest or peace that God promises. We'll consider these passages together to see what common elements appear in them. The first passage comes from the Gospels.

> *Come to me, all you who are weary and burdened, and I will give you rest. Take my yoke upon you and learn from me, for I am gentle and humble in heart, and you will find rest for your souls* (MATT 11:28–29, NIV).

Another passage that sheds light on the meaning of *rest* comes from the Apostle John:

> *This is the message you heard from the beginning: We should love one another. Do not be like Cain, who belonged to the evil one and murdered his brother. And why did he murder him? Because his own actions were evil and his brother's were righteous. Do not be surprised, my brothers, if the world hates you. We know that we have passed from death to life, because we*

love our brothers. Anyone who does not love remains in death. Anyone who hates his brother is a murderer, and you know that no murderer has eternal life in him.

This is how we know what love is: Jesus Christ laid down his life for us. And we ought to lay down our lives for our brothers. If anyone has material possessions and sees his brother in need but has no pity on him, how can the love of God be in him? Dear children, let us not love with words or tongue but with actions and in truth. This then is how we know that we belong to the truth, and how we set our hearts at rest in his presence whenever our hearts condemn us. For God is greater than our hearts, and he knows everything (1 JOHN 3:11–20, NIV).

We must examine one more passage, this one by the Apostle Paul, for a complete picture of rest. Though Paul doesn't use the word *rest* per se, the idea of "peace" is in keeping with this concept. Plus, much of what may be learned from the previous passages is repeated here.

But I say, walk by the Spirit, and you will not carry out the desire of the flesh. For the flesh sets its desire against the Spirit, and the Spirit against the flesh; for these are in opposition to one another, so that you may not do the things that you please. But if you are led by the Spirit, you are not under the Law (GAL 5:16–18, NASB).

But the fruit of the Spirit is love, joy, peace, patience, kindness, goodness, faithfulness, gentleness, self-control; against such things there is no law. Now those who belong to Christ Jesus have crucified the flesh with its passions and desires. If we live by the Spirit, let us also walk by the Spirit. Let us not become boastful, challenging one another, envying one another (GAL 5:22–25, NASB).

Several truths about the "life of rest" can be gleaned from these passages.

- *Rest,* as defined in these passages, is something that is given as a gift from God. In the Matthew passage, Jesus says "I" am the One who gives rest. Paul also speaks of peace as something that originates with God, not from within ourselves. The "fruit of the Spirit" might be better translated as the "fruit produced by the Spirit." Just as Jesus said "I will give you rest," here we learn that peace is provided by the Spirit as well.

- Although this rest is a gift, it requires our participation. A "yoke" is a wooden crosspiece that fastens across the neck of two oxen so that they may cooperate in the work of pulling something, like a cart or a plow. In this context, we are to yoke ourselves to Jesus Christ for His assistance in our lives. The yoke, though, implies our active participation in the work that is done.

- Rest is something that is enhanced by learning over time. The reason we are to yoke ourselves to Jesus is so that we might learn from Him. For training purposes, it is common to yoke an experienced ox to a younger one. While they are yoked together, the older ox demonstrates to (and thus trains) the younger one how to respond to signals from the reins or voice. In this analogy, God gives us a dramatic illustration of how we must stay step by step with Christ to learn what is necessary to find rest. Keeping in step with Christ fits well with the biblical picture of walking through life. As we walk, we need to stay "tied" to Christ, so to speak, so that we will be led in the right direction. Even the word *find* suggests that "rest" is something that we will not acquire on our own. Instead, finding rest requires sustained effort while being yoked to the correct guide.

Just as we are to be yoked to Christ, we are to walk by the Spirit. Again, the idea is that we are to move toward a destination side-by-side with God. We are to be led by Him. This certainly implies what has been stated directly in the Scripture quoted here: namely, that we don't know the correct way to go and must be shown what is correct.

This is the same formula, by the way, that is given in the Old Testament. "This is what the LORD says: 'Stand at the crossroads and look; ask for the ancient paths, ask where the good way is, and walk in it, and you will find rest for your souls'" (JER 6:16, NIV). If you want to find "rest for your souls," a learning process is necessary. Notice the order of these commands.

- *Stand:* The image is of one who is traveling down a certain path and comes to a crossroad. Instead of blindly choosing which road to follow, the traveler stops and considers which way to go.

- *Look:* Carrying the idea of a traveler a bit further, we have the command not only to stand but also to look around to determine our location. We need to know where we are if we are to get where we want to go.

- *Ask:* The fact that we are commanded to ask implies that we need direction in this area, that sometimes our own experience isn't enough. Sadly, we live in a day when people question whether the old ways are the best ways, whether old truths can still be believed, whether old ideas are still to be trusted. And yet God clearly instructs us, in spite of the prevailing mood of the age, to ask for the ancient paths. These ancient paths are identified in the text as the "good way."

- *Walk:* Merely knowing the right way isn't enough. James warns us to "prove yourselves doers of the word, and not merely hearers who delude themselves" (JAMES 1:22, NIV). Jesus makes the same point in this parable:

> *Therefore, everyone who hears these words of mine and* **puts them into practice** *is like a wise man who built his house on the rock. The rain came down, the streams rose, and the winds blew and beat against that house; yet it did not fall, because it had its foundation on the rock. But everyone who hears these words of mine* **and does not put them into practice** *is like a foolish man who built his house on sand. The rain came down, the streams rose, and the winds blew and beat against that house, and it fell with a great crash* (MATT 7:24–27, NIV).

Notice that the difference between the two men is not what they hear but what they do.

- *Find:* Nearly all translations cast this portion of the verse— find rest—as a result of obeying the previous commands, and so it is. What isn't obvious in our English translations is that this is also a command. In other words, if you don't attain rest, you are breaking a command of God. That might sound harsh, but the implication is that if you obey the other four commands, the command to rest is automatically fulfilled. This is why Jesus could promise that if we take his yoke upon us and learn of him, we *will* find rest for our souls. The fact that so many people do not have this kind of peace shows that rest for our souls isn't automatic.

Therefore, to summarize Jeremiah: we are to stop and examine the paths before us, yet we are not to rely on our own wisdom in deciding which way is best. We are to ask for the "ancient paths," which are defined as "the good way." Nonetheless, knowing the path isn't enough; we must walk in it if we are to find rest.

- This rest doesn't reside in the material realm, but is purely spiritual. The rest is for your "souls." There is no hint of material prosperity in these passages. This is not a name-it-and-claim-it item where God is obligated to jump at our whim if we just speak the magic words. There are no material blessings for sale. Instead, a package of spiritual blessings is offered.

When we consider peace as an aspect of the fruit of the Spirit, it's important to note that even though in English the word *fruit* may be singular or plural, it's not so in the original language. The word "fruit" is singular (fruit), not plural (fruits). The best way to imagine the fruit of the Spirit is to think of an orange or a grapefruit. When you peel back the rind, you have only one fruit, but it consists of many segments. In the same way, the peace produced (pun intended) by God the Holy Spirit doesn't exist by itself, but is part of the character of God working in us. If you have peace produced by the Spirit, you will also have joy. If you have love, you will be gentle. If you have faithfulness, you will have self-control. This list should not be considered exhaustive, but merely a sample of what it means to be like Christ, to "learn of Him."

This is why conflict in this world does not stop us from possessing rest. John as much as promises that if we live righteously, the world will hate us. In doing this, he is merely echoing the words of Jesus (JOHN 15:18–19). Therefore, it's possible to be surrounded outwardly by conflict and hatred and inwardly have rest.

- Rest is provided by God, so the author of Hebrews stresses that one important aspect of rest is being at rest with God. No one can ever escape the presence of God (Ps 139:7–11), because He is without limits and fills all of time and space. In a special way, though, the believer is always in the presence of God, because every believer is indwelt by God the Holy Spirit. Because of His indwelling presence, when we sin, we are convicted of our guilt immediately. Therefore, the child of God can have no rest while in rebellion against God, because His Holy Spirit is present constantly to prove us wrong and prompt us to repentance. It doesn't matter if this sin is internal (hatred) or external (murder). Sin in the life of the believer guarantees that he will not have rest. We will not have peace if we are engaged in satisfying the flesh, for the flesh and the Spirit are in opposition to one another. They reside at opposite ends of the road. You are walking either one way or the other; you can't do both. When we sin, our hearts condemn us so that we need to have our hearts set at rest once again.

- Related to the preceding point is the natural conclusion that rest is found in behaving correctly. This is a recurring theme in each of these passages. Whether you call it walking the ancient paths, being yoked to Christ, or loving with actions and truth, our behavior is a significant factor in our having rest.

  Correct behavior is defined as acting like Christ. For example, we are to love one another, but how do we know what love is? We learn about love, not just in theory but in practice, by observing the life of Christ. To put it another way, we are to learn of Him. This learning is not limited to superficial actions, but extends to the very issues of life and death itself. Just as Christ died for you, you are to be willing to die for the brothers. There is no "reasonable" limit upon our obedience.

Now that our investigation is complete, what conclusions may we draw that help us define the term *Sabbath*-rest? What do we know about "rest"?

1. It is provided by God as we walk with Him.
2. It requires our participation.

3. It is enhanced by learning over time.

4. It is spiritual in nature, not material.

5. The conflict around us doesn't affect God's rest.

6. Sin is incompatible with rest.

7. Correct behavior is essential to rest.

8. Correct behavior consists of conforming to the character of God.

It might be helpful at this point to refresh our memories about spiritual maturity:

Definition: The spiritually mature are those who, through the power of the Holy Spirit, both understand God's Word well enough and have consistently put its truths into practice long enough that they are capable of distinguishing good from evil in practical circumstances and are competent in teaching others to do the same.

When this definition is compared with the preceding list, some remarkable similarities between maturity and rest appear:

1. Both are commanded.

2. Both are provided by God.

3. Both require our participation.

4. Both require learning over time.

5. Both are incompatible with sin.

6. Both are exhibited by correct behavior.

Considering these points of comparison, we can derive that spiritual maturity and the Sabbath-rest are related. In fact, it seems that *spiritual maturity* and the *Sabbath*-rest are speaking of the same condition, with one important distinction: the Sabbath-rest appears to be permanent.

When a believer has entered the Sabbath-rest, he has become mature to the point that he will remain mature.

Although we cover this passage of Scripture in greater detail later, it might be helpful to briefly review HEBREWS 4:9–10 (NIV):

> *There remains, then, a Sabbath-rest for the people of God; for anyone who enters God's rest also rests from his own work, just as God did from his. Let us, therefore, make every effort to enter that rest, so that no one will fall by following their example of disobedience.*

This passage teaches that there remains a Sabbath-rest for the people of God today. Unfortunately, the author of Hebrews doesn't define the term *Sabbath*-rest for us. This is why we had to derive the meaning from the passages just discussed. The one clue he gives us regarding the meaning is the comparison he makes between God's rest after creation and the rest God promises us. Hence, if we want to learn the nature of this Sabbath-rest, we should closely examine God's rest.

Entering this Sabbath-rest takes effort. But when we enter, we rest from our labor just as God did from His. When God created the world, He didn't take a short rest and then start creating again. No, He finished his creative activity and then merely maintained what He had created. If we rest as God rested, then when we enter the Sabbath-rest, we maintain the maturity that has been achieved. We continue to grow in understanding and insight, certainly, but we rest from our work and maintain our maturity in imitation of God.

Please notice that I did *not* say we can achieve sinlessness. That cannot be substantiated anywhere in Scripture. It does mean that when the mature believer sins, he will be quick with confession and restoration so his fellowship with God doesn't remain broken for long. He maintains his maturity by habitually walking in the Spirit. With this in mind, we can derive the following definition of the Sabbath-rest:

Definition: The *Sabbath-rest* is a state of permanent spiritual maturity.

Discussion Questions

In each of chapters 10–13, we will be revisiting your answer to the question: "Where do you want to go?" Please look back at your answer to that question and examine it in light of this chapter.

1. How can God the Father's revealed plans for our life give us confidence that our salvation is secure?

2. How does the Lord Jesus' ministry give us assurance of salvation?

3. How do the Holy Spirit's activities assure us of the permanence of our salvation?

4. Describe the "Sabbath-rest" in your own words.

5. Has this chapter brought any questions to mind, or any thoughts you would like to discuss with the group?

6. Is there any issue you would like prayed for, or accountability in, over the course of this week?

7. Please note any other group members' answers that you would like to follow up on this week, either by praying for them or by making an encouraging contact.

THE RED QUEEN INSTRUCTS ALICE

It's time for you to answer now," the Queen said, looking at her watch; "open your mouth a LITTLE wider when you speak, and always say 'your Majesty.'"

"I only wanted to see what the garden was like, your Majesty—"

"That's right," said the Queen, patting her on the head, which Alice didn't like at all; "though, when you say 'garden,'—I'VE seen gardens, compared with which this would be a wilderness."

Alice didn't dare to argue the point, but went on: "And I thought I'd try and find my way to the top of that hill—"

"When you say 'hill,'" the Queen interrupted, "I could show you hills in comparison with which you'd call that a valley."

"No, I shouldn't," said Alice, surprised into contradicting her at last: "a hill CAN'T be a valley, you know. That would be nonsense—"

The Red Queen shook her head, "You may call it 'nonsense' if you like," she said, "but I'VE heard nonsense compared with which that would be as sensible as a dictionary!"

—*Looking-Glass*, ch. II, "The Garden of Live Flowers"

Chapter 12
Living in the Wilderness

Jefferson Hunt, a Mormon battalion captain, knew the Old Spanish Trail.[1] That made him the ideal choice to lead a caravan of pilgrims to the promised land of California. Gold fever was running rampant in 1849. Hunt's party, consisting of pioneers primarily from Illinois, Michigan, and Iowa, was embarking late. Prior to their October 1 departure, more than 50,000 people had already started the trek overland, and hundreds more crowded aboard 61 ships sailing from the East Coast around the Horn to San Francisco.

Starting overland so late in the year was a risky business. Everyone knew the story of the Donner Party. It was in October, just two years earlier, that their doomed expedition, trapped by snow in the Sierra Nevada Mountains, encountered such deprivation and hunger that they ultimately resorted to cannibalism. That's why Hunt wisely decided to lead the wagon train south, through Utah.

While stopped near what is now Cedar City, a passing wagon train gave a map (of unknown and dubious origin) to some in Hunt's caravan; this map revealed a shortcut through the mountains. Not only was this trail shorter, it brought them out of the mountains in Tulare Valley, much closer to the gold fields than Los Angeles, the termination of the Old Spanish Trail.

Hunt knew better than to trust a map he didn't know that pointed to a trail he'd never heard of. He warned his group that following this map might well be "walking into the jaws of Hell."

The Reverend John Wells Briar, a stubborn, greedy, and persuasive man, disagreed. He urged others in the party to join him in following the map. "Go west . . . and in six weeks we will be loaded with gold," he promised.

Leaving Hunt's wagon train, dozens of wagons struck out on their own. After three days of following the map, however, Briar's party caught sight of mountains ahead. Realizing their mistake, more than half the wagons turned back and rejoined Hunt's expedition. Seven weeks later, those wagons arrived in Los Angeles without problem. Those that stayed with Briar, about 27 wagons total, ended up crawling through cactus-studded terrain and barren salt wastes on an agonizing trek.

When Juliette Brier, the good reverend's wife, walked into the valley that day in 1849, it looked just like another desert sink, only more terrible than the rest. Meandering westward, they couldn't find a pass out of the valley. Hemmed in by mountains and dangerously short of supplies, most of the families hunkered down for the winter while a two-man scouting crew pushed on westward for help. Returning in late January, the scouts found that one man had died. The rest of the group survived by burning their wagons and slaughtering the oxen.

On February 4, exactly 134 days after their pilgrimage began, the Briers and those who were left in their party were rescued. They stumbled, sunken-eyed, little more than walking skeletons, out of the desert. Juliette weighed a mere 75 pounds, Reverend Brier had lost more than 100. They left behind more than just four dead companions; they also left behind a name for that terrible place. According to legend, when Juliette looked back as the party was leaving, she said, "Goodbye, Death Valley."

Death Valley: the statistics really don't do it justice. It's the lowest point in the Western hemisphere (282 feet below sea level), one of the driest (average annual rainfall of 1.8 inches), and one of the hottest places on earth (record high: 134°F). When my wife and I drove through it, the temperature was a balmy 117°F.

One of the most memorable places in Death Valley is Badwater Basin. It is a vast salt waste where nothing grows. In fact, it was the most absolutely silent place I have ever been. There literally was no sound at all—no wind, no cars, no people, no birds, no insects. Absolute silence. The air weighs heavy upon you as you stand in the burning sunlight. Despite appearances, some things evidently live there. There is a minute snail in the briny pool for which the area is named, and at certain times pickleweed will appear—but that's about it. It is one of the most inhospitable places on the planet. Not only would no one want to live there, I'm not at all certain any human could.

Unfortunately, this wilderness is a picture of one of the possible spiritual destinations that a believer can inhabit in this life. It is possible to remain in rebellion against God for so long that He confirms your choice of sin over Himself and condemns you to live with the consequences. If that scares you, it should. It is the constant warning of the book of Hebrews.

Hebrews is a tightly-argued letter that is punctuated from time to time with warning passages. As you work through the argument, these warning passages become longer and more severe. The obvious question is: What is the author warning us about? To answer that question, let's walk through one of the warning passages together: HEBREWS 3:7–19. To aid our understanding, we will divide the passage into two parts and look at each in turn.

> So, as the Holy Spirit says: "Today, if you hear his voice, do not harden your hearts as you did in the rebellion, during the time of testing in the desert, where your fathers tested and tried me and for forty years saw what I did. That is why I was angry with that generation, and I said, 'Their hearts are always going astray, and they have not known my ways.' So I declared on oath in my anger, 'They shall never enter my rest.'"

The author begins by recounting the tragic events surrounding the nation of Israel's failure at Kadesh Barnea, as recorded in NUMBERS 14. The reason he recalls this past judgment is that it is possible to repeat the failure and suffer the same results. Therefore, if we are to understand this passage, we must understand what happened at that place so long ago.

God made two promises to the nation of Israel. "So I have come down to rescue them from the hand of the Egyptians and to bring them up out of that land into a good and spacious land, a land flowing with milk and honey—the home of the Canaanites, Hittites, Amorites, Perizzites, Hivites and Jebusites" (Ex 3:8, NIV). These two promises were to (1) "rescue them" from their slavery in Egypt and (2) "bring them into a good and spacious land."

The first promise was fulfilled when God redeemed them as a nation on the night of the first Passover (ISA 43:1). Since God kept the first promise, it's only reasonable to assume that He intended to keep the second one as well.

After they traveled through the wilderness from Egypt to Mount Sinai, God gave His redeemed people the Law. He then led them to the border of the land He had promised to give them. He told them to "[s]end some men to explore the land of Canaan, which I am giving to the Israelites. From each ancestral tribe send one of its leaders" (NUM 13:1–2). In obedience to the Word of the LORD, 12 men, one from each tribe, scouted out the land.

Interestingly, all 12 men agreed concerning the facts of the situation: "We went into the land to which you sent us, and it does flow with milk and honey! Here is its fruit. But the people who live there are powerful, and the cities are fortified and very large. We even saw descendants of Anak there. The Amalekites live in the Negev; the Hittites, Jebusites and Amorites live in the hill country; and the Canaanites live near the sea and along the Jordan" (NUM 13:27–29,

NIV). All in all, a very realistic report. Yet, while they agreed on the facts of the case, their conclusions were poles apart. The majority report (10 out of 12) said, "We can't attack those people; they are stronger than we are. . . . The land we explored devours those living in it. All the people we saw there are of great size. . . . We seemed like grasshoppers in our own eyes, and we looked the same to them" (NUM 13:31–33, NIV).

The minority report, however, was vastly different. Joshua and Caleb reported, "The land we passed through and explored is exceedingly good. If the LORD is pleased with us, he will lead us into that land, a land flowing with milk and honey, and will give it to us. Only do not rebel against the LORD. And do not be afraid of the people of the land, because we will swallow them up. Their protection is gone, but the LORD is with us. Do not be afraid of them" (NUM 14:7–9 NIV). Joshua and Caleb issued a call to faith, but the people refused to believe. In fact, their fearful unbelief was so strong that the people threatened to kill Joshua and Caleb (NUM 14:10).

We must always remember that God takes rebellion seriously. He took this rebellion so seriously that if Moses hadn't directly interceded for the people, God was going to judge them all with physical death on the spot! (NUM 14:11–19). Nevertheless, because of the faithfulness of Moses, God spared the people from the judgment He had threatened. In relenting from His previous judgment, however, God imposed another: He did not allow His redeemed people to enjoy the blessings He had promised. Their rebellion caused them to have to wander in the wilderness until that entire generation, save for Joshua and Caleb, died. God waited until the next generation before He kept his promise of bringing them into the land of plenty.

This incident has been kept before the eyes of God's people as a warning against rebellion. PSALM 95:7–11 warns the people of that day against the dangers of rebellion. The author of Hebrews quotes that psalm to warn the believers of his day—and ours—that rebellion against God results in not entering His rest. We are not to harden our hearts or we will not enter into His rest.

At this point, someone might ask, "How do I know this warning is directed to me?" The second part of this passage makes it clear:

> *See to it, brothers, that none of you has a sinful, unbelieving heart that turns away from the living God. But encourage one another daily, as long as it is called Today, so that none of you may be hardened by sin's deceitfulness. We have come to share in Christ if we hold firmly till the end the confidence we had at first. As has just been said: "Today, if you hear his voice, do not harden your hearts as you did in the rebellion."*
>
> *Who were they who heard and rebelled? Were they not all those Moses led out of Egypt? And with whom was he angry for forty years? Was it not with those who sinned, whose bodies fell in the desert? And to whom did God swear that they would never enter his rest if not to those who disobeyed? So we see that they were not able to enter, because of their unbelief.*

After reviewing the historical precedent, the author explains that unbelief leads to rebellion. This rebellion has five specific consequences associated with it.

1. **We are in danger of turning away from the living God** (v. 12). Two elements of this verse show that this passage is directed to believers: (a) He addresses them as brothers, a term used only for those truly born again, and (b) he warns them not to "turn away," which indicates that they have previously turned to the living God. Therefore, this warning is for believers. You see, even though we have been saved by grace through faith, it is still very possible to choose to live, not by faith, but by unbelief, because of a sinful heart. As we have seen, it's not salvation that's at issue here. Rather,

it's the blessings that flow from fellowship with God, in this life, that we are in danger of losing.

2. **We are in danger of being hardened by sin's deceitfulness** (vv. 13–16). When we break fellowship with God through sin, it is just one more step to become hard or stubborn in our sin. At this point, we've decided that our sin is the course of action we will follow no matter what. When that happens, our hearts become insensitive to the promptings of God the Holy Spirit.

It is interesting to notice the change that occurs between verses 12 and 13. In verse 12, each believer is responsible for his own conduct; in verse 13, this responsibility is also placed upon the entire family of believers. Although it remains true that we are responsible for our own behavior, we share a responsibility with other believers for their behavior as well. In the same way, our brothers and sisters aren't necessarily being nosey when they inquire about our spiritual life, because they have a responsibility to us as well.

This joint responsibility stems from the fact that we have come to share in Christ (v. 14). Because we have a common bond with Christ, we automatically have a common bond with each other. Also, we should recognize that this bond isn't just with the people we like or who are like us. *Anyone* who is born again shares in Christ, and therefore we share in them and they share in us.

But what does the Hebrews author mean when he says, "if we hold firmly till the end the confidence we had at first"? To understand this phrase, we need some help from the original language. There are several ways to say *if* in the original Greek:[2]

- You could say, "if and we'll assume it to be true for the sake of argument." This is like saying, "If it rains today" when the forecast calls for rain and the clouds overhead appear grey and heavy.

- Or you could say, "if and it's not true." This would be the case if you made the same statement, but were in the middle of a drought and the sky was blue from horizon to horizon.
- Another meaning of *if* could be expressed as "if, and it might be true depending on the circumstances." An example of this case is when someone says "if it rains" while talking about an event two months away. There is no way of knowing if it will be raining or not.

The meaning of *if* in each of these cases depends on what words and verb tenses are used in combination in the original Greek. In this case, the original language uses the last option.

Just in case things haven't gotten complicated enough, this last option isn't really quite as simple as I've just described it. It has a few variables of its own:

- If it's talking about the present, it's most often used as a simple logical connection (if A then B).
- Sometimes it's used to express a merely hypothetical situation that probably won't happen.
- Sometimes this Greek structure is used to talk about the future, as it is here. Then it takes on a different meaning. In this case, the *if* expresses what is most likely to occur.

So the argument goes something like this: The fellowship that we share with Christ is in danger if we harden our hearts through unbelief. But that sharing together with Christ will be maintained if you hold onto the confidence you had at first, which you will most likely do, although you should be aware that it's not a certainty.

3. **We are in danger of open rebellion** (v. 17). Quoting PSALM 95, the author repeats the word *today* both in verse 7 and in verse 15. What does the word *today* mean? It means today! Right here, right now,

in the circumstances you're currently facing. You could be in a state of affairs similar to that of Israel at Kadesh Barnea. You could be in a situation that calls for faith and obedience, but you could give way to fear and sin. This would be open rebellion as certainly as it was rebellion in Israel so long ago.

4. **We are in danger of losing the blessings God has promised in this life** (vv. 18–19). Now, at this point we must be careful. The blessings referred to here are not physical or material. It is true that God often blesses us materially, but He hasn't promised this to the church. Instead, the promises of this passage refer to those spiritual blessings that flow from being in fellowship with Him. Rebellion causes the loss of those blessings.

There is a downward progression in this passage that should not be missed. We must avoid complaining as they did at Kadesh Barnea, because complaining leads to a hardening of our hearts. Hardening our hearts (v. 8) causes them to go astray (v. 10). When our hearts go astray, open acts of rebellion follow (vv. 8, 15). Open and persistent rebellion leads to a loss of God's promised blessings (vv. 14, 18–19).

It is important to remember that all of these warnings are based on the experience of Israel at Kadesh Barnea. The ones who sinned were God's redeemed people (v. 17). Yet, even though they rebelled, they never stopped being His people! When they wandered in the wilderness, God was still their God. He protected them and provided for them. "For forty years you sustained them in the desert; they lacked nothing, their clothes did not wear out nor did their feet become swollen" (Neh 9:21, niv). Even in the midst of their punishment, God continued His watchful oversight of His people. In the same way, when we rebel, we do not lose our salvation.

Remember God's two promises to the nation of Israel: to (1) "rescue them" from their slavery in Egypt and (2) "bring them into a good and spacious land." The first promise He fulfilled. In the same way, when we come to Christ, we become His redeemed people. Nothing we do after that ever changes our fundamental status. It is the second promise that is conditional, not the first. Like Israel, we will remain God's redeemed people, but—also like Israel—we can experience the loss of God's planned blessings for us.

5. **We are in danger of that loss becoming permanent** (vv. 18–19). God said that the rebellious generation would never enter into His rest. Why? Because of their unbelief! God has promised, "If we confess our sins, he is faithful and just and will forgive us our sins and purify us from all unrighteousness" (1 JOHN 1:9, NIV). Evidently, though, there comes a point at which we have remained in our stubborn rebellion for so long that God in essence says, "Fine, if you want to remain in sin, that's exactly what will happen." For it is an established fact that sin is often its own punishment. For vivid examples of this, we can look at the alcoholic or drug addict, the person who can't control his anger, or the person who has an affair. Just as fire always changes what it touches, so sin destroys the life of the one who indulges in it. Therefore, God's punishment for sin often takes the form of condemning us to remain in our sin.

We see this pattern throughout the Scriptures. Pharaoh hardened his heart (EX 8:15, 19, 32; 9:7), then God confirmed Pharoah's choice and hardened his heart as well (EX 10:1; 11:10; 14:4, 8). The Jewish leadership *would not* believe (JOHN 12:37), therefore they *could not* believe (JOHN 12:39). In the same way, if we persist in unbelief, God evidently hardens our hearts as part of His temporal judgment of sin. We will remain in our choice of unbelief, so we will never enter into the rest He has available for us in this life.

I realize this sounds harsh, but I believe a moment's reflection will reveal its truthfulness. You don't have to have been in the church very long to have met some older believer in whose life the works of the flesh are obvious. We've all known Christians who have notebooks overflowing with sermon notes and tablets filled with Bible study outlines but who cause trouble everywhere they go. Their bitterness about something, often a long time in the past—how they were wronged at church by someone, or by a family member, or friend—has never gone away. Instead of forgiving, they remain stubborn in unbelief and rebellion. As a result, they have never entered God's rest. Their sin robs them of the joy that could be theirs. The peace they might enjoy never comes. Their hearts are hard. They have been condemned to wander in the wilderness, and since their hearts are hard, it's almost certain that they don't even know their true condition.

Some Final Thoughts

After reading this frightening warning, it's important that we remember who God is and what He is like. We should not conclude that you've got just one chance at this, so don't mess up or you've blown it! That's just not in keeping with God's character.

The standard Old Testament description of the character of God calls Him "gracious and compassionate, slow to anger, abounding in love." Some variation of this phrase occurs at least seven times in the Old Testament (Ex 34:6; Neh 9:17; Ps 86:15; 103:8; 145:8; Joel 2:13; Jonah 4:2). When we remember that God Himself inspired the writers of Scripture, so that they wrote exactly what He wanted them to, it becomes clear that this is the way God wants us to think about Him. Fear of the Lord is important, but that doesn't mean we should live cringing in terror of God's impending judgment if we aren't perfect. David summed it up well:

> The Lord is compassionate and gracious, slow to anger, abounding in love. He will not always accuse, nor will he harbor his anger forever; he does not treat us as our sins deserve or repay

us according to our iniquities. For as high as the heavens are above the earth, so great is his love for those who fear him; as far as the east is from the west, so far has he removed our transgressions from us. As a father has compassion on his children, so the LORD has compassion on those who fear him; for he knows how we are formed, he remembers that we are dust (Ps 103:8–14, NIV).

Let's take a quick mental tour through the Bible to illustrate this point.

Jonah is commanded to go and preach to the greatest city of his time: Ninevah, the capital of Assyria. Instead of heading overland to the west toward Ninevah, he heads in the opposite direction by boat. When the storm comes, he readily admits that he is the cause of the storm, but instead of repenting, he tells the sailors to murder him by throwing him into the churning waters.

You see, Jonah knew God. He hated the Assyrians (in fairness to Jonah, everyone else did too), and he was afraid that God would give them grace when he wanted them judged. He says as much in his prayer at the end of the book after Ninevah repents and is spared.

> *O LORD, is this not what I said when I was still at home? That is why I was so quick to flee to Tarshish. I knew that you are a gracious and compassionate God, slow to anger and abounding in love, a God who relents from sending calamity. Now, O LORD, take away my life, for it is better for me to die than to live* (JONAH 4:2–3, NIV).

But God doesn't give up on Jonah. He sends a huge sea creature to swallow Jonah and, after he finally repents, vomit him onto dry land. It was only then that Jonah obeyed, and even then he did it grudgingly. Still, God used him instead of casting him aside. God didn't give up on Jonah.

Abraham was an idolater, which means that really he was a devil worshipper; Paul states that the sacrifices of pagans are offered to demons, not to God (1 COR 10:20). The story of Rachel hiding her father's idols (GEN 31) shows that idolatry was still in the family three generations after God called Abraham out of Mesopotamia.

In spite of this, God called him out of Ur of the Chaldees (ACTS 7:2–3), which is in modern-day Iraq. Initially he obeyed, but not completely. He traveled only as far as Haran in Syria, where he stopped when he was still hundreds of miles from the promised land. That's where he settled down. So God came to him a second time.

> The LORD had said to Abram, "Leave your country, your people and your father's household and go to the land I will show you. I will make you into a great nation and I will bless you; I will make your name great, and you will be a blessing. I will bless those who bless you, and whoever curses you I will curse; and all peoples on earth will be blessed through you" (GEN 12:1–3, NIV).

God didn't give up on Abraham.

God showed his character to Moses in a similar way. Moses murdered an Egyptian. He assumed that this was acceptable, because, after all, surely his own people would recognize that God was going to use him to save them (EX 2:11–13; HEB 11:23). Moses had a plan, but it wasn't God's plan. So he was forced to flee to Midian, where he lived in obscurity for the next 40 years. We might think Moses ruined his chances for ministry. Obviously, God had rejected him forever, leaving him to spend the rest of his days in the wilderness. When Moses was 80 years old, though, God appeared to him in a burning bush and said, "So now, go. I am sending you to Pharaoh to bring my people the Israelites out of Egypt" (EX 3:10, NIV). God didn't give up on Moses.

The same thing happened to Peter. You remember the story. Peter boasted to Jesus that he was ready to go to prison and even to death for his Lord (LUKE 22:33), and he ended up denying Him three times before morning came. He couldn't even stand up to a little girl (JOHN 18:17).

What should have been done with Peter then? Should he be cast off forever? Was he disqualified from future service? Was he condemned to wander in the wilderness? No. Jesus comes to him after His resurrection and asks the same question three times, once for each denial: "Do you love me?" And after each question Peter gives the same answer, "Yes, you know that I love you." Then, Jesus says the most remarkable thing, "Feed my sheep." God didn't give up on Peter.

Isn't that good to know? How many times have we been like Jonah, refusing to do as God commands? How many times have we been like Abram, stopping short of what God desires? How many times have we been like Moses, doing God's work our own way? How many times have we been like Peter, having our courage fail us? Oh, how many times?

Does God cast us off? Does he disown us? No, for even when we are faithless, God is faithful, for He cannot deny Himself (2 TIM 2:13). What amazing grace is ours.

We need to realize that when we speak of God as the God of second chances, we fail to give God the glory that is rightfully His. In reality, God doesn't just come to us a second time, but a third and a fourth, and a tenth and a thousandth time.

What made the Israelites at Kadesh Barnea different was their sustained, consistent rebellion against God. He gave them chance after chance, and yet they never learned. While God was giving them His holy Law, they were making an idol out of gold. Just as Moses was coming down from the mountain with the tablets, they were evidently engaged in a drunken orgy. So Moses smashed the tablets of the Law, ground the idol to powder, scattered the powder on the water, and made them drink it (Ex 32:1–19). They were disciplined, but they weren't rejected. They complained about the manna God provided and wanted to go back to Egypt (Num 11:4–6). God disciplined them, but didn't reject them. The Israelites rejected God's designated leadership (Num 16:1–6), and God disciplined them again, but He didn't reject them.

At least four times, the people complained and wanted to go back to Egypt (Num 11; 14; 20; 21). It was after the second time (Num 14) that the decision to reject them was finalized. It wasn't merely that they were complaining again. This time their violent refusal to enter the land of rest was the issue. After all that God had done to show how they could trust Him, after all the rebellions He had forgiven, they rejected God's promised rest. Therefore, God confirmed their choice and gave them what they wanted. He didn't allow them to go back to Egypt, because He had redeemed them from that slavery, but He did confirm their choice of not entering His rest.

As noted earlier, the Israelites remained His people even in their wilderness wanderings. It's interesting to notice, though, that they never changed their behavior. At least twice after their confinement to the wilderness, they still longed to go back to Egypt. Evidently they never learned.

If you are worried that God has condemned you to the wilderness, that you have been confirmed in immaturity, then set your heart at ease. If you were wandering in the wilderness, such spiritual matters would either be of little concern to you, or you would have convinced yourself that your sins are minor and you're doing fine. But you're not. Those who believe these lies are the ones who *should* be concerned —and yet they are the ones who will not be.

Perhaps you're facing the choice today of acting in faith and obedience or hardening your heart against what God commands. Be careful how you choose! Choices become habits, and habits turn into character, and there comes a time when God will give you exactly the sinful lifestyle you desire. What a terrifying thought! Never let it be said of you, "He will never enter My rest."

Discussion Questions

In each of chapters 10–13, we will be revisiting your answer to the question: "Where do you want to go?" Please look back at your answer to that question and examine it in light of this chapter.

1. Read NUMBERS 13 AND 14. In your own words, recount the incident in these chapters, which is referred to in HEBREWS 3, that causes the Lord to declare that Israel "shall never enter my rest."

2. List the five consequences of rebellion discussed in this chapter, and explain how they would cause a person to remain (or become) carnal.

3. Explore the idea that we are responsible to, and for, one another, as believers, regarding sin in our lives. Can you think of any cross-references that discuss this?

4. Some variation of the phrase that the Lord is "gracious and compassionate, slow to anger, abounding in love," appears in the following places in the Bible: EX 34:6; NEH 9:17; JOEL 2:13; JONAH 4:2. Look up these verses, read them in context, and share the situations surrounding each version of this declaration. How can this be an encouragement when we have sinned?

5. Has this chapter brought any questions to mind, or any thoughts you would like to discuss with the group?

6. Is there any issue you would like prayed for, or accountability in, over the course of this week?

7. Please note any other group members' answers that you would like to follow up on this week, either by praying for them or by making an encouraging contact.

QUEEN ALICE

I hope it encouraged him," she said, as she turned to run down the hill; "and now for the last brook, and to be a Queen! How grand it sounds!" A very few steps brought her to the edge of the brook. "The Eighth Square at last!" she cried as she bounded across, . . . threw herself down to rest on a lawn as soft as moss, with little flowerbeds dotted about it here and there. "Oh, how glad I am to get here! And what IS this on my head?" she exclaimed in a tone of dismay, as she put her hands up to something very heavy, that fitted tight all around her head.

"But how CAN it have got there without my knowing it?" she said to herself, as she lifted it off, and set it on her lap to make out what it could possibly be.

It was a golden crown.

—*Looking-Glass*, ch. VIII, "It's My Own Invention"

Chapter 13
Enjoying the Sabbath-rest

One of the many things that sets Christianity apart from other world religions is that it is a singing religion. Central to the idea of Christian worship is the idea of congregational singing, and that sets us apart from nearly all other religions. Why are we a singing religion? Well, one reason is that our singing is commanded by God.

> *Let the word of Christ dwell in you richly as you teach and admonish one another with all wisdom, and as you sing psalms, hymns and spiritual songs with gratitude in your hearts to God* (Col 3:16, niv).

Have you ever thought about why we sing? I'm not talking about why we sing during our worship services, but why we sing at all. After all, music is a distinctly human expression.

We have no proof that anything else in God's creation sings. I'm not convinced that the angels sing. There is only one place in the Scriptures that even hints at angels singing (Rev 5:9), and that passage is ambiguous at best. This surprises some people, but the fact is that every time in Scripture we are told of angels clearly uttering praise, the Bible says that they "said," not that they sang. There are a few cases where our English Bibles do us a disservice by translating the word *said* as "sing" (Rev 5:12, niv, is an example); in the original languages, angels are always portrayed as having spoken. Music is something distinctly human. Have you ever wondered why?

Because we are created in the image of God, we could conjecture that we sing because God sings, and in fact, the Bible bears witness to that.

> *The LORD your God is with you, he is mighty to save. He will take great delight in you, he will quiet you with his love, he will rejoice over you with singing* (ZEPH 3:17, NIV).

Even beyond our likeness with our Creator in this capacity, music performs a valuable service. Music is a unique instrument (pun intended) for instilling a message into the heart. If you've ever tried to remember the words of a song, you will know that it is much easier to recall them if you actually sing the song instead of merely reciting the lyrics. Therefore, music helps drive the truths of God's Word into our hearts in a way that no other medium can.

Music also is a unique way of expressing joy or gratitude to God. Thus, when we sing, we are not only moving the truths of God's Word into our hearts, we are responding to those truths with our whole hearts.

Music is a vehicle for allowing the word of Christ to dwell richly in us. As a pastor, I have come to the conclusion that the purposes of the sermon and of our singing are very closely related. While the sermon is to lift up Christ, it is also to allow the word of Christ to dwell richly within us. In the same way, while the singing is to lift up Christ and give glory to His name, it is also to allow the word of Christ to dwell richly within us.

Unfortunately, this beneficial function of music carries with it a danger. What happens when the songs we sing are theologically incorrect? The result is that they fill our hearts and minds with incorrect thoughts and/or false expectations. As you might expect, I have one particular example in mind on this topic. Some of our oldest, most beloved hymns use the promised land of Canaan as a symbol of heaven. Here is just one example:

On Jordan's Stormy Banks

On Jordan's stormy banks I stand
And cast a wishful eye
To Canaan's fair and happy land
Where my possessions lie.
All o'er those wide extended plains
Shines one eternal day;
There God the Son forever reigns
And scatters night away.

The problem with these hymns is that the reality of Canaan doesn't even come close to the promises God has for His people in eternity. To be sure, Canaan was a land "flowing with milk and honey, the most beautiful of all lands" (EZEK 20:15, NIV), but it wasn't a safe land. The spies all agreed that "the people who live there are powerful, and the cities are fortified and very large" (NUM 13:28, NIV). God's promises to the Israelites were that they would enjoy the land, defeat their enemies, and dwell in safety. Notably, He never promised them freedom from conflict or attack. Quite the contrary: They were charged with destroying the inhabitants of the land and taking possession of it by force. God promised that He would enable them to do this, but they actually had to go out and do the fighting (DEUT 7:17–24). In fact, God informed the people of Israel that the conflict would be an extended one. There would be no quick victory. This may seem counterintuitive, but God was doing this for their own good. "The LORD your God will drive out those nations before you, little by little. You will not be allowed to eliminate them all at once, or the wild animals will multiply around you" (DEUT 7:22, NIV).

Rather than the blessings of eternity, the promised land better represents the life that a believer lives in this world. God has promised us victory over our three enemies—the world (1 JOHN 5:4), the flesh (GAL 5:16), and the devil (1 PET 5:8–10)—but those enemies remain. We live in a land of conflict.

Attaining the Promise

In spite of our enemies, regardless of our struggles, we can enjoy the "rest" that God promises. This is the promise of HEBREWS 4:1–11 (NIV):

> *Therefore, since the promise of entering his rest still stands, let us be careful that none of you be found to have fallen short of it. For we also have had the gospel preached to us, just as they did; but the message they heard was of no value to them, because those who heard did not combine it with faith.*

This chapter opens with the word *Therefore*. This word shows that there is a connection between what he is about to say and what he has just said. In this chapter, the author is drawing a conclusion from the truths he taught in the previous chapter.

Immediately prior to this passage, the author recalls how the Israelites rebelled at Kadesh Barnea. They started for the land of promise, but because of unbelief, they were not able to enter the land of rest. They were instead condemned to wander in the wilderness until the next generation grew old enough to enter in belief.

"Therefore"—since it's possible that the recipients of this letter could fall into the same pattern of unbelief and rebellion—they should "be afraid" (the NIV is too weak with "be careful") of falling short of that promise. Instead, they should recognize that the "promise of entering his rest still stands." Simply put, there is a rest that is promised to the believer, and we don't want to miss it!

When we read text, whether it be the Bible or the newspaper, it's clear that we must define (and understand) each word by its use in a particular context. This is because words have multiple meanings, and only the context determines and reveals the meaning the author intended. Consider the statement: "I fought with Joe." Without a larger context, that statement is ambiguous. It could mean, "I fought alongside of Joe," or it could mean "I fought against Joe." The problem in this case is the word *with*. It has multiple meanings, and given such a limited context, it's impossible to know which one to assign here. This type of ambiguity has been the engine for countless jokes down through the years: "My uncle fought with the 1st Infantry, the 2nd Artillery, and the 5th Armored Division. He couldn't get along with anyone!"

In the same way, we must define the word *gospel* according to the context surrounding its use. The word *gospel* simply means "good news." Often it's used to describe the "good news" of salvation from God's wrath through Christ's work on the cross. That's not the way it's used here, however.

In this case, the "good news" is the same "good news" that was preached to the people of Israel after they were redeemed from slavery. The "good news" they heard was of a land flowing with milk and honey, where God would give them His rest. In this context, the "good news" we have received is the same gospel they received. It is the "good news" of a promised rest that we may enter in this life. To say it another way, we have the promise of a life of rest offered to us—and that's good news.

Notice, though, that merely hearing the "good news" regarding this promised rest isn't enough for us to enter it. The hearing must be combined with faith. Just as faith is required in the sinner's life to be born again, so faith is required in the believer's life to enter God's rest. We could state this concept in two simple sentences:

1. Acting in faith allows us to enter God's promised rest.

2. Acting in unbelief keeps us from God's rest.

It's really as simple as that.

Entering His Rest

> *Now we who have believed enter that rest, just as God has said, "So I declared on oath in my anger, 'They shall never enter my rest.'" And yet His work has been finished since the creation of the world. For somewhere He has spoken about the seventh day in these words: "And on the seventh day God rested from all his work"; and again in the preceding passage He says, "They shall never enter my rest"* (HEB 4:3–5, NIV).

The Greek verb translated as "enter" shows a continuous action. Thus, we could translate verse 3 this way: *Indeed, we who have believed are now entering that rest.* In this context, the promised rest is viewed not as an instantaneous act, but rather as a progression. Just as Israel took the land "little by little," so we grow into this rest in the same incremental fashion. It shows the progressive nature of the believer's life as he moves gradually from immaturity to maturity.

Nevertheless, even while we are in the process of entering the rest God promises, that Sabbath-rest can be permanent. To illustrate this, the author of Hebrews refers to God's rest after creation. The divine pattern set by God Himself shows that after the work of creation was finished, there was no need to resume that activity. No additional work was required. The application of this principle is that once we have entered a life of rest, there is no need to enter it again. Just as God rested yet maintains His creation, so the believer can enter into rest and maintain that rest through continued faith. This pattern is restated in verse 10. We can rest from our labors, just as God did from His!

It still remains that some will enter that rest, and those who formerly had the gospel preached to them did not go in, because of their disobedience. Therefore God again set a certain day, calling it Today, when a long time later he spoke through David, as was said before: "Today, if you hear his voice, do not harden your hearts." For if Joshua had given them rest, God would not have spoken later about another day. There remains, then, a Sabbath-rest for the people of God; for anyone who enters God's rest also rests from his own work, just as God did from his.

One of the fundamental truths expressed in this passage is that the offer of rest is a perpetual, continuing offer. It would be easy to conclude that the sinful generation that forfeited its rest moved God to withdraw His offer permanently. Clearly, that wasn't the case, because God allowed the next generation to enter His promised rest. Still, doesn't the fact that God fulfilled His promise in that generation mark the end of the offer? After all, when a promise has been fulfilled, there's no more obligation.

To counter this line of thinking, the author goes back to Psalm 95:7–8: "for he is our God and we are the people of his pasture, the flock under his care. Today, if you hear his voice, do not harden your hearts as you did at Meribah, as you did that day at Massah in the desert . . . ." King David, the author of this psalm, encourages his generation not to harden their hearts like the sinful generation in the wilderness, for "he is our God and we are the people of his pasture, the flock under his care" (Ps 95:7, NIV). The author of Hebrews quotes David's warning to his generation (Heb 4:7) to show that the promise of rest was still offered generations after Israel entered into the land.

When David was anointed King (1 Sam 16:1, 16), it would have been great if, just like Alice, he had suddenly discovered a crown magically on his head. Of course, that's not what happened. Instead, David's life was one of almost constant conflict. In fact, David was responsible for so much bloodshed in his life that God declined his request to build the Temple (1 CHRON 28:3, NIV). In his very first battle, he faced a nine-foot-tall giant who terrified everyone else (1 SAM 17:1–51). He endured persecution from Saul while Saul was alive (1 SAM 18–30). After Saul's death, David was made King of Judah (2 SAM 2:4), but there was still warfare between the house of David and the house of Saul (2 SAM 3:1). Eventually, the latter was defeated and David was made king over all Israel (2 SAM 5:3), yet even after he became king, David spent most of his reign in conflict with the surrounding nations. It is true that "[t]he LORD gave David victory everywhere he went" (1 CHRON 18:6), so that he subdued all the nations around him, but these victories were accomplished through conflict.

Like all of us, King David didn't merely live unto himself. When he went to war, the entire nation engaged the enemy. Nevertheless, in the midst of all this conflict, David wanted to assure his generation that God's promised rest could still be entered by faith.

Since the promise remained even after the first generation took possession of the land, the author of Hebrews conveys a very simple message in verse 9: "There remains, then, a Sabbath-rest for the people of God."

Let us, therefore, make every effort to enter that rest, so that no one will fall by following their example of disobedience.

For the word of God is living and active. Sharper than any double-edged sword, it penetrates even to dividing soul and spirit, joints and marrow; it judges the thoughts and attitudes of the heart. Nothing in all creation is hidden from God's sight. Everything is uncovered and laid bare before the eyes of him to whom we must give account.

After demonstrating that there is in fact a life of rest available to believers today, the author urges us to enter that rest. We are to make not some effort, not a lot of effort, not even nearly every effort, but *every* effort to enter that rest. As has been demonstrated through our earlier discussion, this rest is provided by God but requires our participation. This isn't something we can just drift into without a concerted effort. Again, we don't suddenly discover a crown on our heads.

Instead, entering the rest of God requires an active faith. Faith isn't exhibited by passively sitting around waiting to see what happens. No, faith is an active obedience to God as He reveals His will to us. Furthermore, because faith is so contrary to our nature, we must maintain a careful attention to our lives to ensure that we are exercising it. We can't be like water, taking the path of least resistance, for there is a real danger that we might fall like those in the wilderness through disobedience. Remember: their disobedience was simply a lack of faith that God would do as He promised!

At this point, the question that some may be asking is, "Can someone know if they have entered that rest?" In other words, is it possible to know if you have entered into that permanent state where you are mature and will remain mature? While this text doesn't directly address the issue, I believe from other Scriptures that the answer is no. So let's examine together what can and cannot be known about our own personal maturity.

It seems clear that we can know if we are moving toward maturity and if we are, in fact, among the mature. Paul makes this evident in PHILIPPIANS 3:15–16:

> All of us who are mature should take such a view of things. And if on some point you think differently, that too God will make clear to you. Only let us live up to what we have already attained.

If it were impossible to know if one were mature, then verse 15 would have no meaning. Paul's statement, "All of us" indicates that he includes himself as one of the mature. So whether or not we have attained maturity is something that is knowable, at least to some extent.

However, immediately previous to Paul's confident assertion of his own maturity, he states (PHIL 3:12–14, NIV),

> *Not that I have already obtained all this, or have already been made perfect, but I press on to take hold of that for which Christ Jesus took hold of me. Brothers, I do not consider myself yet to have taken hold of it. But one thing I do: Forgetting what is behind and straining toward what is ahead, I press on toward the goal to win the prize for which God has called me heavenward in Christ Jesus.*

Notice that Paul, although mature, didn't consider himself to have become what he should be as a believer. Instead, he forgets all the things he has achieved and makes a concerted effort to become more mature, "to take hold of that for which Christ Jesus took hold of me." He is "straining toward" the "goal." Picture a runner with complete concentration straining every muscle to reach the goal line and you have the picture. Even though Paul counted himself among the mature, he kept up his intensity with regard to maturity. He didn't let down or slack off. It also seems clear that Paul doesn't expect to reach that goal this side of eternity. The prize he is striving for is "heavenward."

Why would God reveal to us that a state of permanent maturity—the Sabbath-rest—is available, but not allow us to know when we've arrived? The answer seems to be that no matter how mature we become, we will still fall far short of what God desires us to be. So, though we may reach a state of maturity that is permanent (in that we will confess our sins relatively quickly and continue being filled with the Spirit), God withholds that knowledge from us so that we will remain spiritually diligent. We must continue to strain toward the goal, and as long as there is still sin in our lives, we haven't arrived yet.

Spiritual diligence is also required because of the revelation God has provided. Our lives are judged by the Word in the here-and-now. Oh, certainly we will all stand before the judgment seat of Christ (2 Cor 5:10), but even in this life we can know God's assessment of our behavior through His Word.

The way the Bible is described in this passage is fascinating. It seems to be written in such a way that we won't be tempted to try and pull a spiritual fast one. The temptation is always there to try to rationalize that our sin really isn't that bad, or that God couldn't really require this painful a sacrifice. As we try to convince ourselves, we might also be tempted to think that we can convince God as well. That just isn't going to happen.

Look at the way the Bible is described:

- *It is living.* The Bible is literally "God-breathed" (2 Tim 3:16) and therefore exhibits the character of God Himself. As God lives, so His Word lives. These aren't ordinary words on a page, but words brought to life by God Himself in our hearts.

- *The Word is active.* It does something to those who read it. For some, it shames them into repentance. For others, it stiffens their rebellion against God. Still, no one reads the Bible and remains unchanged. As it enlightens our minds, it also changes our behavior because it reveals what is really going on inside of us.

- *It is a sharp sword.* Some have restricted this to mean that it penetrates us easily so as to distinguish good from evil within our hearts—the part no one but God can see. I find this too limiting, though: a sword doesn't merely penetrate, it wounds. If you've ever read the Word and been found guilty of an attitude or action that you've denied or covered up or ignored, if you've ever burned with shame because of the testimony of Scripture, you know what I mean.

God is gracious, compassionate, slow to anger, and abounding in love. This is true of the Bible as well, because God reveals Himself in its pages. But God is also the Holy God full of glory! At the sight of Him, Isaiah could say nothing but "Woe is me!" because of his consciousness of his sin (Isa 6:3–5). Because the Bible reveals God, it produces the same response. It allows no excuses, it grants no exceptions, it permits no delay. It demands obedience and humble submission to the living and active words we read.

- *It is a discerner of our hearts.* In connection with the preceding point, nothing can be hidden from its piercing gaze. Everyone is naked and laid bare before Him to whom we must give an account.

Is it any wonder, then, with so much at stake, that the author of Hebrews commands us to make "every effort" to enter the rest God has provided? And why wouldn't we want to? Don't you desire peace and joy that this world can never give? Don't you long for self-control over those sinful areas of your life that are so destructive? Have you forgotten the glory of God's person and the intimate fellowship we can have with Him?

Do you want to know what peace in the midst of conflict looks like? On Thanksgiving Day, my father was eating the traditional meal at my sister's house. I've been told that the food was great, but he couldn't keep any of it down. So they took him to the hospital. After the doctors ran a series of tests, we were informed that the problem could be cancer. Still, they wouldn't know for sure until they'd done one or two more tests.

When all the information was in, the family was summoned to the doctor's office. Before he could speak, my dad said, "I want you to know that you can't give me any bad news, so don't worry about what to say. If you tell me that I'm going to die, then I get to go and be with my Savior, for to be absent from the body is to be present with the Lord. If you say that my condition is treatable, then I get to stay here and spend more time with my children and grandchildren. I'm really in a win-win situation here. So don't worry about anything, just tell me the truth."

The doctor informed us that my dad had pancreatic cancer and the prognosis was grim. When we asked about treatment, he said, "If you were ten people, it wouldn't help nine of you." My father shrugged his shoulders and said simply, "Well, okay then. I know what I've got to look forward to."

As a pastor, I've dealt with numerous people who have found themselves in similar situations. My dad's peaceful attitude, which is the product of faith, isn't exactly rare among believers, but I confess it is uncommon. Would you have responded that way? When serious conflict comes here in Canaan, how do you react?

Oh, dear one, make every effort to enter that rest and move on toward maturity. If you keep walking in that direction long enough, you'll arrive at the place of rest—and when you settle there and make it your home, you'll find it's the most wondrous place this side of eternity.

What's amazing is that it's available now.

Discussion Questions

1. In each of chapters 10–13, we have revisited your answer to the question: "Where do you want to go?" Now that we've completed this section of the book, please rewrite your answer to that question and compare it to your original answer.

2. Describe the nature of the Sabbath-rest, and how one enters it.

3. What do you imagine this rest would "look like" in your life?

4. Discuss the nature of the Scriptures, and how they affect a person's entry into rest.

5. Has this chapter brought any questions to mind, or any thoughts you would like to discuss with the group?

6. Is there any issue you would like prayed for, or accountability in, over the course of this week?

7. Please note any other group members' answers that you would like to follow up on this week, either by praying for them or by making an encouraging contact.

Living in Canaan Part Five

As she'd expected, Christine found the next four months horrible. Ben seemed to take perverse delight in making her life difficult. Her work was never sufficient, no matter how hard she tried. His off-hand comments were calculated to wound as deeply as possible. "How'd you ever get this job? What did they do, feel sorry for you?" "Christine, you can stay late. The rest of us have plans and you never go out anyway."

Once, when leaving for the day, she heard his voice among others coming from around the corner near the employee exit. She stopped and listened, even though she was under heavy conviction to keep walking. The voices were lowered, but she was able to hear her name once or twice. Then she heard laughter. The blood rushed to her face as she started off again, her heels clicking on the concrete. Just after she passed, someone let out an "Oops" and the laughter began again.

"Serves me right," she thought. "I know better than to do that."

"Lord, forgive me," she prayed as she continued to the parking lot. "The consequences of sin are never worth it and You've just taught me that once more. Please remind me again next time." She knew there would be a next time.

As Ben became more arrogant, he began to experiment with physical intimidation when it suited him. To his (small) credit, it was never when Christine was alone. That would have genuinely frightened her. No, his specialty was humiliation.

The first instance was on a Tuesday afternoon. Everyone was at their desks preparing for the budget review meeting. "Mr. Ackerman" (as he insisted he be addressed) marched to her desk and snatched a piece of paper from the folder he was carrying. He slammed the folder on top of the filing cabinet just outside her cubicle. The hollow frame of the cabinet let out a metallic boom and all eyes snapped to the source of the sound. Holding the paper aloft in his right hand, he howled, "We don't allow shoddy work around here!" With that he tore the paper into tiny bits, which showered down into her cubicle, and snarled, "Fix it!" Christine thought she saw an ever-so-slight smirk on his face as he stalked back to his office.

All eyes were on her as she quietly put down her work, got down on her hands and knees, and began picking up the pieces. The silence of those few moments was deafening. Slowly people began to return to their tasks as Christine retook her seat and began assembling the puzzle before her. It turned out to be a routine memo that had nothing to do with the budget process. When she opened the memo on her computer, she had to read it twice before she found the lone typo.

Steve did his best to cheer her up when times got particularly tough, but his hatred for Ben made her conversations even with him less than encouraging. Still, she was determined to maintain as good a Christian witness as she knew how.

Thankfully, she didn't have to go it alone. Christine remembered the night at church during the ladies' Bible study, when it all came spilling out. As usual, when the lesson was over they began to take prayer requests. She had meant simply to ask prayer for work, but she didn't make it past the first few words. Without warning, she began to sob uncontrollably. She buried her eyes in her handkerchief, clenched tightly in her fists, and rocked back and forth. She tried to speak, but every breath she took was expended on her loud cries. Her sisters hurried around her with hugs, tears, and prayers. Nearly unable to speak, it took some time for Christine to get the story out, but when she faltered, one or two would pray until she could continue. After that night, she became a special object of prayer and love. Those in the study group often sent her short notes of encouragement and reassurance. Someone, it seemed, was in contact with her every couple of days. And they all were praying for her earnestly. She wasn't perfect, and she knew it. She was, however, deeply thankful that God, through the prayers of His people, graciously gave her strength when she needed it the most, so that her testimony remained unsoiled.

One day Steve stopped by her desk with a cheery, "What's up, kid? How's things?"

"Oh, about the same," she said flatly. Earlier that morning, Ben had ceremoniously dropped a huge stack of folders on her desk, loudly proclaiming that she had done them all wrong.

"Well, I've been thinking," Steve whispered as he leaned in closer. "I think there's a way to finally stick it to ole Benedict over there." He found the comparison with the famous traitor funny every time he said it.

"Knock it off," Christine snapped, in a sudden fit of temper that surprised even her. Drawing a deep breath, she asked, "Do you think this has been easy for me? You are not helping make it any easier."

"I want to make it easier," said Steve genuinely. "That's why I've been thinkin'—"

"About what?" she asked sharply. "About how to sabotage Ben? About how to lie and swindle just like he did? About how to tempt me to sin when I so desperately . . . " Christine bit her lip and snapped her gaze across the room.

"Don't want to?" Steve suggested, shifting his weight as he spoke.

"No!" Then her tone softened as she turned her head back. "No, Steve, when I so desperately *do* want to. When I want revenge more than anything in the world." She began tapping her desk with a pen. "But I can't take it." Her jaw was set and her eyes resolute.

"Well, well, well, my little angel," Steve said with a twinkle in his eye as he leaned in a little closer, "you don't have to. I know you well enough to know that you wouldn't stoop to his level. I wouldn't ask you to do that." He was lying and he knew it, but it sounded good.

Christine cocked her head slightly to one side and studied him closely. "What are you talking about?"

"Oh, nothin'," Steve said with a sly grin. "But I bet if you pulled the sales receipts from last month and checked them against the inventory report, you'd find some very entertaining reading." With that he turned on his heel and walked away, cheerfully whistling some nameless tune.

FASTER! FASTER!

Now! Now!" cried the Queen. "Faster! Faster!"
And they went so fast that at last they seemed to
skim through the air, hardly touching the ground
with their feet till, suddenly, just as Alice was getting
quite exhausted, they stopped, and she found
herself sitting on the ground, breathless and giddy.

The Queen propped her up against a tree, and said
kindly, "You may rest a little now."

Alice looked round her in great surprise. "Why, I do
believe we've been under this tree the whole time!
Everything's just as it was!"

"Of course it is," said the Queen, "what would you
have it?"

"Well, in OUR country," said Alice, still panting
a little, "you'd generally get to somewhere else—
if you ran very fast for a long time, as we've been
doing."

"A slow sort of country!" said the Queen. "Now,
HERE, you see, it takes all the running YOU can
do, to keep in the same place. If you want to get
somewhere else, you must run at least twice as
fast as that!"

—*Looking-Glass*, ch. II, "The Garden of Live Flowers"

Chapter 14
How Do You Get There?

I n 1995, McArthur Wheeler walked into two Pittsburgh banks and robbed them in broad daylight, with no visible attempt at disguise. He was arrested later that night, less than an hour after videotapes of him taken from surveillance cameras were broadcast on the 11 o'clock news. When police later showed him the surveillance tapes, Mr. Wheeler stared in incredulity. "But I wore the juice," he mumbled. Apparently, Mr. Wheeler was under the impression that rubbing one's face with lemon juice rendered it invisible to videotape cameras.

That amazing story is the opening paragraph of a scientific study, conducted by researchers at Cornell University,[1] with a surprising conclusion: *Incompetent people don't know they're incompetent.* According to these investigators, the skills it takes to be competent are the same skills it takes to recognize competency. The authors state: "[W]hen people are incompetent in the strategies they adopt to achieve success and satisfaction, they suffer a dual burden: Not only do they reach erroneous conclusions and make unfortunate choices, but their incompetence robs them of the ability to realize it."[2]

The report details four studies that tested the participants' ability in humor, logical reasoning, and English grammar. The participants were then asked to predict how well they had done on these tests overall and how well they had done in comparison with others. Based on this research, Kruger and Dunning reached the following three conclusions:

1. Incompetent people tend to grossly overestimate their own abilities. People scoring in the bottom 25 percent of these tests overestimated their performance by an average of 45 to 50 percent. People in the top 25 percent routinely underestimated their scores.

2. Incompetent people do not get a truer picture of their own incompetence by observing the behavior of others. When given the opportunity to review the test results of all the participants, those in the bottom 25 percent actually did worse in estimating their own abilities, whereas those in the top 25 percent improved their estimates.

3. The way to make incompetent people recognize their own incompetence is to help them become competent. The bottom 25 percent in the tests improved their ability to recognize their own competence only when they were trained in the subject in which they were being tested. When they were given training in English grammar, not only did their test scores in that area improve, but their ability to see their actual competence in that area improved as well.

Now, I don't know about you, but I find the results of that study unsettling. I say that because, according to this study, I could be grossly incompetent and not know it! This study shows us that we must rely heavily on the assessment of others regarding our abilities if we are to have a true picture of ourselves.

This is just as true in the spiritual realm as in the physical realm. Because the carnal man is relying on the flesh for his judgments concerning right and wrong, he will be convinced of the correctness of his behavior, not realizing his incompetence in spiritual matters.

He will observe his own jealousy and quarreling, his division of the church by encouraging factions, his lack of faith—and be convinced that he is exercising the appropriate behavior for the circumstances. He will continue to believe this even if he is surrounded by mature believers whose behavior is directly contrary to his own.

The only way to convince a carnal believer to behave differently from the world is to make him competent in righteousness. He must be trained to distinguish good from evil (HEB 5:14). But how, exactly, is such training accomplished? We have seen that we must spend hours in the gym, so to speak, to train for righteousness. Still, what exactly are we to practice?

If the truth were told, many of us would have to admit that we have no idea. Like Alice, we run as fast as we can, and yet it seems we stay in the same place. Then we're told that our problem is we're just not running fast enough!

An often-used illustration is of two dogs fighting within you: a good dog and a bad dog. The one that wins is the one you feed the most. So, we resolve to read our Bible more, pray more, give more, . . . (fill in the blank), but it never produces the results we hope for. We run as fast as we can and yet stay in the same spot. Anyone who has ever seriously attempted to live righteously will immediately identify with Paul when he speaks of this problem:

> *We know that the law is spiritual; but I am unspiritual [literal translation: fleshy], sold as a slave to sin. I do not understand what I do. For what I want to do I do not do, but what I hate I do. And if I do what I do not want to do, I agree that the law is good. As it is, it is no longer I myself who do it, but it is sin living in me. I know that nothing good lives in me, that is, in my sinful nature [lit., flesh]. For I have the desire to do what is good, but I cannot carry it out. For what I do is not the good*

I want to do; no, the evil I do not want to do—this I keep on doing. Now if I do what I do not want to do, it is no longer I who do it, but it is sin living in me that does it. For in my inner being I delight in God's law; but I see another law at work in the members of my body, waging war against the law of my mind and making me a prisoner of the law of sin at work within my members (Rom 7:14–23, NIV).

What Paul is saying here is that spiritual growth isn't just a matter of making up our minds, trying harder, or catching the White Rabbit! If it were that easy, there would be no problem. We would just say the magic words, or pray the correct prayer, and our struggle with sin would be solved, over and done with. Instead, what we discover is that the story about the dogs is just so much hokum. The reality is that I don't do the good I want to do, the evil I despise is what I end up doing, and trying harder doesn't get the job done! I'm sold as a slave to sin! I've lost the war with sin and have been taken prisoner! I've been thrown in the dungeon of sin, and I don't know how to get out!

The great thing about ROMANS CHAPTER 7 is that it is followed by ROMANS CHAPTER 8 (profound observation, I know). The reason this is great news is because the answer to the problem described in ROMANS 7 is found in ROMANS 8:

Therefore, there is now no condemnation for those who are in Christ Jesus, because through Christ Jesus the law of the Spirit of life set me free from the law of sin and death. For what the law was powerless to do in that it was weakened by the sinful nature, God did by sending his own Son in the likeness of sinful man to be a sin offering. And so he condemned sin in sinful man, in order that the righteous requirements of the law might be fully met in us, who do not live according to the sinful nature but according to the Spirit (Rom 8:1–4, NIV).

Romans 8:1 is one of the most misunderstood verses in the Bible. Most people read the phrase "no condemnation" and conclude that it is referring to our salvation from condemnation in hell. It's true that we are saved from such condemnation, but that interpretation doesn't fit the context of Paul's argument. The word *condemnation* in the original language doesn't merely declare someone guilty. It refers to penal condemnation or the punishment of being confined to prison.[3] What Paul is saying is that we are no longer condemned to prison. What prison? Why, the prison of sin (Rom 7:24)! The doors have been unlocked and thrown open. We no longer have to live in the squalor of the dungeon.

So, how do we become practically righteous? Not by living according to law. The law demanded righteousness from us, but it was powerless to help us in that it was "weakened by the sinful [literally, *flesh*] nature." Nevertheless, the righteousness that the law demands can be, not partially, not even mostly, but "fully" met in us, "who do not walk according to the flesh, but according to the Spirit" (Rom 8:4, NASB).

The careful reader at this point will notice that Paul is speaking about the difference between the carnal man (walking according to the flesh) and the spiritual man (walking according to the Spirit). Hence, the question at this point is simply this: What does it mean to walk according to the Spirit? What we will discover is that walking in the Spirit is one of the qualifications for being "filled with the Spirit" (Eph 5:18). When we are filled with the Spirit, He is accomplishing in and through us all He desires at that moment, so we lead holy lives.

So, what are the requirements for being filled with the Spirit? What does being filled with the Spirit look like, anyway? What's the remedy when the believer sins? These questions and more are answered in the following chapters.

Discussion Questions

In each of chapters 14–20, we will be revisiting your answer to the question: "How do you get there?" Please look back at your answer to that question and examine it in light of this chapter.

1. Using the version of your choice, write ROMANS 8:1–4 out on a card and post it where it can be an encouragement to you as you face temptations. Consider memorizing this chapter.

2. Write in your own words what this chapter teaches you about your battle with sin.

3. Has this chapter brought any questions to mind, or any thoughts you would like to discuss with the group?

4. Is there any issue you would like prayed for, or accountability in, over the course of this week?

5. Please note any other group members' answers that you would like to follow up on this week, either by praying for them or by making an encouraging contact.

THE WHITE KNIGHT

Of all the strange things that Alice saw in her journey Through The Looking-Glass, this was the one that she always remembered most clearly. Years afterwards she could bring the whole scene back again, as if it had been only yesterday—the mild blue eyes and kindly smile of the Knight—the setting sun gleaming through his hair, and shining on his armour in a blaze of light that quite dazzled her—the horse quietly moving about, with the reins hanging loose on his neck, cropping the grass at her feet—and the black shadows of the forest behind—all this she took in like a picture, as, with one hand shading her eyes, she leant against a tree, watching the strange pair, and listening, in a half dream, to the melancholy music of the song.

"But the tune ISN'T his own invention," she said to herself: "it's 'I GIVE THEE ALL, I CAN NO MORE.'" She stood and listened very attentively, but no tears came into her eyes.

—*Looking-Glass*, ch. VIII, "It's My Own Invention"

Chapter 15
Through the Looking-Glass

Have you ever noticed that couples who have lived together a long time tend to look alike? Sometimes the resemblance might tempt you to mistake them for siblings. There are several theories as to why this happens, but one of the most interesting involves what is called "mirroring."[1]

Evidently, certain neurons in the brain are triggered when we watch someone else. If that person shows disgust, your face moves to mirror the emotion you are witnessing. If you see someone smile, you tend to mirror that smile. This mirroring appears to help us enter the emotional state of another person and more thoroughly understand it.* So, when two people look at one another and mirror the emotions expressed, they use the same facial muscles. Over time, continuous exercise of these muscles tends to produce the same set of automatic facial responses and even the same set of wrinkles. Couples married

---

*When I see the facial expression of someone else, and this perception leads me to experience that expression as a particular affective state, I do not accomplish this type of understanding through an argument by analogy. The other's emotion is constituted, experienced and therefore directly understood by means of an embodied simulation producing a shared body state. It is the activation of a neural mechanism shared by the observer and the observed to enable direct experiential understanding" (Gallese, 2008).

fifty years look alike because they've been making the same faces at one another for a long time!

In the same way, walking with God over time makes us more like Him. You might say we begin to look like Him because we mirror—we reflect—what He looks like. Here is Paul's description of this phenomenon:

> *And we, who with unveiled faces all reflect the Lord's glory, are being transformed into his likeness with ever-increasing glory, which comes from the Lord, who is the Spirit* (2 COR 3:18, NIV).

In other words, just like couples here on earth, we begin to look like God. We are "transformed into his likeness."

The fact that we are "being" transformed indicates that this is a process, as we noted earlier. It also indicates that not all Christians are the same. Employing a number of different phrases to distinguish them, the Bible teaches that there are two varieties of Christians:

- Those who remain in Christ and those who do not remain in Christ (JOHN 15:4, 6)

- Those who walk in light and those who walk in darkness (1 JOHN 1:6, 7)

- Those who are slaves to sin and those who are slaves to righteousness (ROM 6:16)

- Those who walk according to the Spirit and those who walk according to the flesh (ROM 8:4)

- Those who walk according to the Spirit and those who walk as men (GAL 5:16; 1 COR 3:3)

- Those who are spiritual and those who are carnal (1 COR 2:15, 3:1)

Remember two important facts when considering these distinctions: (1) these contrasts describe the quality of life that believers experience, and (2) in each case there is a command, either explicit or implicit, to live one way and not the other.

Knowing this to be true, we may say that the Bible *commands* a great transformation in the life of every believer. This transformation should not be considered a second work of grace, but rather the growth that occurs when we move from walking by the flesh to walking in the Spirit; that is, when we move from immaturity to maturity.

We should be quick to remember that merely possessing intellectual knowledge concerning these distinctions is not enough to move us in the right direction. Similarly, enjoying the blessings of walking in the Spirit, at least to some degree, doesn't require the ability to pass a theology exam. Although the Bible speaks at length about this stage in the believer's life, this great transformation is more experiential than academic. Knowing what the Bible has to say is part of becoming mature, but knowledge by itself does not enable one to become mature. Likewise, the lack of knowledge doesn't completely prevent spiritual living. This is due to the nature of the change God demands.

The great transformation that God demands is based upon a relationship, not the accumulation of facts. This is not to say that knowledge isn't important. The means by which "the man of God may be thoroughly equipped for every good work" is through Scripture's role in "teaching, rebuking, correcting, and training in righteousness" (2 TIM 3:16–17, NIV). If knowledge were completely unnecessary for spiritual growth, then the Bible could have been made much shorter without harming God's people. I'm sure the essential facts required for salvation would fit within the pages of an average magazine. Nevertheless, God has revealed so much more of Himself, because we need that knowledge to grow. We thus see a mutual dependency: knowledge by itself cannot strengthen a relationship, nor can a relationship thrive without knowledge.

If you were to ask me to describe my wife, I could give you a list of facts about her. I could list her height (but not her weight, if I know what's good for me), her age, place of birth, favorite colors, and so forth. But I couldn't describe what it's like to touch her hand, see her smile, hear her laugh, smell her hair, or taste her lips. Any attempt to place into words these wondrous joys would be laughably inadequate. Nor could I chronicle the sweet communion we enjoy after spending most of our lives together. Words fail when asked to convey too much.

If I really have close communion with my wife, I will know certain facts about her. I'll know what she likes and dislikes. I'll be aware of what to say (and definitely what not to say), and when to say it. I'll be conscious of what makes her happy, and if I love her, I'll do those things.

In the same way, our relationship with the Spirit is not reducible to knowledge, yet as that relationship grows and flourishes, we gain knowledge that is necessary for and suitable to moving the relationship deeper. Even though we can't completely describe the peace, the power, and the blessings that come from yielding to God, we can know the source of it. God the Holy Spirit is the One who produces these qualities in our lives.

In the same way, though we can't completely describe the qualities the Holy Spirit imparts to our lives, we can detail some of these blessings, because God has given clear revelation concerning these things. The fact that we aren't completely able to describe what God does in the life of the believer doesn't mean we are completely unable, either. Incomplete descriptions aren't the same as no descriptions at all.

For example, the child of God is able to "test and approve" God's "good, pleasing and perfect will" for us (ROM 12:2, NIV). This means that when we are led by the Spirit, we will be able to know and do those "good works, which God prepared in advance for us to do" (EPH 2:10,

NIV). By the power of the Holy Spirit, we can have reproduced in us the "mind of Christ" (1 COR 2:16, NIV) and "participate in the divine nature" (1 PET 1:4, NIV).

These "very great and precious promises" (1 PET 1:4, NIV) are fulfilled when one is "filled with the Spirit" (EPH 5:18).

Filled with the Spirit

Just as we had to derive the definitions discussed earlier, we must also investigate the exact meaning of being "filled with the Spirit." There is only one direct command in the New Testament concerning this phenomenon: "And do not get drunk with wine, for that is dissipation, but be filled with the Spirit" (EPH 5:18, NIV). Actually, the tense of the verb in the original language shows a continuous action, so a better translation might be "keep on being filled with the Spirit." Also notice that this is a command. Therefore, not to be "filled" is disobedience, otherwise known as sin.

The problem we face at this point is that, although being Spirit-filled is compared to getting drunk, no formal definition is given. We can't be certain, but one possible reason for this omission could be that the Spirit does "not speak on His own initiative," but instead speaks on behalf of the Son in order to bring Him glory (JOHN 16: 12–15).

I remember one time I was ministering in a little village in Bolivia. The thatched-roof church was full of native South Americans known as Quechua. My missionary host, who had been in the field longer than I had been alive at the time, was translating my sermon into Spanish, so that the pastor of the church could understand and repeat it in Quechuan. I began to suspect that something was being lost in translation, however, when I would speak only a phrase or two of a sentence and the missionary would continue for two or three minutes. Then, when I finished the sentence, he would merely say, "Sí." I don't know what sermon the congregation was hearing, but I'm fairly certain it wasn't the one I was preaching.

Well, unlike the missionary translator I worked with, we might think of the Spirit as the perfect translator. He only speaks what He hears (JOHN 16:13). One strong piece of evidence of His complete faithfulness to this mission is that we don't know His name. We know the name of the Father, because He has disclosed it to us. "God, furthermore, said to Moses, 'Thus you shall say to the sons of Israel, The LORD, the God of your fathers, the God of Abraham, the God of Isaac, and the God of Jacob, has sent me to you. This is My name forever, and this is My memorial-name to all generations'" (Ex 3:15, NASB). The word "LORD" (in all capital letters in the Old Testament) is a translation of God's name, usually pronounced *Yahweh.* We know the name of the Son because God has likewise revealed that name as well: "And she will bear a Son; and you shall call His name Jesus, for it is He who will save His people from their sins. . . . [S]he gave birth to a Son; and he called His name Jesus" (MATT 1:21, 25, NIV). In contrast, the Spirit is only revealed to us by descriptive terms such as "the Holy Spirit," or "the Spirit of God," or simply "the Spirit."

The Spirit doesn't seek His own glory, but He does seek to glorify Christ (JOHN 16:14). An example of this truth can be found in the conversion of the Apostle Paul. We read in ACTS 9:17 (NIV) that Paul was "filled with the Holy Spirit." The result of that filling was that, after eating, "immediately he began to proclaim Jesus in the synagogues, saying, 'He is the Son of God'" (ACTS 9:20, NIV). There is no evidence that Saul (Paul's name before it was changed) was conscious of the filling of the Spirit, but there is evidence that his preoccupation was with the person of Jesus Christ. So we see that the Spirit was the cause of the preaching that glorified Christ.

Because the Spirit speaks only what He hears and His passion is with Christ's glory, it isn't surprising that His own work is mentioned without formal definition. Nevertheless, we are not left entirely in the dark as to how to fulfill the command to "keep on being filled with the Spirit." Three times in the New Testament, being filled with the Spirit is contrasted with being drunk:

> [F]or he will be great in the sight of the Lord. He is never to take wine or other fermented drink, and he will be filled with the Holy Spirit even from birth (LUKE 1:15, NIV).

> All of them were filled with the Holy Spirit and began to speak in other tongues as the Spirit enabled them. . . . Some, however, made fun of them and said, "They have had too much wine" (ACTS 2:4, 13, NIV).

> Do not get drunk on wine, which leads to debauchery. Instead, be filled with the Spirit (EPH 5:18, NIV).

In LUKE 1:15, alcohol is shown to be incompatible with being filled with the Spirit. John the Baptizer was to "never" take either wine or any other fermented drink. Instead, he would be filled with the Spirit "from birth." The absolute nature of his life should be noted. Evidently, all his life he was "filled with the Holy Spirit," which precluded his drinking alcohol.

In ACTS 2, the disciples are given the miraculous ability to speak known languages that they had not previously learned (the list of the languages is in verses 9–11). The theme of their preaching was Christ (vv. 22–36). Their boldness in professing Him was mistaken for being drunk. It seems there is a pattern of behavior that is similar to drunkenness when one is filled with the Spirit.

This pattern of behavior doesn't lead to the same result, however. Paul tells us why we're not to get drunk: it leads to "debauchery." In English, this word usually is defined as excessive indulgence in sensual pleasures. The original language, however, provides a wealth of information concerning what it means to be filled with wine. The word translated as "debauchery" refers to "behavior which shows lack of concern or thought for the consequences of an action—'senseless deeds, reckless deeds, recklessness.'" That's why this word is translated in some languages as "what one does without being able to think about it" or "what one does when the mind is absent."[2]

This is a good description of the effect of alcohol on a person's inhibitions. According to the Nineteenth Judicial Circuit Court of Illinois, "The first area of the brain [that] alcohol affects is the area which regulates inhibitions, judgment, and self-control. It is the lack of such restraints that causes the apparently 'stimulated' or uninhibited behavior and people may do things they might not otherwise do."[3] It is this lack of inhibition, or the loss of the ability to say no, that causes "debauchery." So when we drink (as little as .05% blood alcohol content), we begin to lose the ability to say no to the flesh. The more we drink, the less we say no. The result is that we end up doing things when we are drunk that we wouldn't dream of doing had we remained sober. We also say things we wouldn't normally say. This is the meaning of the old Latin phrase *in vino veritas* ("in wine there is the truth"). People have fewer inhibitions when they drink, so they say what they really think.

When we compare this understanding of drunkenness to being filled with the Spirit, a clear picture begins to emerge. People don't say no to the flesh when they are drunk, and the opposite is true when they are filled with the Spirit. Not only do they say no to the flesh (GAL 5:16), but they don't say no to the Spirit. Their inhibitions concerning the things of God go away and they have power from above to obey. Given all this, we can derive the following definition for "being filled with the Spirit":

Definition: The filling of the Spirit is the spiritual state attained when the Holy Spirit is accomplishing in and through us all that He desires.

Although this definition is complete, several aspects of it require further explanation:

- There is no such thing as being partially filled with the Spirit. It may be true that there are different levels of drunkenness; however, the believer is either filled with the Spirit or he is not. The Spirit is either accomplishing what He desires in our lives or He is not.

   Consider it this way: The filling of the Spirit is like an on/off switch. Moving toward maturity is like a dimmer switch. Only two states are possible regarding the filling of the Spirit: on or off. You're either filled or you're not; there is nothing in between. In contrast, like a dimmer switch, many levels of maturity are possible as we grow in Christ and move toward the Sabbath-rest—and the amount of "light" may increase or decrease at any time.

- The "filling" issue isn't one of our getting more of the Holy Spirit, but of the Holy Spirit getting more of us. The term *filling* might conjure a mistaken mental image. When we are filling a glass with water, we are adding more water to the glass. This isn't the case with God the Holy Spirit. Every believer is indwelt by the Spirit from the moment of salvation. He "is a deposit guaranteeing our inheritance until the redemption of those who are God's possession" (EPH 1:14, NIV). We will never have more of the Spirit than at the moment of salvation. What is at issue is how much we allow the Spirit to control us.

- Even the newest believer can be (and in fact is commanded to be) filled with the Spirit. Although the time we spend being filled with the Spirit moves us closer to maturity, maturity is not a prerequisite to being filled. To state it more plainly, you can be filled with the Spirit right now as long as you accept and trust Christ as your Savior.

- When we are filled with the Spirit, He is able to display in us the life and character of Christ. Being filled with the Spirit is the only way a believer may say, "For me to live is Christ, and to die is gain" (PHIL 1:21, NIV). The character produced in us will be that of Christ. The cause of that godly character, however, is the unhindered indwelling Holy Spirit working within us. "And we, who with unveiled faces all reflect the Lord's glory, are being transformed into his likeness with ever-increasing glory, which comes from the Lord, who is the Spirit" (2 COR 3:18, NIV).

What should be our response to this? Obviously, we need to be filled with the Spirit. We need to say, like Paul:

Brothers, I do not consider myself yet to have taken hold of it. But one thing I do: Forgetting what is behind and straining toward what is ahead, I press on toward the goal to win the prize for which God has called me heavenward in Christ Jesus. All of us who are mature should take such a view of things. And if on some point you think differently, that too God will make clear to you (PHIL 3:13–15, NIV).

Now, how exactly does one press toward the goal? We should note at this point that there are three qualifications for being filled with the Spirit:

1. Do not grieve the Spirit (EPH 4:30).
2. Do not quench the Spirit (1 THESS 5:19).
3. Walk by the Spirit (GAL 5:16).

In other words, there are three requirements the believer must fulfill in order to be filled with the Spirit. We will see that we must:

1. Confess every known sin. Unknown sin isn't an issue, because it doesn't affect the attitudes of our heart. It is our willingness to cease our rebellions by confession that is important.

2. Yield ourselves to the will of God, as well as we can know it.

3. Walk in conscious dependence upon the power of the Holy Spirit to produce in us a life pleasing to God.

We will also see that trying to live according to a list of rules does not contribute to a righteous life. In fact, it brings about just the opposite. These are the issues we turn to next.

Discussion Questions

In each of chapters 14–20, we will be revisiting your answer to the question: "How do you get there?" Please look back at your answer to that question and examine it in light of this chapter.

1. Discuss how knowledge of God promotes spiritual maturity. How can a person's relationship with a spouse illustrate this?

2. How does intellectual knowledge figure into our growth in maturity?

3. In your own words, discuss what we can learn about the filling of the Spirit by its contrast with drunkenness.

4. Has this chapter brought any questions to mind, or any thoughts you would like to discuss with the group?

5. Is there any issue you would like prayed for, or accountability in, over the course of this week?

6. Please note any other group members' answers that you would like to follow up on this week, either by praying for them or by making an encouraging contact.

A MAD TEA PARTY

The Hatter was the first to break the silence. "What day of the month is it?" he said, turning to Alice. He had taken his watch out of his pocket, and was looking at it uneasily, shaking it every now and then, and holding it to his ear.

Alice considered a little, and said, "The fourth."

"Two days wrong!" sighed the Hatter. "I told you butter wouldn't suit the works!" he added, looking angrily at the March Hare.

"It was the BEST butter," the March Hare meekly replied.

"Yes, but some crumbs must have got in as well," the Hatter grumbled; "you shouldn't have put it in with the bread knife."

The March Hare took the watch and looked at it gloomily; then he dipped it into his cup of tea, and looked at it again; but he could think of nothing better to say than his first remark, "It was the BEST butter, you know."

—*Wonderland*, ch. VII, "A Mad Tea Party"

Chapter 16
Butter Won't Suit the Works

Every genuine believer understands the fact that we are saved by grace apart from works, so that no one can boast (EPH 2: 8, 9). What is less understood is that, just as we can't be saved by a list of do's and don'ts, we don't grow in righteousness that way either. For some strange reason, we have the tendency to think that, while our salvation must be a work of God, our practical, day-to-day righteousness is up to us. So we struggle; we make resolutions; we promise to do better; we grit our teeth and sweat and strain—all to no avail. Why is this?

Paul answers this question by explaining the true nature of the Law and the terrible effect it has on us:

For while we were in the flesh, the sinful passions, which were aroused by the Law, were at work in the members of our body to bear fruit for death. But now we have been released from the Law, having died to that by which we were bound, so that we serve in newness of the Spirit and not in oldness of the letter.

What shall we say then? Is the Law sin? May it never be! On the contrary, I would not have come to know sin except through the Law; for I would not have known about coveting if the Law had not said, "You shall not covet." But sin, taking opportunity through the commandment, produced in me coveting *of every kind; for apart from the Law sin is dead. And I was once alive apart from the Law; but when the commandment came, sin became alive, and I died; and this commandment, which was to result in life, proved to result in death for me; for sin, taking opportunity through the commandment, deceived me, and through it killed me. So then, the Law is holy, and the commandment is holy and righteous and good. Therefore did that which is good become a cause of death for me? May it never be! Rather it was sin, in order that it might be shown to be sin by effecting my death through that which is good, that through the commandment sin might become utterly sinful* (ROM 7:5–13, NASB).*

The terrible reality of trying to live by the law works (whether it is the Law of Moses or any other system of rules) is that it is ultimately self-defeating. For while our set of rules demands a certain type of behavior, it doesn't provide the power necessary to produce that behavior. Instead, rule books stir up the sinful rebellion in our hearts so that they produce the very behavior that they prohibit. Our sinful passions are aroused by the Law (ROM 7:5). Sin takes advantage of the opportunity that the Law produces to increase and express our natural wickedness.

You know this to be true, don't you? What's the quickest way to get someone to do something? Tell them they can't. Immediately, the desire for the forbidden springs to life. I'm convinced that if you posted the sign: "Tar consumption absolutely prohibited here!," people would suddenly have the strong urge to eat tar. (I used this illustration in church and an older woman came to me and stated that she used to eat tar. When she was young and on the farm, there was some sort of work being done with tar, and she would go the edge of the work after the tar had cooled, pull off a piece, and chew it like gum. When she told me this, all I could think of to say was, "Well, I'm glad you kicked the habit.")

Not convinced that the law incites us to sin? Consider the Volstead Act (1920–1933), the piece of federal legislation that outlawed the manufacture, transport, and sale of alcoholic beverages. The period of time this law was on the books is commonly known as Prohibition. Against expectations and intentions, Prohibition stimulated even greater levels of alcohol consumption in America (along with a large increase in associated law-breaking, such as manufacture, distribution, and sale of alcoholic products); the social experiment was finally abandoned with repeal of the Volstead Act in 1933.

Before Prohibition, Times Square, between 34th and 52nd Streets in New York City, offered approximately 300 saloons. By 1925, just five years after America went "dry," there were more than 2,500 speakeasies in the same area. There were approximately 177,000 taverns in the entire nation before 1920. By 1925, there were an estimated 3 million "booze joints." The unfortunate result of trying to legislate morality was that a nation of relatively moderate drinkers turned into a nation of tormented alcoholics (and, by default, lawbreakers).[1]

When alcohol was made illegal, an enormous black market arose to meet the ever-increasing demand. This black market affected the nation's economy for decades and led to the establishment of organized crime, which quickly and easily changed its "business plan" from alcohol to drugs after 1933. With the inception of organized crime on such a massive scale, other social ills followed: there was a corresponding increase in murder, fraud, extortion, and the ever-present corruption of government at all levels.[2] Prohibition is exhibit "A" when speaking of our hearts' natural rebellion against law.

In fact, Paul makes an interesting observation about life and death. He states that he was alive until the Law came alive, and then he died. When the Law came alive, sin came alive with it (Rom 7:9–10). But when we serve in the power of the Spirit, the Law dies, and sin dies with it (Rom 7:6).

So what does this say about the Law? Is there something wrong with it? Absolutely not! It is holy and righteous and good because it is given by God, Who is holy and righteous and good (Rom 7:12). The problem isn't with the Law, the problem is with us. Just as butter is good in its place, it's not suitable for lubricating watches. It doesn't even matter if it's the best butter. Butter wasn't made for watches. In the same way, the Law is holy and righteous and good, but it's not intended to produce righteousness in sinful humanity. In fact, it was designed to do just the opposite, in one respect at least. It is through the commandment that sin becomes utterly sinful.

Well, if the Law isn't what is needed to bring about a righteous life, what is? As you might expect, it is the power of the Holy Spirit in our lives.

> For what the Law could not do, weak as it was through the flesh, God did: sending His own Son in the likeness of sinful flesh and as an offering for sin, He condemned sin in the flesh, in order that the requirement of the Law might be fulfilled in us, who do not walk according to the flesh, but according to the Spirit (Rom 8:3-4, nasb).

My wife is an excellent cook. In fact, I can personally provide more physical evidence than is necessary to back up that claim. Suppose my wife cooks a small turkey for Thanksgiving (which really takes some imagining, because my wife's Thanksgiving dinners are always sufficient to feed the ship's complement of an aircraft carrier—but I digress). The smell of the turkey permeates the house until at last she pronounces it "done." Not willing to serve it from the roaster, she takes the large fork that's used for our outdoor grill and sticks it in the turkey. She begins to lift the turkey from the pan when, splash, the meat gives way, and the turkey falls back into the drippings. Undaunted, she tries again, with the same result. By this time, turkey drippings are all over the stove, on her apron, and even a few drops on the floor (for which the dogs are grateful). But my wife is a valiant woman. Never one to give way in the face of adversity, with the back of her wrist she brushes back the wisp of hair that has fallen into her face, and tries again, this time piercing the pesky poultry closer to the bone. Alas, the now-shredded bird stubbornly refuses to leave the roaster.

So she puts aside the fork, and instead reaches for the large spatula we also use for grilling. She slides the spatula underneath the (extremely tender) bird and lifts it lovingly to the serving platter.

At this point a question must be asked: Was there anything wrong with the fork? No, it was a perfectly good fork. The problem is that it was unsuited to the job because of the condition of the turkey. If the turkey had been uncooked, it might have worked, but cooking made the flesh tender, which is just another way of saying "weak."

So we could summarize the story this way: what the fork could not do, in that it was weak through the flesh, the spatula did. The same task for which the fork was initially chosen was accomplished by the spatula. The standard didn't change (in this case, the goal of getting the turkey out of the roaster and onto the platter); rather, we had to use the right tool to accomplish that goal. In the same way, there is nothing wrong with the Law. The problem occurs because of the condition of the flesh.

So, what was it the Law could not do? The Law was unable to produce the righteous life it demanded. Therefore, God did what the Law could not do, by (1) taking the Law out of the way, by giving His Son as a sin offering; and (2) providing His Spirit so we could walk in Him and not in the flesh. Notice that the goal—the righteousness the Law requires—never changed, but the means of accomplishing that goal did. We become practically righteous through the power of the Holy Spirit.

The Holy Spirit performs at least seven ministries to the believer. Through these activities, God the Holy Spirit brings about the righteous life the Law requires.

At this point, a clarification is probably in order. When we speak of the "righteous life that the Law requires," we are not referring to the ceremonial aspects of the law, such as clean and unclean animals, ritual sacrifices, or wearing different types of cloth in the same garment. Rather, we are referring to the moral requirements of the Law. An expanded summation of the Law can be found in the Ten Commandments (DEUT 5:1–22), but Jesus gave a more succinct summary when he responded to the question, "Which is the greatest commandment?" Jesus replied: 'Love the Lord your God with all your heart and with all your soul and with all your mind.' This is the first and greatest commandment. And the second is like it: 'Love your neighbor as yourself.' All the Law and the Prophets hang on these two commandments" (MATT 22:37–40, NIV). What is especially noteworthy about this divine overview of the Law is that it revolves around a character trait that is available only through the power of the Holy Spirit: love.

There is, of course, a human love, which is very real and very powerful. This can be seen, for instance, in countless hospital waiting rooms around the world. However, true love, as the Bible defines it, is produced through the human heart only as it flows from God the Holy Spirit: "God has poured out his love into our hearts by the Holy Spirit, whom he has given us" (ROM 5:5, NIV). Notice that this true love is poured into our hearts by the indwelling Holy Spirit. Without the work of the Spirit, there is no true biblical love. When Jesus prayed for His disciples and those would believe in Him through their testimony, he prayed "that the love you have for me may be in them and that I myself may be in them" (JOHN 17:26, NIV). Here again, love is described as something that must originate with God Himself. True love occurs only when the Spirit is working in and through the believer to produce the love that is naturally foreign to the heart. We may experience this love that God gives, but we cannot generate it.

What is true love? How is the love produced in the believer's heart by the Holy Spirit different from the very real and proper love that a husband and wife or parent and child without the Spirit feel for one another? The answer is found in the nature of God as contrasted with our own.

John tells us that "God is love" (1 JOHN 4:8, 16). This means that an attribute of God's person is that He loves. Thus, when He loves, He doesn't need to work at it; He expends no effort at all. When God loves, He is simply being Himself. Put another way, God loves in the same way that I have a Y chromosome. For those of you who slept through high school biology (not that I'm one to judge, mind you), women have two X chromosomes, whereas men have an X and a Y. In other words, I don't have to try to be male, I just am. In fact, I couldn't stop being male (as defined by the Y chromosome) if I tried. It is merely something that is true of me. In the same way, God loves because that's who He is. He cannot *not* love.

Please note that the statement "God is love" describes only one attribute of God, so it can't be turned around to say, "Love is God." This reduces God to only one aspect of His being, and ignores the other attributes of God, such as His holiness, omnipotence, and so forth.

Definition: God's love can be defined as his yearning for and delight in the well-being of those he loves. This love is so completely self-forgetful that God is willing to express it even if it involves self-sacrifice (1 JOHN 3:16–18; 4:8–10; 1 COR. 13:4–6).

How does this love work out in practice?

- When the members of the Trinity took counsel together in eternity past concerning the salvation of mankind, it was in love that He determined to adopt as sons those whom He chose (EPH 1:4–5). God's love is what enables us to become the children of God (1 JOHN 3:1). This shows the desire of the Godhead for the absolute best for the objects of His love, for what could be better than being adopted as a child of God?

- It was also determined that the Father would send the Son to be a satisfaction for the penalty of sin (1 JOHN 4:10–11). This gives evidence of the willingness of the Father to sacrifice. What loving Father willingly lays down the life of his Son?

- The Son showed his love for the Father by submitting to His will (JOHN 14:31). Again, the aspect of self-sacrifice can be seen, not just in the laying down of His life, but in His taking upon Himself the awful burden of all the sin of the entire world down through time.

This type of sacrificial love shows that God's love is not just different in scope, but also different in kind from mere human love. The love that the natural man is capable of shares some of the qualities of God's love, but is lacking in key areas.

First of all, our love is never self-forgetful. That's not to say that natural love can't be sacrificial, for there is clear evidence that it can be. But it is never self-forgetful, in that it takes into consideration the worthiness of the object loved. This isn't the way God loves. In fact, Paul argues:

You see, at just the right time, when we were still powerless, Christ died for the ungodly. Very rarely will anyone die for a righteous man, though for a good man someone might possibly dare to die. But God demonstrates his own love for us in this: While we were still sinners, Christ died for us (ROM 5:6–8, NIV).

Second, our love is limited to those who please us in one way or another. Parents love their children because there are those moments from birth forward when that love is returned. Even if children become rebellious later in life, that love remains because of the hope that one day things will be as they were before. Very often, however, human love grows cold. Why is the divorce rate so high? Because one spouse is not pleasing the other in some fashion and the love disappears.

God doesn't love that way. He is unchanging in every aspect of His being (MAL 3:6). Thus, if He has ever loved, which is an essential characteristic of who He is, then He continues to love, because He does not change. We should be quick to note that this unchanging love doesn't hinder any other aspect of His being, such as His righteous judgment of sin. That said, even in the midst of judgment, God's love remains. If you want to hear the heartbeat of God, then listen to His pleading through the prophet Ezekiel (33:11):

> *Say to them, "As surely as I live, declares the Sovereign LORD, I take no pleasure in the death of the wicked, but rather that they turn from their ways and live. Turn! Turn from your evil ways! Why will you die, O house of Israel?"*

I keep repeating this same theme over and over again, but I truly believe it is necessary because this is so counterintuitive to us. We want to believe that we can love without any action of the Spirit, even if it's at a lesser level. Nothing could be further from the truth. Consider the following biblical statements concerning love:

- **The natural man doesn't experience the love that God supplies to the believer.** "[B]ut I know you. I know that you do not have the love of God in your hearts" (JOHN 5:42, NIV). The phrase "love of God" can be translated two different ways, but each makes the same point. It could be translated "the love that God supplies," with Jesus being the object of that love; or as "love for God," which causes them to reject Jesus. In either case, God's love is set apart as something they don't possess, with the evidence of this being their rejection of Christ.

- *God's love reaches out to the whole world.* "For God so loved the world that he gave his one and only Son" (JOHN 3:16, NIV). Motivated by this love, He tasted death for everyone (HEB 2:9), and became the atoning sacrifice for our sins (1 JOHN 2:2). This divine love is directed toward a world that hates God and is in constant rebellion against Him (JOHN 15:18). While "we were still sinners, Christ died for us" (ROM 5:6, NIV). So, whenever we call someone a sinner, we are by definition calling him an object of God's love.

- *Although God loves the world of people, His love is not directed at the world system.* In the same way, love for the things of this world do not come from the Father. "Do not love the world or *anything in the world.* If anyone loves the world, the love of the Father is not in him. For everything in the world—the cravings of sinful man, the lust of his eyes and the boasting of what he has and does—comes not from the Father but from the world" (1 JOHN 2:15, NIV, emphasis mine).

- *Christ loves His church so much that He gave Himself up for her.* "Christ loved the church and gave himself up for her" (EPH 5:25, NIV). This statement answers the why and the how regarding our love toward one another. "This is how we know what love is: Jesus Christ laid down his life for us. And we ought to lay down our lives for our brothers" (1 JOHN 3:16, NIV).

- *God's love is never exhausted.* "Jesus knowing that His hour had come that He should depart out of this world to the Father, having loved His own who were in the world, He loved them to the end" (JOHN 13:1, NASB).

So, what conclusions should we draw concerning love?

- Those who don't know Christ don't really know how to love. When we expect that kind of love from them, we expect too much.

- Just as God loves lost people, so we should love lost people—not just the lost people we happen to like or the ones who look like us, but *all* lost people.

- We should not love the world system or anything associated with it. That system, even though it is composed of the very people we are to love and try and reach with the gospel, is the believer's enemy. The power, position, pleasures, and possessions that the world system produces should not be loved.

- We should love God's people in a special way, such that we should desire their fellowship. In fact, we are called upon to die for our brothers and sisters in Christ if that is necessary (1 JOHN 3:16). Such should be the extent of the love that God produces in us (JOHN 15:13).

- We should love without end, just like God does.

As God's love interacts with creation, we experience several other characteristics that flow from His love.

- *God's patience* is a manifestation of His love toward those who deserve His wrath (1 COR 13:4). In other words, God's righteous anger is slow to act against those who fail to listen to His warnings or to obey His commands. His eternal longing for the highest good for His creation holds back, for a time, His holy justice (NUM 14:18; 2 PET 3:9).

- *God's kindness* (ROM 2:4; 1 COR 13:4) moves Him to act toward others in a way that has no ulterior motive and is not limited by what the object of His love deserves (TITUS 3:4–5).

- *God's grace* is the expression of God's kindness toward His undeserving creation after His righteousness and holiness have been satisfied (EPH 2:6–9).

As you can see, this type of love is supernatural in origin and does not originate within ourselves. This is why we need the ministries of God the Holy Spirit in our lives. We will examine these ministries next.

Discussion Questions

In each of chapters 14–20, we will be revisiting your answer to the question: "How do you get there?" Please look back at your answer to that question and examine it in light of this chapter.

1. Explain in your own words how the law relates to our desire to sin.

2. If we cannot be made righteous through following the law, explain how we can be righteous.

3. Explore the differences between the biblical love described in this chapter and produced by the Holy Spirit, and our culture's popular conception of the nature of love.

4. Has this chapter brought any questions to mind, or any thoughts you would like to discuss with the group?

5. Is there any issue you would like prayed for, or accountability in, over the course of this week?

6. Please note any other group members' answers that you would like to follow up on this week, either by praying for them or by making an encouraging contact.

PAINTING THE ROSES

*A large rose tree stood near the entrance of the garden;
the roses growing on it were white, but there were three
gardeners at it, busily painting them red. Alice thought this a
very curious thing, and she went nearer to watch them, and
just as she came up to them she heard one of them say, "Look
out now, Five! Don't go splashing paint over me like that!"*

*"I couldn't help it," said Five, in a sulky tone; "Seven jogged
my elbow."*

*On which Seven looked up and said, "That's right, Five!
Always lay the blame on others!"*

*"You'd better not talk!" said Five. "I heard the Queen say
only yesterday you deserved to be beheaded!"*

"What for?" said the one who had spoken first.

"That's none of your business, Two!" said Seven.

*"Yes, it is his business!" said Five, and I'll tell him—it was
for bringing the cook tulip roots instead of onions."*

*Seven flung down his brush, and had just begun "Well, of
all the unjust things—" when his eye chanced to fall upon
Alice, as she stood watching them, and he checked himself
suddenly; the others looked round also, and all of them
bowed low.*

*"Would you tell me, please" said Alice, a little timidly,
"why you are painting those roses?"*

—*Wonderland*, ch. VIII, "The Queen's Croquet Ground"

Chapter 17
Painting the Roses

When a person is filled with the Spirit, the Spirit engages in at least seven ministries as He works in and through the believer's life. These ministries are the natural result of the Spirit's filling and are discussed in detail in this chapter.

The Spirit Produces Godliness

There are several lists in the New Testament that might be used to describe what godly character looks like. There is the fruit (singular) produced by the Spirit as discussed earlier: "love, joy, peace, patience, kindness, goodness, faithfulness, gentleness, self-control" (GAL 5:22–23, NIV). This is most likely a summary, not an exhaustive list of the qualities God the Holy Spirit produces in us.

If I were to describe the colors visible to the human eye, my list could be as short as red, green, and blue. If my wife were making the list, it would likely be expanded to include aubergine, azure, bisque, cyan, goldenrod, indigo, magenta, ecru, sienna, and puce. The point is, just as it is impossible to codify all the shades and hues of the color spectrum, so there is no way to describe in finite terms the infinite perfections of God's character.

Nevertheless, God has revealed enough of His character that we may know what general qualities should be produced in us if we want to be pleasing to Him. These character traits are universally attributed to the work of God in the life of the believer, not to the independent effort of the believer himself.

God's divine power has given us everything we need for life and godliness through our knowledge of Him Who called us by His own glory and goodness. Through these He has given us His very great and precious promises, so that through them you may participate in the divine nature and escape the corruption in the world caused by evil desires.

> *For this very reason, make every effort to add to your faith good-*
> *ness; and to goodness, knowledge; and to knowledge, self-control;*
> *and to self-control, perseverance; and to perseverance, godliness;*
> *and to godliness, brotherly kindness; and to brotherly kindness,*
> *love. For if you possess these qualities in increasing measure,*
> *they will keep you from being ineffective and unproductive in*
> *your knowledge of our Lord Jesus Christ* (2 PET 1:3–8, NIV).

Notice that, just as with the fruit produced by the Spirit, these character traits are available to us because God's divine power has given us every-thing we need for life and godliness (2 PET 1:3). There is still a need for exertion on our part ("make every effort"), but the power for such effort is divine, not human. We must never forget that these virtues are completely foreign to the natural man. There is no way to cultivate these character traits apart from the work of the Holy Spirit.

There are four reasons why such godly character is important:

1. **Godly character is important so that we might participate in the divine nature.** Now, by all accounts, this statement is less than clear. Still, two applications flow from the interpretive options avail-able to us.

On the one hand, when a person is born again, that new believer is indwelt by God the Holy Spirit. Therefore, that "new man" can now participate in the divine nature, because he now experiences the constant presence of God. As Christians, we have His Spirit testifying with our spirits that we are the children of God (Rom 8:16). We can know the thoughts of God because we share His Spirit (1 Cor 2:12).

Please don't misunderstand. This in no way means that we become "little gods," as some teach, nor does it mean that we in any way stop being human. What it does mean, however, is that God the Holy Spirit indwells us so that in a real way we are partnering with Him in our lives. That's what the word *participate* means: to partner or be an associate.

On the other hand, we become participants in the divine nature when that nature is being worked out—being allowed to express itself —in our lives. When the Spirit begins to produce this fruit in our lives, we are really participating in the divine nature, in that we are having His nature lived through us.

When we examine these two options, we find that they are both true. We have the indwelling Holy Spirit, Who is producing fruit that causes us to act in accordance with the divine nature. When we understand who God is and what is required to have fellowship with Him, not only are both options true, they are both necessary.

Christians have a tendency to casually use words that they really don't understand. One of those is the word *holy*. We tend to think of this word as expressing some truth about righteous living, but that is far too narrow a meaning. The word *holy* actually means "to be separate." The opposite of the word *holy* isn't "unholy," it is "common." That's why places (Ex 3:5), objects (Ex 29:37), time (Gen 2:3), activities (Joel 1:14), people (Matt 27:52), and God (Rev 4:8) can all be holy. When we say that someone is "holy," what we are really stating is that he is separated to God and separated from anything that is ungodly. *Ungodly* means "not like God."

This raises an interesting question, though: What do we mean when we call God holy? Well, we mean that God is separated from everything that is unlike Himself. He remains completely true to His own nature; He does not change or compromise His essential being. God is completely true to His moral character and abhors anything that lacks His essential purity. It is this aspect of God's nature that requires both perspectives on participating in the divine nature to be true if we are to have fellowship with God.

For God to have fellowship with us, He must find something like Himself in us if He is to remain holy. But, since there is no trace of God's divine perfections in our character, God must place it there Himself. The amazing thing is that God does indeed desire fellowship with us and, therefore, chooses to make it possible! "I no longer call you servants . . . . Instead, I have called you friends" (JOHN 15:15, NIV). He has given us everything we need for a life of godliness—a life that is separate from whatever is unlike God and is separated to Him.

It is vital to understand that, although nothing in the believer himself can produce such character, God utilizes every energy of the believer as He places him in circumstances designed to bring about maturity. In the midst of those circumstances, God provides what is needed to produce godly character. We see this pattern clearly illustrated in JAMES 1:2–5 (NIV). Notice that we are to have pure (not diluted) joy when facing trials, because the end result is maturity. In other words, maturity is worth the short-term pain. Also, if, in the midst of trials, we need God's wisdom, it is generously available to us:

> *Consider it pure joy, my brothers, whenever you face trials of many kinds, because you know that the testing of your faith develops perseverance. Perseverance must finish its work so that you may be mature and complete, not lacking anything. If any of you lacks wisdom, he should ask God, who gives generously to all without finding fault, and it will be given to him.*

2. **Godly character is important if we are to escape the corruption in the world caused by evil desires.** This is a natural extension of the preceding discussion, only viewed from the opposite perspective. We want to participate in the divine nature, but we also want to escape the corruption in the world.

During my time in the Navy, we frequently ran drills on how to fight fires. Everyone on board ship, from the Old Man on down, was expected to know how to fight a fire. There was one very simple and practical reason for this: if a fire breaks out, there is no way to escape it—it's a "sink or swim" situation, so to speak.

We learned all about fire. I could tell you what kind of fire it was by observing the color of the smoke (white = things that leave an ash, black = chemical, blue = electrical). I knew the fire triangle (fuel, oxygen, heat) and that if any one of the three was removed, the fire would go out. One of the most important lessons we learned was that fire destroys all it touches. As I've stated several times, sin is exactly like that. It is not without reason that Peter uses the word *escape*. Just as we must escape a fire or be burned, so we must escape the corruption in the world that is so attractive to our own evil desires.

3. **Godly character is important so we won't be ineffective in our knowledge of Christ.** This is a bit tricky: the word *ineffective* can be misleading in English. We label someone "ineffective" when he's trying his hardest but just isn't able to get the job done. That's not the idea here, however. Here the word means "unworking." Jesus uses this word in MATTHEW 20:1–6 when he describes a landowner who goes early in the morning to hire men to work in his vineyard. He goes again at the third, sixth, and ninth hours. When he goes at the eleventh hour, he still finds people standing around. "He asked them, 'Why have you been standing here all day long doing nothing?'"

(MATT 20:6, NIV). It's that idea of idleness, of doing nothing, that is expressed here by the word *ineffective*.

James uses this term to describe a faith that fails to produce works. He says that faith without works is useless (JAMES 2:20). It's unworking, it's idle. It doesn't do what it is designed to do. It is a faith that does nothing.

If we are to accomplish anything productive for Christ, we must have the character of Christ—and that is produced only by God the Holy Spirit.

4. **Godly character is important so we won't be unproductive in our knowledge of Christ.** This word, *unproductive*, literally means "unfruitful." It brings to mind a picture of a tree that remains without fruit even under the most favorable conditions. Jesus spoke to a fig tree in that condition, remember?

> *Early in the morning, as he was on his way back to the city, he was hungry. Seeing a fig tree by the road, he went up to it but found nothing on it except leaves. Then he said to it, "May you never bear fruit again!" Immediately the tree withered* (MATT 21:18, NIV).

I can't contemplate this idea of being unfruitful without thinking of the parable of the soils:

> *"A farmer went out to sow his seed. As he was scattering the seed, some fell along the path, and the birds came and ate it up. Some fell on rocky places, where it did not have much soil. It sprang up quickly, because the soil was shallow. But when the sun came up, the plants were scorched, and they withered because they had no root. Other seed fell among thorns, which*

grew up and choked the plants. Still other seed fell on good soil, where it produced a crop—a hundred, sixty or thirty times what was sown. He who has ears, let him hear" (MATT 13:3–9, NIV).

Then he explained the parable:

"Listen then to what the parable of the sower means: When anyone hears the message about the kingdom and does not understand it, the evil one comes and snatches away what was sown in his heart. This is the seed sown along the path.

"The one who received the seed that fell on rocky places is the man who hears the word and at once receives it with joy. But since he has no root, he lasts only a short time. When trouble or persecution comes because of the word, he quickly falls away. The one who received the seed that fell among the thorns is the man who hears the word, but the worries of this life and the deceitfulness of wealth choke it, making it unfruitful. But the one who received the seed that fell on good soil is the man who hears the word and understands it. He produces a crop, yielding a hundred, sixty or thirty times what was sown" (MATT 13:18–23, NIV).

Did you see what makes someone unfruitful? It is trouble or persecution, the worries of this life, and the deceitfulness of wealth. What do you need to combat these things? You need perseverance, you need self-control, you need godliness, you need the knowledge of right and wrong in all circumstances. If you have these virtues, then the seeds that sprouted but bore no fruit will not be you.

You need the character of Christ in order to bear fruit. Otherwise, the corruption in the world will choke off anything you attempt in your own strength.

The Spirit Enables Service

The Spirit enables service. Not only that, but without His empowerment, no service rendered by the believer is acceptable before God. This includes activities that might be behind the scenes and considered (by some who are unlearned) unimportant. For example, if you work in the church kitchen preparing meals for funeral dinners or organizing potlucks, you cannot do your work acceptably unless you are filled with the Spirit. If that sounds like an incredible claim, consider the qualifications listed for those who would deliver food to widows. From outward appearances, there doesn't seem to be a lot of spiritual activity involved in this ministry: You just get a list of names, make out a schedule, pick up the groceries, and drop them off. Nevertheless, when considering who would perform this function, the Twelve demanded men who were "known to be full of the Spirit and wisdom" (ACTS 6:3, NIV). Evidently, not just anyone can carry loaves of bread. To minister in the name of God—in *any* way—the primary qualification is to be filled with the Spirit.

The reason Spirit-filling is necessary for even apparently menial tasks is straightforward but not obvious. It has to do with the eternal plan of God. The service of every believer has been designed and planned by God for the working out of His own purposes. "For we are God's workmanship, created in Christ Jesus to do good works, which God prepared in advance for us to do" (EPH 2:10, NIV). In other words, one of the reasons we were saved was for the accomplishment of good works that God has planned for each of us to do. He left nothing to chance. No one will be able to stand before the judgment seat of Christ and complain, "There was just nothing for me to do!" God plans good works specifically for every believer.

Knowing this to be true, no act of service is really acceptable to God unless it was also foreordained by Him. Anything else we do is just painting the roses. It ultimately comes to nothing. This is why we need to be filled with the Spirit, so that we may have the mind of Christ and "be able to test and approve what God's will is—his good, pleasing and perfect will" (ROM 12:2, NIV).

Now, at this point someone might object, saying, "If you perform a good work, it's still good even if God didn't specifically plan it for you. It's not God's plan that makes a work good, but the nature or quality of the work itself, right?" Well, no. That's not correct. Look at what Jesus said:

> *"Not everyone who says to me, 'Lord, Lord,' will enter the kingdom of heaven, but only he who does the will of my Father who is in heaven. Many will say to me on that day, 'Lord, Lord, did we not prophesy in your name, and in your name drive out demons and perform many miracles?' Then I will tell them plainly, 'I never knew you. Away from me, you evildoers!'"* (MATT 7:21–23, NIV).

Notice what is important to Christ: *doing the will of the Father,* which means doing those things that He has prepared ahead of time for us to do. If someone doesn't do the will of the Father, but does other good things instead (prophesying in His name, driving out demons, performing miracles), Jesus won't commend them for such actions. He will call them "evildoers" or, more literally, "you who practice lawlessness." It is the prerogative of God, and God alone, to state what is good and what is not according to His holy character. In this case, those claiming the good works aren't even saved, because Jesus states "I never knew you." All the time they were doing these "good works," they had no relationship with Christ.

How is it any different for those who are born again? Certainly, Jesus knows us as His own, but unless what we perform is the will of the Father, we are acting like those who are lost—acting independently of His will and making ourselves the judges of correct behavior, the deciders of good and evil.

This might sound a bit scary at first. You may think, "Oh, great! I have good works to do but I have no idea what they are! What if I miss them?" Well, don't be too worried. God the Holy Spirit is available to every believer to lead them in the way they should go (Rom 8:14). Not only that, but if we have the mind of Christ, we will be motivated to do the good works God desires. So, there is no need to fear. Quite frankly, God desires you to know and do His will more than you want to know it. Plus, He is so gentle with us: "He tends his flock like a shepherd: He gathers the lambs in his arms and carries them close to his heart; he gently leads those that have young" (Isa 40:11, niv).

Not only does God lead us to the good works He has planned for us, but He also enables us to perform them. God gives two types of gifts to His church. The first type is gifted men to fill the offices necessary to equip His people.

It was he who gave some to be apostles, some to be prophets, some to be evangelists, and some to be pastors and teachers, to prepare God's people for works of service, so that the body of Christ may be built up until we all reach unity in the faith and in the knowledge of the Son of God and become mature, attaining to the whole measure of the fullness of Christ (Eph 4:11–13, niv).

Although the offices of apostle and prophet are no longer being filled today, God gives evangelists and pastors/teachers to the church. I find it interesting that the Greek word for "shepherd" is the same word from which we get the word *pastor*, and I think the parallel is an fascinating one.

Sheep aren't able to exist for very long on their own. They need someone to protect them, someone to help them find pasture, someone to lead them to water. It's easy to find wild goats, but wild sheep are very unusual. Sheep need a shepherd.

Just as sheep need a shepherd, God's people need pastors and teachers. Because of this need, God gives men to the church. Perhaps we should take this opportunity to stop and examine the way we view the job of the pastor. The pastor is not just some hired man. He isn't just a trained professional. He is a gift from God, sent by God to shepherd His people.

These gifted men are to fulfill a purpose that God has foreordained for them. They are to "prepare God's people for works of service." The word translated "prepare" means "to make adequate, to furnish completely, to cause to be fully qualified."[1] It's a general word that means "to supply what is missing." It's used to describe the mending of nets or the supplying of an army. This idea of "making adequate" finds its use in a medical sense by referring to the setting of a broken bone.[2]

The pastor is to completely furnish God's people through preaching of the Word. If there is a broken bone, he must endeavor to set it. If he sees a brother or sister in sin, he is required to confront and attempt to restore that person. Sometimes that hurts, but if the bone isn't set, that person will remain a cripple for the rest of his life. If some virtue is missing from their lives, he is to encourage its cultivation. He is to provide, through the Word, what is lacking in people's lives.

Whereas it is the pastor who does the equipping, it is the people who do the works of service. These works of service have as their goal the building-up of the body of Christ. When this goal is kept in view, it becomes easier to see why God has prepared beforehand works of service for each of us. Only He is qualified to know what the body as a whole requires, so He places us in the body to build it up until "we all reach unity in the faith and knowledge of the Son of God."

Once again we see the interdependence of faith and knowledge. A flaw in faith affects our ability to discern spiritual truth. A flaw in knowledge affects our faith because we cling to mistaken and wrong ideas. God is not indifferent to weaknesses in either our faith or our knowledge. Therefore, He provides gifted men to supply what is necessary in both areas.

The purpose of building up the body is that we might "become mature, attaining to the whole measure of the fullness of Christ." God gives gifted men to the church so that His people will be equipped for service in building up the body so that we might all become mature.

God gives gifted men to the church, and he also gives each individual a "grace" gift. This gift shouldn't be confused with the natural abilities that people possess. No one would deny that the ability to sing well is a gift from God. But it is a gift, like the sun and the rain, that God gives to both the evil and the good, the righteous and the unrighteous (MATT 5:45). In contrast, "grace" gifts are given by the Spirit for the common good of the church.

> *There are different kinds of gifts, but the same Spirit. There are different kinds of service, but the same Lord. There are different kinds of working, but the same God works all of them in all men. Now to each one the manifestation of the Spirit is given for the common good* (1 COR 12:4–7, NIV).

Even though no two believers perform the exact same function, they share in common the Holy Spirit Who gives them the ability to serve. Their exercise of their gifts is described as a "manifestation of the Spirit." There can be no service that is pleasing to God, therefore, if you aren't in fellowship with the Spirit. Likewise, if you are doing something that God hasn't called you to do, there is no giftedness for that task. Without such giftedness, there is no manifestation of the Spirit in your work. This means, despite all outward appearances, that whatever "good work" you're doing isn't really a good work at all.

Notice that, just as the works of service in Ephesians 4 are for the building-up of the body, here the gifted service of the believer is for the common good. In other words, the equipped believer has the same goal as the gifted believer: the common good of the church.

At this point, a few observations about spiritual gifts are in order, as there is so much confusion on the subject. It is beyond the range of this discussion (and this book) to do a complete examination of spiritual gifts, but it really takes only three short paragraphs to make practical sense of them.

- No one is ever commanded to find out what their gift is. So relax. When God leads you into a ministry, you can be sure it is in accordance with the way He has gifted you. After all, He gave you the gift for the ministry to which He calls you.

- There are only three lists of gifts in the New Testament: Rom 12:4–8, 1 Cor 12:7–11, and 1 Pet 4:10–11. Though there is some overlap, these three lists don't match. This implies that, like the colors we discussed earlier, there is an infinite variety of "shades" to the gifts that God gives. We can be sure that whatever God calls us to do, He also gives us the ability to do it. Isn't that good news?

- Exercising our giftedness for the building-up of the body requires faith. The more faith we exercise, the more effective we are in utilizing our gift. Faith is necessary so that we won't become proud and think of ourselves more highly than we ought (Rom 12:3), and so that we may exercise our gift to the fullest (Rom 12:6). The relationship between these ideas seems to be this:
  - The more faith we exercise, the more we think of ourselves correctly.
  - The more we think of ourselves correctly, the more we will consciously depend upon the power of the Holy Spirit in exercising our gifts.

☐ The more control the Holy Spirit exercises in your life, the greater the effectiveness of your ministry (whatever form it takes).

After reviewing the role of the Spirit in Christian service, we may derive the following definition:

Definition: *Christian service* is a manifestation of the Spirit through the individual believer for accomplishing the good works that God has prepared in advance for that believer to do, utilizing the gifts He has given.

With this definition in mind, what exactly is it that you are doing? If you were called to testify in court concerning your work for Christ, would it measure up to this definition? Would you be able to name any activity that God the Holy Spirit has led you to and has empowered you to do? If not, you might want to start praying that God will show you His will with regard to building up the body for the common good. But don't start praying unless you're ready to be surprised.

"For my thoughts are not your thoughts, neither are your ways my ways," declares the LORD. "As the heavens are higher than the earth, so are my ways higher than your ways and my thoughts than your thoughts" (ISA 55:8, NIV).

The Spirit Teaches

The teaching ministry of the Spirit to the believer was described by Jesus to His disciples when He was in the Upper Room.

"I have much more to say to you, more than you can now bear. But when he, the Spirit of truth, comes, he will guide you into all truth. He will not speak on his own; he will speak only what he hears, and he will tell you what is yet to come. He will bring glory to me by taking from what is mine and making it known

to you. All that belongs to the Father is mine. That is why I said the Spirit will take from what is mine and make it known to you" (JOHN 16:12–15, NIV).

Some interpret this passage to refer only to the Spirit's role in the writing of the New Testament. I agree that the passage teaches at least that much, but find their interpretation too limiting. When this passage is compared to other statements in the New Testament, it seems to be teaching about more than just the inspiration of the New Testament.

For example, Paul teaches that "We have not received the spirit of the world but the Spirit who is from God, that we may understand what God has freely given us" (1 COR 2:12, NIV). God the Holy Spirit is not only the author of the New Testament (as well as the Old Testament), but He also acts as the divine interpreter, so that the believer can understand and put into practice what is taught in Scripture.

At this point we need to learn a new vocabulary word. The fact that we need to learn new vocabulary shouldn't surprise us, because we need to do it all the time. If I went to your work or school or club or nearly any other activity you could name, I'd be forced to learn new terms if I were to participate fully. That's because words act like a form of shorthand, which distills complex concepts into a few syllables. For example, instead of saying, "I need the form that allows me to schedule a time to take a certain piece of machinery off-line for routine maintenance," we say, "I need Form 210." See how new vocabulary makes life simpler?

For this discussion, the new vocabulary word is *perspicuity*. It means "clarity." (I know, I know, there's no way to get "clarity" out of "perspicuity." But then again, why is "abbreviation" such a long word?) At any rate, here's what we mean by "the perspicuity of the Scriptures."

Definition (of *perspicuity*): The Bible is sufficiently clear and complete in context to express the message that God desires to communicate.

First, let's make sure we understand what is, and what is not, being stated in this definition. We are *not* saying that every passage of Scripture is as easy to understand as all the others. That clearly isn't so. What we *are* stating is that the Bible is written in such a way that an ordinary, normal understanding of the text is enough to get the main idea that God wants to communicate. For example, consider the following passage:

> *When men began to increase in number on the earth and daughters were born to them, the sons of God saw that the daughters of men were beautiful, and they married any of them they chose. Then the LORD said, "My Spirit will not contend with man forever, for he is mortal; his days will be a hundred and twenty years."*
>
> *The Nephilim were on the earth in those days—and also afterward—when the sons of God went to the daughters of men and had children by them. They were the heroes of old, men of renown.*
>
> *The LORD saw how great man's wickedness on the earth had become, and that every inclination of the thoughts of his heart was only evil all the time. The LORD was grieved that he had made man on the earth, and his heart was filled with pain. So the LORD said, "I will wipe mankind, whom I have created, from the face of the earth—men and animals, and creatures that move along the ground, and birds of the air—for I am grieved that I have made them"* (GEN 6:1–7, NIV).

To understand this passage, I don't need to know who the "sons of God" are or be able to identify the "Nephilim." (Actually, there is great debate among scholars as to the identity of both groups.) What I do need to know is plainly stated: the earth was filled with violence, which filled God's heart with pain, so He decided to destroy the world. That much is crystal clear. That's the clarity that we speak of when we use the word *perspicuity.*

Knowing that the Bible is sufficiently clear (or "perspicuous," if you want to impress your friends) for anyone to understand, the question that immediately pops to mind is: "Why do we need a teacher at all?" Why do we need a human pastor/teacher and why do we need a divine teacher? The answer to both these questions lies in the nature of the human heart.

We need a divine teacher because the Bible speaks of realities that are unseen, and are therefore unavailable to the human senses and intellect. As discussed earlier, the natural man may understand the concepts being taught, but he will never accept them as true. Similarly, the carnal man, the one who relies on the flesh, will resist those teachings that run counter to what his flesh can confirm. Only through faith will he be able to move to the deeper things of God.

The role of the Holy Spirit as teacher, then, is to press home the reality of those things that are clearly taught in the Scriptures, so that we might live a godly life. This is why John says:

> *And as for you, the anointing which you received from Him abides in you, and you have no need for anyone to teach you; but as His anointing teaches you about all things, and is true and is not a lie, and just as it has taught you, you abide in Him* (1 JOHN 2:27, NASB).

The focus for John is your relationship with the Spirit—that you abide in Him. Notice that this teaching concerns "all things," just as

Paul wrote about the spiritual man: "The spiritual man makes judgments about all things" (1 COR 2:15, NIV). The clear word of God is applied to all circumstances by the Holy Spirit Who teaches us.

Why, then, do we need God's gift of the pastor/teacher? There are at least two reasons, both of which are related to our behavior.

When we realize the limits of perspicuity—that is, that not all portions of the Bible are as easy to understand as others—it becomes clear that we need someone to do the hard work of digging deep into the Scriptures so the more difficult passages become understandable. We need someone to compare Scripture with Scripture to see the big picture and to analyze the argument of a book to understand what the author meant in an individual verse. Otherwise, we could wrest a verse from its context and make it say something that God never intended.

This type of study takes time that most people do not have and effort that they cannot make. Thus, God has given us specially gifted men to accomplish these tasks and to pass that knowledge on to others. However, this knowledge isn't merely to satisfy intellectual curiosity. It is intended to equip the saints—believers—to do works of service so that the body of Christ may be built up and all of us become mature.

In the same way, since "all Scripture" (not just the clearer parts) is "useful for teaching, rebuking, correcting, and training in righteousness, so that the man of God may be thoroughly equipped for every good work" (2 TIM 3:16–17, NIV), God gives the pastor/teacher to the church to actually do the rebuking when required, to correct when necessary, to teach and train so that good works follow. The pastor/teacher puts legs, so to speak, on the Bible, applying it according to the need of the moment.

We should be quick to remember that even when God is using a chosen human instrument, it is still the work of God the Holy Spirit enabling this person to exercise his giftedness as God directs. Ultimately, it is God the Holy Spirit Who teaches His church so that they may become mature.

The Spirit Encourages Praise and Thanksgiving

Immediately after the command to "be filled with the Spirit" (EPH 5:18, NIV), there is a description of what that filling should look like:

Speak to one another with psalms, hymns and spiritual songs. Sing and make music in your heart to the Lord, always giving thanks to God the Father for everything, in the name of our Lord Jesus Christ (EPH 5:19–20, NIV).

This aspect of the filling of the Spirit makes perfect sense when you consider who God is. He is the ultimate in perfection, the sustainer of the universe, the compassionate and gracious God, Who is slow to anger and abounds with love. In addition, God doesn't change; thus, He is always worthy of our adoration and praise. Therefore, if we take on the mind of Christ, we will think rightly about God and be filled with praise.

We will also recognize that "Every good and perfect gift is from above, coming down from the Father of the heavenly lights, who does not change like shifting shadows" (JAMES 1:17, NIV). Hence, we will ever be thankful for the blessings, both material and spiritual, that God provides.

The praise and thanksgiving that result from the Spirit's filling take two forms, one public, one private. We are to "speak to one another" with different kinds of music, evidently to build one another up in the faith and to encourage those who are going through tough times. (Remember the discussion of music and singing in Chapter 13?) However, we are not to limit our music-making to the corporate worship of the gathered church. We are, instead, directed to make music in our hearts in private worship as well.

It's worth remembering that praise and thanksgiving to God are completely foreign to the natural heart. In fact, the lack of gratitude seems to be one of the most elemental sins a person can commit. Even though God has revealed Himself to all humankind through His creation, people do not respond appropriately, because of their wicked hearts. "For although they knew God, they neither glorified him as God nor gave thanks to him, but their thinking became futile and their foolish hearts were darkened" (ROM 1:21, NIV).

In contrast, the Spirit-filled believer recognizes God for who He is and realizes that He doesn't change; such a believer is therefore eager to give God glory and praise with thanksgiving no matter what the current circumstances. Our circumstances change; God does not.

The Spirit Leads

This manifestation of the Spirit in the believer's life is connected to the larger ministry of building up the church and bringing the believer to Christlikeness. In this case, the Spirit leads the believer according to God's ways and away from the ways of the flesh.

> [F]or if you are living according to the flesh, you must die; but if by the Spirit you are putting to death the deeds of the body, you will live. For all who are being led by the Spirit of God, these are sons of God (ROM 8:13–14, NASB).

> For the flesh sets its desire against the Spirit, and the Spirit against the flesh; for these are in opposition to one another, so that you may not do the things that you please. But if you are led by the Spirit, you are not under the Law (GAL 5:17–18, NASB).

In these two passages, we see seven truths about the leading ministry of the Spirit.

1. **There are two principles resident in the believer that are in opposition to one another: the flesh and the Spirit.** As a result, the

believer's life is one of internal conflict, at least at one level. Yes, we can have peace in the midst of external conflict, but the internal struggle against the flesh never goes away. Until our bodies are redeemed, either by resurrection or Christ's return for His church, the flesh will stand in opposition to whatever the Spirit attempts to do in our lives. In the same way, when the flesh tries to make a move, the Spirit stands opposed to it.

When I think of the flesh and Spirit in opposition to one another, the picture that comes to my mind is the trenches of World War I. In France, the two opposing forces built strongly fortified trenches that connected to one another in an intricate network. During the years 1914–1917, the lines barely moved at all. There were attacks and defenses, to be sure, but the basic structure of the trenches and the battle lines remained fixed. When one army tried to make a move, the other army was right there to to stop it. It was a war of attrition, in which each side tried to grind down the resources of the other until it was no longer able to fight. When the stalemate finally broke, with the British advance of July 31 to December 7, 1917, the British still averaged only 68 yards per day.

Thankfully, the believer has the winning power in this struggle available to him at all times. Such a stalemate should never be a reality to the believer, but the unfortunate truth is that the trenches never go away. The flesh never gives up. It stands in constant opposition to the Spirit.

2. **The flesh isn't assisted in becoming better by the Spirit.** Instead, all that is good within us is by the direct accomplishment of the Spirit in spite of opposition by the flesh.

3. **The believer doesn't need to wait for growth to occur in order to have the virtues of Christ lived out in his life.** From the moment of salvation, the Holy Spirit stands ready to lead us while putting

to death the deeds of the flesh. You don't have to wait. You have victory available to you right now because of the indwelling Holy Spirit. There will be a struggle, but the victory is available.

4. **Being led by the Spirit sets us free from the "don'ts" of the Law.** Real spirituality is found in what you do, not what you don't do. It is not a holding back of the flesh, but a yielding to the Spirit so that He can accomplish in and through us what He desires. It is living out the life of Christ.

5. **What God desires from us is an eternal preoccupation with Himself,** so that the world and the flesh are merely forgotten. When we focus our attention upon the Spirit as He leads, we develop an absent-mindedness regarding the things of the flesh.

6. **Being led by the Spirit should be the normal experience of the believer.** The book of Romans equates being led with being a son of God. The fact that it is not the normal experience for so many believers is an entirely avoidable tragedy.

7. **The Spirit enables us for service through the bestowal of grace gifts.** Nevertheless, the believer must be led into those ministries by the Spirit in order to exercise those gifts. Therefore, He doesn't lead all believers down the same path. He leads us where He desires us to exercise our gifts for the building-up of the body.

The leading of the Spirit, therefore, is God's method for putting to death the deeds of the flesh and developing His character within us.

The Spirit Testifies about Our Salvation

It is the rare believer who has never doubted his salvation. Sometimes these doubts are mere fleeting annoyances, but sometimes they can become a debilitating cancer that steals our joy, removes our ability to serve, and paralyzes us into fearful inaction. God, however, "knows how we are formed, he remembers that we are dust" (Ps 103:14, NIV). Therefore, one of the ministries of the Holy Spirit is to testify to us that we really are saved. "The Spirit himself testifies with our spirit that we are God's children" (ROM 8:16, NIV).

Unfortunately, some are so distrustful of anything subjective in the Christian life that they refuse to listen to the voice of the Spirit. Any suggestion that God actually speaks with His people today is reviled as an error derived from the Charismatic movement. (Just for the record, although I love my brothers and sisters who are in this movement, I disagree with their theology of modern-day miracles and grace gifts.) Paul states that the Spirit "testifies" with our spirit. Clearly, there is communication between the Spirit of God and our spirits.

Up until now, we have merely assumed that the Spirit speaks to us. How else could we be led or taught by Him, for example? Some, however, do not accept this concept. They reject any form of communication from God to the individual that is outside the pages of the Bible. In doing so, they take the "personal" out of the relationship. This viewpoint is shown to be false by ROMANS 8:16. He "testifies." He speaks concerning our salvation. I just do not see any other way to read this passage.

We are persons because we are created in the image of God, Who is a person. We speak, because we are created in the image of God, Who speaks. Why then should we be surprised that God speaks to us on a personal level? The simple fact that the Holy Spirit speaks to us assures us of our salvation, because only the saved have access to the Holy Spirit.

It is one thing to know a truth intellectually. It is another to experience it. I may know that I have been forgiven by faith in the finished work of Jesus Christ on the cross, but it is something else entirely to have an experience in my heart where the Holy Spirit makes real what I already accept as true. Because of the Holy Spirit's testimony to us, we can have certain knowledge that moves beyond the intellectual and into the heart's experience.

To put it another way, we can have the prayer of Paul answered in our own lives:

> *I pray that out of his glorious riches he may strengthen you with power through his Spirit in your inner being, so that Christ may dwell in your hearts through faith. And I pray that you, being rooted and established in love, may have power, together with all the saints, to grasp how wide and long and high and deep is the love of Christ, and to know this love that surpasses knowledge—that you may be filled to the measure of all the fullness of God* (EPH 3:16–19, NIV).

The Spirit Intercedes for Us

Have you ever prayed for something and then later rejoiced that you didn't get what you prayed for? I think that's a rather common experience. The truth is we don't know what's best for us or for others. Fortunately, because of the intercessory ministry of the Spirit, prayer is the one activity we can't foul up.

> *In the same way, the Spirit helps us in our weakness. We do not know what we ought to pray for, but the Spirit himself intercedes for us with groans that words cannot express* (ROM 8:26, NIV).

Some have taken this verse to refer to a secret prayer language that exists between the believer and God. This is praying in an unknown tongue, we are told. A simple reading of the verse, however, makes that interpretation impossible. If the Spirit intercedes for us with "groans that words cannot express," why do some people think that we can use words (known or unknown) to express them? That doesn't make any sense. Instead, this verse teaches that our human limitations do not limit the effectiveness of our prayers, precisely because of this ministry of the Spirit on our behalf.

We are weak. The context of this verse suggests that this weakness is due to our bondage to decay, like the rest of creation. Haven't you noticed that it's harder to pray when you're tired or sick than when you're rested and well? The condition of our physical bodies often makes prayer even more difficult than it normally is. And if you think prayer isn't difficult, then I suggest you haven't really made a serious effort at it.

Not only are we weak, but our knowledge is limited. We don't know the beginning from the end. We can't see all the consequences that result from our actions. But God knows.

That's why the Holy Spirit helps us in our weakness and intercedes for us with the Father. He makes sure that our prayers are in accordance with God's will. This is a wonderful truth. You may be walking in the Spirit and praying for something with all earnestness, all the while not knowing that what you are praying for would result in disaster. God the Holy Spirit takes those earnest prayers, intensifies them, and prays for us what we would have prayed if only we knew what God knows.

This should encourage us to pray! Even when we feel the feeblest in prayer, our prayers become mighty before the throne, because of the interceding work of God the Holy Spirit on our behalf.

Conclusion

God the Holy Spirit works in the believer's life to produce godly character by energizing and enabling us for service for the building-up of the body, equipping us for service by teaching us from His Word, and leading us in the way we should go. He prompts us to praise and thanksgiving by making known to us the reality of who God is, by testifying to our spirits, and by interceding for us in prayer.

God does all this because of His great love for us. Knowing all of this to be true, the only appropriate way to end this chapter is with the outburst of praise from the pen of Jude:

> *To him who is able to keep you from falling and to present you before his glorious presence without fault and with great joy—to the only God our Savior be glory, majesty, power and authority, through Jesus Christ our Lord, before all ages, now and forevermore! Amen* (JUDE 24–25, NIV).

Discussion Questions

In each of chapters 14–20, we will be revisiting your answer to the question: "How do you get there?" Please look back at your answer to that question and examine it in light of this chapter.

1. This chapter discusses the meaning of the word *holy*. Please think of a way you could illustrate the meaning of this word if you were teaching a class of children or young people.

2. As we look at where we are, where we're going, and how we intend to get there, it's helpful to remember why we are on this journey. This chapter lists four reasons why godly character is important. List them, and add any thoughts that come to mind about how these motivations apply in your own life.

3. What is the nature and purpose of service that is acceptable to God?

4. Discuss the working of the Holy Spirit with regard to our assurance of salvation and our prayer life.

5. Has this chapter brought any questions to mind, or any thoughts you would like to discuss with the group?

6. Is there any issue you would like prayed for, or accountability in, over the course of this week?

7. Please note any other group members' answers that you would like to follow up on this week, either by praying for them or by making an encouraging contact.

THE BLACK KITTEN

*One thing was certain, that the WHITE kitten had
had nothing to do with it—it was the black kitten's
fault entirely. For the white kitten had been having
its face washed by the old cat for the last quarter
of an hour (and bearing it pretty well, considering);
so you see that it COULDN'T have had any hand
in the mischief. . . .*

*But the black kitten had been finished with earlier
in the afternoon, and so, while Alice was sitting
curled up in a corner of the great armchair, half
talking to herself and half asleep, the kitten had
been having a grand game of romps with the ball
of worsted Alice had been trying to wind up, and
had been rolling it up and down till it had all come
undone again, and there it was, spread over the
hearthrug, all knots and tangles, with the kitten
running after its own tail in the middle.*

—*Looking-Glass,* ch. I, "Looking-Glass House"

Chapter 18
When Temptation Is a Kitten

Recently a woman came to see me in my study to discuss some issues in her marriage. After we had talked for a while, she said, "Well, there is just one more thing, but this is kind of stupid." She rolled her eyes and her face turned slightly pink as she let out a little laugh.

"My daughter and I were walking down the road about a week ago—I can't believe I'm bringing this up—anyway, we were taking a walk when out of the weeds by the side of the road stumbled a little black kitten. She was soaking wet, had her fur all matted, and looked really hungry. So we took her home. We do that all the time," she added. "We pick up strays, get them healthy, and then drop them off at the pet store for adoption."

"Well," here she rolled her eyes again, "I don't know why, but I've become really fond of this particular kitten. She just has so much personality, I really want to keep her. But my husband won't hear of it." She turned her head to look straight at me. "I think he's saying no just because he knows I want it."

"Have you named the kitten yet?" I asked.

"No. Why?"

"Well, I have the perfect name for it—Temptation."

"What?" she asked, laughing as she had before.

"Darlene,* the Bible is quite clear in its commands regarding your responsibility to your husband. The way you respond to your husband has a direct bearing on your relationship to God. You know that."

"Okay. So?"

"Well, this little kitten is disrupting that relationship. I mean, you're not exactly submitting to your husband in everything as unto the Lord [EPH 5:22–24], now are you?"

She sighed heavily and looked away. "No."

"Darlene, it may look like a cute little kitten, but the kitten is actually a temptation to get you to disobey the clear teaching of Scripture."

Sometimes temptation is obvious. Other times it's subtle. But the reality of temptation is that it's never very far away. Because temptation is such a constant companion to the believer, the sad fact is that sin is present in the life of the believer as well.

As Christians, we are called to spend our lives being filled with the Spirit. Moment by moment we are called to be in sweet communion with the One Who is infinitely holy. You can see, then, that sin in the life of the believer automatically disrupts that communion: when the believer sins, God the Holy Spirit is no longer able to work in and through him. Now He must minister to that believer to bring him to repentance.

It is important to note that sin doesn't cause the Spirit to depart the believer—but it does grieve Him. Obeying the command "Do not grieve the Holy Spirit of God" is the first condition necessary to be filled with the Spirit.

Do not let any unwholesome talk come out of your mouths, but only what is helpful for building others up according to their

---

* This is a false name to protect the privacy of the individual telling the story. This story was used by permission.

needs, that it may benefit those who listen. And do not grieve the Holy Spirit of God, with whom you were sealed for the day of redemption. Get rid of all bitterness, rage and anger, brawling and slander, along with every form of malice. Be kind and compassionate to one another, forgiving each other, just as in Christ God forgave you (EPH 4:29–32, NIV).

Just as the believer is either "filled" or "unfilled," so he is either in a state of "grieving" or "not grieving" the Spirit of God.

Exactly what does it mean to "grieve the Holy Spirit of God?" In the context, grieving the Spirit is equated with all manner of different sins. There are the things we do (unwholesome talk, bitterness, rage and anger, brawling and slander, and every form of malice), as well as what we refuse or fail to do (being kind, compassionate, and forgiving of each other). Given this, we can state the following definition:

Definition: *Grief* is the emotion that God the Holy Spirit feels when the believer *knowingly* sins. The believer cannot be filled with the Spirit as long as the Holy Spirit is grieved.

Even though the quoted passage lists specific sins to be avoided, we cannot limit the grieving of the Spirit to these few, or to those on any other list. Any and all known sin grieves the Holy Spirit.

At this point we need to refine our understanding. *Sin* is often defined as any lack of conformity to the character of God. Therefore, whenever we do something God wouldn't do, think something God wouldn't think, or even feel something emotionally that God wouldn't feel, we are sinning. In the same way, when we fail to do what God would do, fail to think what God would think, fail to feel what God would feel, we are also sinning.

It should become immediately evident from this definition that we sin all the time and don't even know it! In fact, in LEVITICUS 4 the

Old Testament Law lays out a whole series of sacrifices for those who sin unintentionally. When you consider that the first and greatest commandment is to "Love the Lord your God with all your heart and with all your soul and with all your mind," the situation becomes even more dire—who can say that he has ever obeyed that command completely?

Therefore, grieving the Spirit must be limited to those sins (as listed above) that are known to the believer. If this weren't the case, the believer would never be filled, since the Spirit would be continually grieved! So we don't need to worry about dredging up every sin that we can possibly imagine. If you're at all like me (and I know you are), you will have your hands full with sin that you know all too well.

God desires that sin be prevented or avoided, but when someone does sin, God has also provided a remedy. The Bible uses two words to offer God's remedy for our sin. The first is *believe*. This calls out to all who have not yet come to the cross for salvation. The second word is *confess*. This is the remedy for those who have already trusted Christ. Let's look at each in turn.

When we believe, we enter into God's gracious salvation, of which forgiveness of sins is only a part. We have received "great and precious promises" (2 Pet 1:4, NIV) that go far beyond removal of sin. Most believers tend to view salvation as subtraction. Christ paid the penalty of our sins so that "as far as the east is from the west, so far has he removed our transgressions from us" (Ps 103:12, NIV). This is certainly true, but it is not nearly expansive enough. If all that had occurred on the cross was the removal of our sins, we would just be brought back to moral zero, so to speak. All that is negative about us would have been removed, but nothing positive would have been added to our account. If all that were necessary was the removal of sins, then the most practically righteous among us would be those who are comatose. They have no opportunity to sin! But God desires far more from us.

I do not mean to belittle the great subtraction that takes place at the cross, but merely to highlight that there is also a wonderful addition. God's wrath is satisfied by Christ's sacrifice of atonement (usually translated as *propitiation*—the satisfaction of God's wrath by means of a sacrifice), so our sins are removed from us. When we believe, though, there is also the addition of Christ's righteousness to our account.

> *But now a righteousness from God, apart from law, has been made known, to which the Law and the Prophets testify. This righteousness from God comes through faith in Jesus Christ to all who believe. There is no difference, for all have sinned and fall short of the glory of God, and are justified freely by his grace through the redemption that came by Christ Jesus* (ROM 3:21–24, NIV).

Notice that a righteousness originating with God comes to all who believe. We have been "justified" by His grace. Do we know what this means? Actually, several words in this passage require definition. These verses contain a great many terms that believers use regularly without really understanding their meaning. So let's examine a couple of them more closely.

The new birth that results from belief isn't a process, but rather that point in time when God does amazing things in and for the believer. We should be aware that just as we don't remember our physical births, and yet know that they have taken place because here we are, some might not remember their spiritual births either. Nevertheless, the Bible depicts saving faith as an instantaneous event. Here are just some of the things that happen at salvation:

- God sets out for us ahead of time a destination (that's what *predestined* means) that He guarantees we'll reach. Our assured destination is that we will be conformed to the image of His Son (ROM 8:29).

- We are redeemed or purchased by the blood of Christ (ROM 3:24; EPH 1:7; 1 COR 6:20).

- We are reconciled to God (2 COR 5:18). That means that there is now peace between God and the believer.

- Our sins are all forgiven (COL 2:13).

- We die to the Law (ROM 7:2–6).

- We are "born again"(1 PET 1:23) so that we might be the children of God (JOHN 1:12–13).

- The new birth (regeneration) cleanses us (TITUS 3:5) and gives us new life (COL 2:13).

The list could go on and on; this list of highlights is in no way exhaustive. The point is that at the moment of salvation, a complex set of events takes place, even though they happen simultaneously. That being said, each of these events could be taken separately from the others and examined more closely, despite the fact that they make up one united whole.

This is very similar to a slow-motion instant replay in professional football. There is an event—we'll say a caught pass—that happens in a moment of time. For that catch to be considered complete, though, several factors must be true at once. For example, both feet have to touch the ground in bounds, or the catch is incomplete. The receiver has to have "control of the ball" while in bounds. He cannot be pushed out of bounds if he would normally have landed in bounds, and so forth. The instant replay can take this near-instantaneous event and slow it down, enabling us to see if all the conditions were met for the single act of catching a completed pass.

Let's take an "instant replay" look at the word *believe*. This single word is the total of all that a sinner can and must do to be saved. There are no works to be accomplished, no promises to keep, no magic prayer to pray. Belief is the one and only requirement for salvation. But when we slow down the instant replay, we see that belief actually has two parts. If either of these parts is absent, then belief—that is, saving faith—does not exist.

- *First, before there can be saving faith, an intellectual awareness must take place;* this includes a body of knowledge that must be known. In other words, some basic information must be available to the sinner before belief can occur. Paul asks (Rom 10:4, NIV), "How, then, can they call on the one they have not believed in? And how can they believe in the one of whom they have not heard? And how can they hear without someone preaching to them?" This just makes sense. You can't have faith in nothing. There must be some truth, known and understood, in which to have faith. For example, the facts that all people are sinners and that Jesus was the sacrifice for our sins must be known before someone can be saved.

- *Second, after that body of knowledge is gained, there must be an acceptance of that body of knowledge as true.* Someone can receive the information, understand the claims being made, and yet not accept them as true. This happens all the time. People regularly disbelieve the miraculous story of Jesus Christ. Dead people don't come back to life. Virgins don't conceive. God doesn't become man. Everyone knows this. The belief part of faith, however, requires people to, well, believe these things. They must hold these things as true.

The intellectual aspect of belief, however, is not enough to save—in fact, this first aspect of faith is possessed by demons! "You believe that there is one God. Good! Even the demons believe that—and shudder" (JAMES 2:19, NIV). There is one more aspect to saving faith:

- *There must be a trust or reliance upon the knowledge* known and regarded as true. This involves *an act of the will*. It might be thought of as my desire for this truth to be applied to me and then resting in the information based upon my conviction of its truthfulness.

This trust includes the desire for the truths of the gospel, specifically the cleansing from sin it provides, to be personally applied. It is unfortunate but true that many people profess belief in the message of Scripture but, in reality, have no desire for *the essential* element of the gospel—namely, the cleansing from sin—to affect their lives.

Although I agree that at the moment of saving faith, God endows the believer with a new nature (Rom 6:5–7; Gal 2:20; Col 3:9–10) that should result in good works (Eph 2:10), true salvation is in no way dependent upon good works at any time in the life of the believer (Eph 2:8–9). Good works are not the deciding factor of whether someone is saved. Belief, not works, is the sole determining factor.

Unfortunately, many people make some sort of profession or other in their lives yet show absolutely no evidence of the new life that Christ offers. This experience is so common that it demands examination. Charles Ryrie's observation is worth noting at this point: "Every Christian will bear spiritual fruit. Somewhere, sometime, somehow. Otherwise that person is not a believer. Every born-again individual will be fruitful. Not to be fruitful is to be faithless, without faith, and therefore without salvation."[1]

Ryrie then provides three caveats to this statement:

1. This does not mean that a person will *always* be fruitful.
2. This does not mean that a certain person's fruit will necessarily be outwardly evident.
3. My understanding of what fruit is, and therefore what I expect others to bear, may be faulty and/or incomplete.[2]

Clearly, there are some believers who produce so little that is of eternal worth that they are likened to a man escaping a burning building. He has no possessions after the fire, only the smell of smoke on his clothes. Nevertheless, he himself is saved (1 COR 3:12–15). Therefore, it is possible for a person to be a genuine believer but live a life of such little value that one might wonder if salvation has taken place at all. Still, Paul's command and promise in 1 CORINTHIANS 4:5 (NASB) must be remembered.

Therefore do not go on passing judgment before the time, but wait until the Lord comes who will both bring to light the things hidden in the darkness and disclose the motives of men's hearts; and then each man's praise will come to him from God.

First we see that it is not our right to judge someone's salvation. That privilege belongs to the Lord alone. Yet, at the same time there is the promise of each believer bearing some fruit, no matter how miniscule, since each man will be praised by God. In other words, God will produce something in the life of every believer that is praiseworthy, even if it isn't much.

That being said, what of those who claim to have "made a decision" at some point in their lives, but since that time have shown absolutely no evidence whatsoever of the new life that Christ offers? What about them?

Although I certainly cannot say this is true in every case, I do believe that one common cause of this situation is that they have believed something that is not the gospel. Well-meaning individuals often present the saving message of Jesus Christ in such a way that they offer what God hasn't promised and obscure what He has promised.

The gospel, by its very nature, is other-worldly. It is a spiritual message, not a material one. It deals exclusively with salvation. To be saved, though, we must recognize that there is something to be saved *from*. It is at this point that problems arise. Some promise that we will be saved from disease or poverty. Others promise that we will be saved from the difficult circumstances in which we find ourselves. In other words, they say that the things from which we are saved are material and of this world. This could not be more false!

The gospel begins with "The wrath of God is being revealed from heaven against all the godlessness and wickedness of men who suppress the truth by their wickedness" (ROM 1:18, NIV), not "God loves you and offers a wonderful plan for your life."[3] This last statement may or may not be true for someone living in North America, but what about believers in Iran, or India, or Saudi Arabia, or China? Their wonderful plan most likely includes prison, torture, and possibly death. When people place their trust in a gospel centered in this world, they have an intellectual problem, in that the gospel has not been presented correctly; and a volitional problem, in that they are trusting in the wrong object. They are trusting in a God Who makes their life better, not a God Who saves them from their sins.

Perhaps an example will make this clear. Recently I had a man enter my study whose life was a wreck. Sin had so ravaged his past that nearly any relationship possible, regardless of whether it was personal, professional, or legal, was in tatters. He freely admitted that he was miserable and that it was his own fault. I didn't need any time whatsoever to convince him that he was a sinner—that much he knew. From his youthful days in Sunday School, he also knew about Christ's sacrificial death on the cross for his sins. He even "made a decision" for Christ at a Christian camp one year, although he admitted that he really hadn't understood what he was doing and it had no effect whatsoever on his life.

With tears streaming down his face, he told me of his desire to be saved. I sensed, however, that his real desire wasn't what the gospel offers (namely, cleansing from sin), but rather a desire for his problems to start disappearing. I pressed him on the nature of the gospel. We need to be made right in the eyes of God our Creator and Judge. Until we get that relationship right, none of the others will be made right.

Up to this point he had been slumped over in his chair. The mention of "cleansing from sin," however, made him sit up straight and focus on what I was saying. "Does that mean that I'll have to quit doing thus and so?" he asked, his eyes narrowing.

Normally, I never mention what a person must do to exercise saving faith, because the issue isn't works but belief. When someone brings it up on their own, though, I assume that it is God the Holy Spirit working in his life convicting him of sin. So I answered, "Do you think thus and so is a sin that needs cleansing? If the answer is yes, how can you desire that cleansing and still purpose in your heart to continue in it?"

Please notice that I didn't mention anything about promising to do better or cleaning up his own life. I merely asked if this particular sin needed cleansing. He made the obvious connection. If he was going to be cleansed from sin, eventually that sin must be dealt with, along with the others.

"Hmmmm . . . " he mused, his eyes still narrow and his brow furrowed. "I don't want to give that up."

"Then I guess we have a problem with your will, don't we? You want Christ to straighten out your life—something he *hasn't* offered—but don't want cleansing from your sin, which is what he really offers."

"I guess you're right, Pastor," he said seriously. I also detected more than a little sadness in his voice. I prayed with him and told him I would continue to do so, and he left.

So, what was his problem? Intellectually, he accepted as true the message of the gospel, but his will was tied to the fleeting pleasures of this world. In other words, it wasn't that he didn't give intellectual assent to the truths of the gospel, he simply didn't want them.

Belief could be thought of as the combination of the intellect (I believe it to be true that Christ died for my sins) + the will (I place my trust in Christ to save me from my sins). I greatly fear that many who call themselves Christians today have gone as far as the intellect, but have stopped there. They have given theoretical assent to a bunch of facts (learned in Sunday School, confirmation class, Sunday preaching, neighborhood Bible study, etc.), but that intellectual assent hasn't made its way to the will. They believe the facts of the gospel are true, but they don't desire them for themselves.

I see this most often when people who are nominally Christians (in that their church attendance is sporadic, their interest in the things of God low, their character largely unchanged) tell me they're Christians because they went forward, or made a decision at camp, or prayed with the preacher. Unfortunately, these activities often indicate an intellectual assent that has been divorced from the will.

Belief, therefore, is a combination of an intellectual awareness of the facts concerning the gospel, particularly Christ's sacrificial death and His physical resurrection, and a voluntary act of will that desires the cleansing from sin that Christ offers.

My question for you is this: *Do you have saving faith?* Are you stuck in this world, viewing the gospel merely as a means to a better life in the here-and-now? Or have you moved forward to believing the true gospel of salvation from our sins, which is what God really offers?

Now that we have a clear idea of what belief entails, we can return to the fact that righteousness is given to all who have believed in this way. Salvation isn't merely the subtraction of sins, but also the addition of a positional righteousness.

This is why Paul can say we have been "justified freely" by God's grace. *Justification* is another word Christians use regularly without fully understanding what it means. Some, in an attempt to be helpful, say that justification is "just as if I've never sinned." This is an incomplete definition because it speaks only of the subtraction that happened at the cross. It ignores the addition of righteousness that also occurred. Paul helps us understand this concept better in the next chapter in Romans.

> *What then shall we say that Abraham, our forefather, discovered in this matter? If, in fact, Abraham was justified by works, he had something to boast about—but not before God. What does the Scripture say? "Abraham believed God, and it was credited to him as righteousness."*
>
> *Now when a man works, his wages are not credited to him as a gift, but as an obligation. However, to the man who does not work but trusts God who justifies the wicked, his faith is credited as righteousness* (ROM 4:1–5, NIV).

Abraham believed, and as a result of that belief righteousness was "credited to him." We might say it was deposited in his account. It wasn't something he worked for, nor was it something that was automatically acted out in his life. This righteousness is positional, not practical (although we should quickly add that positional righteousness should have practical application). However, the righteousness of God that is given to the believer refers to someone's standing with God, not with how that person actually behaves. Knowing this to be true, we can derive the following definition:

Definition: *Justification* is the judicial act of God whereby He declares the believing sinner righteous.

Two words in this definition are extremely important: *judicial* and *declares*. Justification is a judicial act, in that God brings down the gavel in His courtroom and declares us righteous. This doesn't mean we really are righteous in our behavior, any more than everyone declared "not guilty" in our own courts really didn't commit the charged crime. Instead, in the eyes of the law, our standing is one of righteousness. When God looks at the believer, He no longer sees our sins, but instead sees the righteousness of Christ that has been given to us.

Believing is the first action required to deal with sin in our lives. *Confession* is the word describing the action of a believer who has sinned. The main passage that deals with the issue of fellowship with God and sin in the believer's life is found in 1 JOHN:

> *We proclaim to you what we have seen and heard, so that you also may have fellowship with us. And our fellowship is with the Father and with his Son, Jesus Christ. We write this to make our joy complete.*
>
> *This is the message we have heard from him and declare to you: God is light; in him there is no darkness at all. If we claim to have fellowship with him yet walk in the darkness, we lie and do not live by the truth. But if we walk in the light, as he is in the light, we have fellowship with one another, and the blood of Jesus, his Son, purifies us from all sin.*
>
> *If we claim to be without sin, we deceive ourselves and the truth is not in us. If we confess our sins, he is faithful and just and will forgive us our sins and purify us from all unrighteousness. If we claim we have not sinned, we make him out to be a liar and his word has no place in our lives.*
>
> *My dear children, I write this to you so that you will not sin. But if anybody does sin, we have one who speaks to the Father in our defense—Jesus Christ, the Righteous One* (1 JOHN 1:3– 2:1, NIV).

As we read through this passage, we learn several truths that are important if we are not to grieve the Holy Spirit.

- The word *fellowship* nearly leaps off the page. It's used four times in this section. This makes clear what issue is being discussed. This passage is not instructing us concerning salvation, but about fellowship with God. This, of course, is the issue when we discuss being filled with the Spirit.

- It's also clear that believers are being addressed, because John writes to "My dear children." Another indication that this is written to and for believers is that it speaks of the fellowship we are to have with one another.

- One of the barriers to fellowship is sin. We lose fellowship with God when we sin, because "God is light; in him there is no darkness at all." Therefore, when there is darkness in us, fellowship is broken.

- The believer can make three false claims about sin. (1) If we walk in darkness and claim to have fellowship with God, we are lying. (2) If we claim to be without sin, we are deceiving ourselves. (3) If we claim we have not sinned, we make God out to be a liar.

It's clear, therefore, that sin is still a problem even for the believer. Anyone who tries to make a claim of sinless perfection is making God out to be a liar. (If someone claims to be without sin, my first thought is, "I wonder if their spouse would agree with that claim?")

- When we sin (and we all do!), we don't lose our salvation, because we have One Who speaks in our defense before God. This passage is not threatening the possibility of a loss of salvation. The issue is fellowship and loss of fellowship.

- If we walk in the light—which is another way of stating that we are being filled with the Spirit—the blood of Christ "keeps on" purifying us from "all" sin. The original language again shows continuous action.

- The way to deal with sin and get back into fellowship is to "confess our sins."

It's good to know that sinless perfection isn't demanded of the believer. God doesn't want us to sin, but He recognizes who we are and what we are capable of. He has a very realistic picture of our spiritual life. This is why He has provided a way for us to stay in fellowship with Him, even though we are so prone to sin.

When we sin, the antidote is confession. The word *confess* means "to concede that something is factual or true."[4] This is all that is required. There is no penance to complete, no special ritual to perform: God only asks us to tell the truth about our sin. God desires that we move from falsehood (that it's okay this time, that it really doesn't matter, and so forth) and be honest with Him and with ourselves about who we are and what we have done (or have failed to do, as the case may be).

When we are once again telling the truth, God promises to be faithful and just to forgive our sin and cleanse us from all unrighteousness. Notice that God doesn't promise to be merciful or lenient. God is never lenient with sin. God always judges sin. Leniency is never promised in the Bible.

But what about mercy? God does claim to be a merciful God. Why isn't His mercy mentioned here? The answer is simple: God has already been merciful: He saved us through the blood of Christ. His mercy has already been put on display, so there is no necessity for mercy here.

Instead, God promises to be faithful and just. He is faithful, in that He will fulfill the promise of forgiveness procured by the cross. He will be just, in that He will accept the sacrifice Christ offered in our stead and refuse to punish the same sin twice.

To summarize, the word *believe* involves judicial forgiveness. The word *confess* deals with parental forgiveness. This latter is the word that talks of the child of God's restoration to fellowship as part of the family.

Let me point out once again that this passage only refers to known sin. There is no warrant or command to search every crevice and chink of our lives looking for something that might be an offense against the character of God. Some people become obsessed with continually dredging the depths of their souls, searching for something of which God disapproves. At first, that might sound admirable, but in actual practice it can be paralyzing. It causes the person to live in fear, not faith, and to remain almost immobile out of concern for crossing some line, real or imagined.

Such a view of confession and sin doesn't encourage—or even acknowledge—the joyful, peace-filled life produced by the Spirit. This attitude also lends itself to the mistaken notion that we are so wicked we cannot possibly please God. Though this is certainly true if we are speaking merely of the flesh, it is absolutely false if we are referring to a life lived in the power of the Spirit! If we walk by the Spirit, we will not carry out the desire of the flesh (GAL 5:16, NASB). *It is possible to be pleasing to God!*

Confession is limited to those sins that God the Holy Spirit brings to our attention. Like any good parent, He will correct us when we do what is wrong.

In your struggle against sin, you have not yet resisted to the point of shedding your blood. And you have forgotten that word of encouragement that addresses you as sons: "My son, do not make light of the Lord's discipline, and do not lose heart when he rebukes you, because the Lord disciplines those he loves, and he punishes everyone he accepts as a son.

*Endure hardship as discipline; God is treating you as sons.
For what son is not disciplined by his father? If you are not
disciplined (and everyone undergoes discipline), then you are
illegitimate children and not true sons. Moreover, we have all
had human fathers who disciplined us and we respected them
for it. How much more should we submit to the Father of our
spirits and live! Our fathers disciplined us for a little while as
they thought best; but God disciplines us for our good, that we
may share in his holiness. No discipline seems pleasant at the
time, but painful. Later on, however, it produces a harvest of
righteousness and peace for those who have been trained by it*
(HEB 12:4–11, NIV).

Just as fathers and mothers discipline their children in love, so
God disciplines us to bring about the holiness He desires to share with
us. God's discipline can take as many different forms as He has children, but Scripture contains some hints of the more extreme measures
He uses in particularly troublesome cases.

We read, for example, that gross disobedience when partaking of
the Lord's Supper resulted in many being weak and sick, and a number
who even died (1 COR 11:30). There is a sober warning in 1 JOHN 5:16
that there are sins which lead to death. We aren't told what those sins
are, but it's a safe bet that they went unconfessed for a considerable
period of time, because if confession had been made, God is faithful
and just to forgive. It is when we continuously grieve the Holy Spirit
that such judgments occur.

At the very least, we can say that God's hand weighs heavy on
those who continue in sin and refuse to confess. David testified to this
soul-ache when he wrote, "When I kept silent, my bones wasted away
through my groaning all day long. For day and night your hand was
heavy upon me; my strength was sapped as in the heat of summer"

(Ps 32:3–4, NIV). This is the effect of the Holy Spirit grieving over a soul that refused fellowship with Him.

Of course, there is a way to avoid this kind of discipline. "But if we judged ourselves, we would not come under judgment. When we are judged by the Lord, we are being disciplined so that we will not be condemned with the world" (1 COR 11:31, NIV). Judging ourselves means recognizing when we have sinned (and we know when we've sinned, don't we?) and confessing immediately. When we judge ourselves in this way, we remain filled with the Spirit. The Holy Spirit no longer has to work on or minister to us, but is now able to work in and through us.

When we sin, we need to keep short accounts in order to be filled with the Spirit.

And do not grieve the Holy Spirit of God, with whom you were sealed for the day of redemption (EPH 4:30, NIV).

Discussion Questions

In each of chapters 14–20, we will be revisiting your answer to the question: "How do you get there?" Please look back at your answer to that question and examine it in light of this chapter.

1. As you read about grieving the Holy Spirit, was anything brought to your mind in which you are doing so? If so, what do you intend to do about this?

2. Two different definitions of the word *justification* were mentioned: the commonly used "just as if I'd never sinned," as opposed to the definition used in this book, "the judicial act of God whereby He declares the believing sinner righteous." In your own words, explain why the second definition is preferable.

3. Has this chapter brought any questions to mind, or any thoughts you would like to discuss with the group?

4. Is there any issue you would like prayed for, or accountability in, over the course of this week?

5. Please note any other group members' answers that you would like to follow up on this week, either by praying for them or by making an encouraging contact.

TWEEDLEDEE AND TWEEDLEDUM

Tweedledee smiled gently, and began again:

"The sun was shining on the sea,
*   Shining with all his might;*
He did his very best to make
*   The billows smooth and bright—*
And this was odd, because it was
*   The middle of the night.*

"The moon was shining sulkily,
*   Because she thought the sun*
Had got no business to be there
*   After the day was done—*
'It's very rude of him,' she said,
*   'To come and spoil the fun!'"*

—*Looking-Glass*, ch. IV,
"Tweedledum and Tweedledee"

Chapter 19
The Moon Was Shining Sulkily

J ust as we are not to grieve the Holy Spirit of God, we are also not to "quench the Spirit" (1 THESS 5:19, NASB). The NIV translates this as "Do not put out the Spirit's fire." This is the second condition that must be met in order to be filled with the Spirit.

The word translated "quench" means "to cause a fervent activity to cease."[1] Both the NASB and the NIV are accurate in translating this word as "quench" or "put out the fire," but neither adequately expresses the sense of Paul's original word. Figuratively, it means to "stifle or suppress, to cause an action, state, or faculty to cease to function or exist."[2]

Note that "putting out the Spirit's fire" doesn't mean that He is somehow extinguished or that He simply withdraws from us. We have seen that He indwells us until the "day of redemption" (EPH 4:30). To understand what it means to quench the Spirit, we must remember that we are speaking of *acting out* our salvation, not of our salvation itself. Therefore, we will use the following definition:

Definition: *Quenching* the Spirit is saying "no" to the Spirit's leading.

In the strictest sense, any resistance to the Spirit of God would be "quenching the Spirit." In this regard, quenching the Spirit is somewhat similar to grieving the Spirit, discussed in chapter 18. It is possible, for example, to grieve the Spirit and fall into sin by saying no to what the Spirit demands. In the same way, one may quench the Spirit by saying no to His promptings to abstain from sin. However, the context of 1 THESSALONIANS seems to point particularly to resisting the Spirit as He works to produce Christlike character and prompt us to service:

> *Be joyful always; pray continually; give thanks in all circum-stances, for this is God's will for you in Christ Jesus. Do not put out the Spirit's fire; do not treat prophecies with contempt. Test everything. Hold on to the good. Avoid every kind of evil. May God himself, the God of peace, sanctify you through and through. May your whole spirit, soul and body be kept blameless at the coming of our Lord Jesus Christ* (1 THESS 5:16–23, NIV).

The command regarding quenching is in the midst of a list of appar-ently random commands. Nevertheless, each command is connected to the others in that they all deal with the believer's behavior as it relates to the will of God. Why are we to be joyful, pray, and give thanks? Because it is "God's will for you in Christ Jesus." It is also God's will that you not put out the Spirit's fire or treat prophecies with contempt.

This last phrase is a little difficult. Three options seem to be available, and each option revolves around how you define *prophecy.* Each definition has at its core the idea of "interpreting divine will or purpose,"[3] whether *prophecy* is taken to mean the act of interpreting, the gift of interpreting, or the utterance of someone who interprets. Paul could be talking about the grace gift of prophecy (whether it be supernatural revelation, which has ceased, or the utterance of God's truth as recorded in the Bible), or the prophecies that have been written down for us in the Holy Scriptures. Nevertheless, however you view this command, it's clear that we are to test what God's will is for us and cling to the good while avoiding evil.

The twin ideas of testing what God's will is and not saying no to God are expressed by Paul in another passage as well. Whereas in 1 THESSALONIANS he makes the command negative (Do not quench the Spirit), in ROMANS 12 he states basically the same command, only this time positively:

Therefore, I urge you, brothers, in view of God's mercy, to offer your bodies as living sacrifices, holy and pleasing to God—this is your spiritual act of worship. Do not conform any longer to the pattern of this world, but be transformed by the renewing of your mind. Then you will be able to test and approve what God's will is—his good, pleasing and perfect will (ROM 12:1–2, NIV).

The negative command of "not saying no" becomes the positive command to "offer your bodies as living sacrifices." Whether stated negatively or positively, the idea is clear. Our will is to be put aside so we may perform the will of the Spirit (put another way, so that we allow the Spirit to work through us). In both passages, it is assumed that God the Holy Spirit is making demands upon our lives and that we must yield ourselves to Him. As Paul says in another place, "Do not offer the parts of your body to sin, as instruments of wickedness, but rather offer yourselves to God, as those who have been brought from death to life; and offer the parts of your body to him as instruments of righteousness" (ROM 6:13, NIV).

This all sounds great on paper—but we really have a hard time trusting that God knows what is best, don't we? In public, we would loudly agree with the Prophet Jeremiah: "I know, O Lord, that a man's life is not his own; it is not for man to direct his steps" (JER 10:23, NIV). All too often, though, we're just a bunch of phonies. We are constantly confronted with what our senses tell us and what our minds can reason, and so we struggle with God's direction for us. Like the moon, we shine sulkily when the full light of the sun is where we don't want it.

It's been said that if we knew as much as God knows and were as good as God is, then we would do exactly what God does. The problem is, we *don't* know what God knows and we're *not* as good as He is, so those things that He commands run contrary to what makes the most (natural) sense to us. Once again, to obey this command to offer our bodies—to not say no to the Spirit—requires faith. There's just no getting around it. If you are going to live a life that is pleasing to God, you must exercise faith, regardless of what other people tell you.

A self-guided life is a mis-guided life. God has planned good works for us to do. Therefore, if we are to be filled with the Spirit, we must say yes to God's direction, whether it makes sense to us or not. We must pray like Jesus, "not my will, but yours be done" (LUKE 22:2, NIV).

We must also be careful not to water down what is being commanded. There's always a temptation to take the "all or nothing" statements of Scripture and dilute them with the water of practicality. So, to guard against this very natural tendency, let's take a moment and examine what God desires.

Paul uses the language of the Old Testament sacrificial system to describe what God desires from us. He desires our bodies. The most obvious implication of this is the most jarring for "safety-first" North Americans: It is possible that God could call us to give up our lives in His service. Whether or not something is safe is not the primary issue when it comes to doing the will of God. The Apostle John is quite clear concerning our response to Christ's sacrifice for us. "This is how we know what love is: Jesus Christ laid down his life for us. And we ought to lay down our lives for our brothers" (1 JOHN 3:16, NIV). Read that verse again and let it sink in. Now consider Peter's contribution to this idea:

> *Christ suffered for you, leaving you an example, that you should follow in his steps. "He committed no sin, and no deceit was found in his mouth." When they hurled their insults at him, he did not retaliate; when he suffered, he made no threats. Instead, he*

entrusted himself to him who judges justly (1 PET 2:21–23, NIV).

Again, the clearly expressed idea is that we are to follow Christ regardless of the outcome, having faith as Christ did in God's justice.

The idea that God could lead us somewhere unsafe is so foreign to our minds that we probably need another example. Here is a passage of Scripture that is routinely misread. We pick up the story as Stephen is preaching to the Jewish leadership:

> *"You stiff-necked people, with uncircumcised hearts and ears! You are just like your fathers: You always resist the Holy Spirit! Was there ever a prophet your fathers did not persecute? They even killed those who predicted the coming of the Righteous One. And now you have betrayed and murdered him—you who have received the law that was put into effect through angels but have not obeyed it."*
>
> *When they heard this, they were furious and gnashed their teeth at him. But Stephen, full of the Holy Spirit, looked up to heaven and saw the glory of God, and Jesus standing at the right hand of God. "Look," he said, "I see heaven open and the Son of Man standing at the right hand of God."*
>
> *At this they covered their ears and, yelling at the top of their voices, they all rushed at him, dragged him out of the city and began to stone him. Meanwhile, the witnesses laid their clothes at the feet of a young man named Saul.*
>
> *While they were stoning him, Stephen prayed, "Lord Jesus, receive my spirit." Then he fell on his knees and cried out, "Lord, do not hold this sin against them." When he had said this, he fell asleep* (ACTS 7:51–60, NIV).

The way we normally think of this is that Stephen is preaching the Word, the Jews become incensed, they begin to stone him, and he sees Jesus. But look again; that's not what happens. Yes, he is preaching condemnation to the Jewish leadership. Yes, they are furious at him—but they have not moved across the line to murder yet. It is at this point that Jesus appears to Stephen and he sees "the Son of Man standing at the right hand of God." It is this revelation that pushes the crowd over the edge. Only after he sees Jesus do they begin to stone him.

Here's the burning question: Why did Jesus choose that moment to reveal Himself in such a dramatic way to Stephen? Why give the vision of His glory at that moment? The only possible answer is that Jesus desired for Stephen to glorify God with a martyr's death. Hence, He appeared at just the right time to ensure that it would happen.

Wait!—Are you saying that God desired that Stephen be murdered by an enraged crowd? Yes, that's exactly what I'm saying. There is no other explanation for Jesus' revealing Himself in that way at that time. It was God's will for Stephen that he offer his body as a living sacrifice. So much for practicality!

Although the command to offer our bodies includes the physical aspect, it isn't limited to our physical bodies. Instead, this command extends to the entire person. The word *bodies* is used to emphasize a person's interaction with the world. Our material body is the instrument of our immaterial spirit. Every action we perform must be through the use of the body. Thus, we are forced to ask questions like, "Where do your feet take you? What do you allow your eyes to see? What does your tongue say?" Our inward character is expressed through the use of our bodies.

We should also notice that there are three qualities describing the sacrifice of our bodies:

- In contrast to the Old Testament sacrifices, which died when they were offered, we are to be living sacrifices. This may indeed take us to the point of death, but then again it might not. The point is that every moment of your existence is to be spent yielded to God so that you are an active agent of His will.

- We are to be holy. As we have seen, this means we are to be set apart from all that is common or profane. Instead, we are to be available for God's exclusive use.

- We are to be pleasing to God. Just as the Old Testament's offerings had to be acceptable, so we are to be acceptable before God. We are to be without spot and without blemish, in that our sins are confessed and we have been cleansed from all unrighteousness (1 JOHN 1:9). The combination of living actively for Christ while being set apart from what is sinful results in a sacrifice that is pleasing to God.

It is possible to be so caught up in introspection, to be so appalled by the extent of our sinfulness, that we despair of ever doing or being anything that is pleasing to God. But the promise has been made. *We can please God.*

This type of sacrifice is "spiritual" worship. The word *spiritual* is sometimes translated as "reasonable." It carries the idea of a worship that involves the mind and the heart as opposed to merely going through the motions of a ritual. Spiritual worship is appropriate because it gives God what He truly desires: a life yielded to Him.

We must also notice, however, that there is a danger to avoid.

Do not conform any longer to the pattern of this world, but be transformed by the renewing of your mind. Then you will be able to test and approve what God's will is—his good, pleasing and perfect will (ROM 12:2, NIV).

The word *conform* implies being pushed into a mold,[4] and it's a word that every parent can understand. I remember playing with

Play-Doh when I was young. We would take a brightly colored lump and push it into an opening at the top of an extremely sophisticated contraption. We would then take a plastic stick with holes of various shapes cut out of it and slide it in front of another opening at the front of the apparatus. Then we would push down the handle and—presto!—the Play-Doh would be squeezed through the hole into the shape of a star or a circle or a square. What we had done was to squeeze the material into a mold we had chosen, so that pressure changed the formerly shapeless lump into something completely uniform.

In the same way, the world is trying to squeeze us into its mold, so that we all look the same, act the same, and think the same. If you don't think this is true, try driving the speed limit on the interstate. You can be in the slow lane and most people will just whiz around you. Inevitably, though, someone will come up behind you and refuse to go around you. Instead, he'll ride your bumper trying to get you to go faster. What he's really trying to do is make you speed just like everyone else. These people are trying to push you into the mold.

Instead of being conformed, we are to be transformed. The word for "transformed" occurs only three other times in the New Testament. In MATTHEW 17:2 and MARK 9:2, it's used to describe the transfiguration of Jesus on the mountain. In 2 CORINTHIANS 3:18, it describes the change of believers into the likeness of Christ.

The word itself—*metamorphoō*—is thought-provoking. We get our word *metamorphosis* from it. It refers to a complete change that is effective both inwardly and outwardly.[5] Again, the emphasis is upon the union of purpose between the physical and spiritual parts of the person.

Still, this interplay between the material and the immaterial parts of us raises an interesting question. Why are we to "present" our bodies but "renew" our minds? Why are the commands different?

Simply put, the way we serve God is through our bodies, but the pressure to conform (to be of the world, of the flesh, to sin) comes through the mind. Note that both the negative and the positive commands are passive. The commands don't address what we do, but instead what is done to us. Knowing this, don't allow yourself to be conformed. Instead, allow yourself to be transformed.

The fact that both commands are passive implies that two outside forces are being applied to us. While the world is trying to conform us, we need to allow the Holy Spirit to transform us. We must say no to the world and say yes to the Holy Spirit. To put it another way, we are not to quench the Spirit. We are not to put out His fire!

This is the central issue of the spiritual life. Just as in eternity we will have unbroken fellowship with our Triune God, so on this side of eternity we have the responsibility to maintain unbroken fellowship with God the Spirit who indwells us. This lofty goal sounds completely out of reach, and, in one respect at least, it is, because we will never achieve sinless perfection in this life. That being said, although the confession of every sin of which we are aware and constant dependence upon God the Spirit depend on the action of the (fallen) human will, it is equally true that God the Spirit enables us to do just that, despite our corruption. This isn't some theoretical activity occurring only at the speed of light in a vacuum! This really is the way that God desires us to live in the here-and-now.

Paul writes, "for it is God who works in you to will and to act according to his good purpose" (PHIL 2:13, NIV). The word translated "work" means "to put one's capabilities into operation."[6] So, we could translate this as "God who energizes the will and action" or "God who causes you to be willing."[7] This should not be viewed as any sort of divine coercion or the negation of free will. On the contrary, there is an exercise of human responsibility in not quenching the Spirit. It is our surrender to the will of God that allows us to be filled with the

Spirit. From that point forward, though, God the Holy Spirit so enables our will and empowers our actions that we can indeed lead a life of fellowship with Him. He gives us the freedom to live in a way that we are powerless to live on our own. We really can be the living sacrifices that God desires, because God is "working" within us!

Knowing the Will of God

When we serve God in this way, as living sacrifices, one of the benefits is that we will be able to know God's will. His will is good, pleasing, and perfect, just as God is. There are, however, some prerequisites to knowing the will of God:

- God reveals His will only to those who are already committed to doing it. Only after we offer our bodies as living sacrifices are we able to know the will of God. It has been said that God is able to speak loud enough to make a willing believer hear— but He is silent to those who set preconditions on how they will allow themselves to be used.

- God's will is always in perfect accord with Scripture. This doesn't mean we are to treat the Bible as some sanctified ouija board. We don't just let the Bible flop open and blindly stick our finger on a verse to determine what to do at a given moment. In the same way, there is no warrant for the casting of lots,* or any other form of discerning God's will by chance. Instead, we are to study and know the Scriptures so the Holy Spirit may guide us in His role as teacher.

---

*In the Old Testament, the casting of lots was never used to determine God's will. Instead, this practice was used to make the decision process fair. For examples, see JOSHUA 18:6, 8; 1 CHRONICLES 24:5; 25:8; NEHEMIAH 10:34; 11:1. Even the gentile sailors in JONAH 1:7 cast lots, not to determine guilt, but to make fair the process of who to question first.

- God doesn't lead His children by a set of rules. This doesn't mean that there are no standards of righteousness, for God's character never changes. It does mean, however, that we can't pull out our cookie-cutters and try to make everyone the same. Because God has determined ahead of time different works for each of His children to do, there is no set pattern to be followed. Not everyone is called to the same thing, nor to do it in the same way. Genuine spirituality is free from law of any kind and is lived in a vital personal relationship with God the Holy Spirit.

- Although God often uses providence to direct His people, it is the leading by the indwelling Spirit that provides meaning to providence and actually directs the believer. When we are filled with the Spirit, we have the "mind of Christ." As a result, we have the inward thoughts of God directing our paths.

At this point, be aware of a danger. Satan often attempts to mislead the believer, appearing as an "angel of light" (2 COR 11:14). He will attempt to confuse the mind with counterfeit thoughts cleverly designed to look like God's will. This is a threat to every believer. Satan will make use of a troubled conscience, a false sense of duty, or a lack of understanding of what the Scriptures actually teach to raise serious doubts in the believer and paralyze him into inaction or goad him into false action, whenever possible. We need to be on our guard! This is why we are told to "test and approve what God's will is." We can be deceived.

That being said, it is possible to tell the difference between the lies of Satan and the leading of the Spirit. God's will is good, pleasing, and perfect. There is a sweetness about it that is unmistakable. Satan's counterfeits are designed to wear us down, to weigh heavy upon us, to keep us discouraged and defeated.

- God's leading is not a voice we can hear or a series of signs we can observe, but a knowledge that God provides. It is difficult to explain or describe, but we can describe the times when we have been led by the Spirit in the past. Think of the last time you were tempted. Now remember the struggle that went on inside you. You knew the right thing to do, didn't you? How did you know? How would you describe that knowledge of right and wrong? What words do it justice? I confess there are none I can find—but the knowledge was there, nevertheless.

In the same way, as God the Holy Spirit directs us moment by moment, we can know the right action to take, the correct decision to make by that same sure knowledge. Not a feeling, not a voice, but a knowledge that we may possess because we have the "mind of Christ."

It is worth remembering that God has given other believers to the church in order to build up the body. He has given the pastor/teacher for the equipping of the saints. We have the Scriptures to guide us. There is the hand of God in providence. In short, there are many ways that God the Holy Spirit may make His will known to us, but ultimately it is the interpreting work of the Spirit within us that makes sense of all these external events and guides us in the way we should go so that we will accomplish the good works He has set before us.

Jesus described our yieldedness to God as "remaining in him" (JOHN 15:4, NIV). Three blessings result from our remaining in him:

- *We have a new power in prayer.* "If you remain in me and my words remain in you, ask whatever you wish, and it will be given you" (JOHN 15:7, NIV). This is not a "name it and claim it" promise, whereby God obligates Himself to do whatever we want. It is a conditional promise. *If* we remain in Him and His words remain in us, we can ask what we wish. The implication is that we will be asking in accordance with the will of God, and that we won't be asking to spend what we get on our pleasures (JAMES 4:3). Instead, we will pray as Christ prayed and have the power of the Holy Spirit interceding for us.

- *We will have a joy that is complete.* "I have told you this so that my joy may be in you and that your joy may be complete" (JOHN 15:11, NIV). If you lack joy, then you need to practice remaining in Christ. You need to stop quenching the Spirit. You must say yes to God. The promise is that our joy will be complete when that condition is met.

- *We will have works that endure.* "You did not choose me, but I chose you and appointed you to go and bear fruit—fruit that will last" (JOHN 15:16, NIV). An empty life is foreign to the believer who remains in Christ. The work that we do for Him will be meaningful and lasting because it was designed specifically for us before the world began.

These results are conditioned upon obedience to Christ. "If you obey my commands, you will remain in my love, just as I have obeyed my Father's commands and remain in his love" (JOHN 15:10, NIV). Remaining in Christ, then, is simply obeying the known will of God in the same way that Christ obeyed. We obey by saying yes to the leading of the Spirit. We refuse to put out the Spirit's fire.

When we do not quench the Spirit, we have met one of the qualifications of being filled with the Spirit.

Do not quench the Spirit (1 THESS 5:19, NASB).

Discussion Questions

In each of chapters 14–20, we will be revisiting your answer to the question: "How do you get there?" Please look back at your answer to that question and examine it in light of this chapter.

1. In chapter 18, we looked at "grieve not the Spirit," and in this one, we look at its companion, "quench not the Spirit." As you read through this discussion, did the Holy Spirit bring anything to your mind? Is there some act of service to which He is leading you?

2. The idea was proposed that, sometimes, following God's leading is inherently "unsafe" (by our definition!). Can you give examples of when you, or others, pursued God's will for you, at the expense of what would appear to be the "safe" choice?

3. What did you learn in this chapter about knowing God's will? In chapter 9, "Believing the Impossible," there were four points about knowing God's will (which you copied out and tucked into your Bible). Is there anything from this chapter you would like to add to this card, to guide you in the future?

4. Has this chapter brought any questions to mind, or any thoughts you would like to discuss with the group?

5. Is there any issue you would like prayed for, or accountability in, over the course of this week?

6. Please note any other group members' answers that you would like to follow up on this week, either by praying for them or by making an encouraging contact.

CURIOUSER AND CURIOUSER!

Curiouser and curiouser!" cried Alice (she was so much surprised, that for the moment she quite forgot how to speak good English); "now I'm opening out like the largest telescope that ever was! Good-by, feet!" (for when she looked down at her feet, they seemed to be almost out of sight, they were getting so far off). "Oh, my poor little feet, I wonder who will put on your shoes and stockings for you now, dears? I'm sure I shan't be able! I shall be a great deal too far off to trouble myself about you: you must manage the best way you can; —but I must be kind to them," thought Alice, "or perhaps they won't walk the way I want to go! Let me see: I'll give them a new pair of boots every Christmas."

And she went on planning to herself how she would manage it. "They must go by the carrier," she thought; "and how funny it'll seem, sending presents to one's own feet! And how odd the directions will look:

> *"ALICE'S RIGHT FOOT, ESQ.*
> *HEARTHRUG, NEAR THE FENDER,*
> *(WITH ALICE'S LOVE)."*

"Oh dear, what nonsense I'm talking!"

—*Wonderland*, ch. II, "The Pool of Tears"

Chapter 20
How Odd the Directions Will Look!

The first two conditions for being filled with the Spirit are both negative commands. They are things you must not do. You must not grieve the Holy Spirit of God and you must not quench the Spirit. The third qualification, in contrast, is a positive command. This is something that you must do. To be filled with the Spirit, you must walk by the Spirit.

Several passages speak to this aspect of spirituality, but the most direct is GALATIANS 5:16 (NASB): "But I say, walk by the Spirit, and you will not carry out the desire of the flesh."

It is vital to note that the command is not walk "in" the Spirit (as in the KJV), but walk "by" the Spirit (as rendered by the NIV and NASB). If the command were to walk "in" the Spirit, the implication would be that we are the ones doing the walking. Instead, we are to walk "by the Spirit." We might say walk "by means of the Spirit," or "maintain the walk that the Spirit produces." Just as the fruit of the Spirit is fruit that the Spirit produces, so walking "by the Spirit" is walking with the power that the Spirit provides.

Because this statement is a command, some human activity is necessarily involved, but it is not our activity that produces the walk. Our involvement is a moment-by-moment conscious reliance upon the power of the Holy Spirit. It is this dependency upon the Spirit that is being commanded.

The same idea is found just two verses later: "But if you are led by the Spirit, you are not under the Law" (GAL 5:18, NASB). Being led implies a dependency upon the one doing the leading. Therefore, we may understand "walking in the Spirit" as follows:

> **Definition:** Walking in the Spirit is an unbroken reliance upon God the Holy Spirit to empower us to accomplish what He desires in us.

You may have noticed that this definition is quite similar to being filled with the Spirit, the condition when "the Holy Spirit is accomplishing in and through us all that He desires." The difference between the two concepts lies in which side of this divine equation you are looking at. The filling of the Spirit is God working in us. Walking in the Spirit is our dependence upon Him. They are obviously related ideas, but one stresses human responsibility and the other emphasizes the result.

There are at least three reasons why we so desperately need the power of the Holy Spirit in our lives if we are to defeat sin. Each reason is related to the enemies of the believer: the world, the flesh, and the devil. We will see that in each case, only the power of the Holy Spirit is sufficient to defeat our enemy. This is why we must walk by the Spirit.

A Supernatural Standard

When we are redeemed, God calls us to a supernatural life. If we define *heaven* as "the abode of God," then, one day, after God completely destroys the world and then recreates it (2 PET 3:10–13), God will come to live with us on earth as we enjoy His creation and presence in glorified bodies. Heaven and earth will be the same place.

And I heard a loud voice from the throne saying, "Now the dwelling of God is with men, and he will live with them. They will be his people, and God himself will be with them and be their God. He will wipe every tear from their eyes. There will

*be no more death or mourning or crying or pain, for the old
order of things has passed away"* (Rev 21:3–4, niv).

Because this is the ultimate destiny for God's people, it is no wonder
that He wants us to live according to the standard of being in His holy
presence in the here-and-now. We are "to live a life worthy of the
calling [we] have received" (Eph 4:10, niv). Our lives are to consistently
reflect the values of our native country. Paul reminds us that "our citi-
zenship is in heaven" (Phil 3:20, niv). While we sojourn here on
earth, we are expatriates, so to speak.

God has graciously granted me the privilege of traveling to train
national pastors in many different countries. One of the countries
I've visited several times is Rwanda. While I was there, I found they
used a different currency, spoke a different language, dressed differently, had different customs . . . even the food was different. (Boy, was
it different!) Although I was physically located in the central part of
Africa, that wasn't my home. I held a passport showing that I was a citizen
of another country. Despite my location, my dress, speech, and values
all reflected my native land.

In the same way, I currently hold a passport to a kingdom that
shall never end. One day that kingdom will be here on earth, after
Christ returns, sets foot on the Mount of Olives, and establishes his
thousand-year reign. For now, though, my country is where my king
is: in heaven, the abode of God. When I was in Rwanda, I was separated
from my country by distance. As a believer who will one day rule with
Christ in his Millennial Kingdom (Rev 5:9–10), I am currently separated from my homeland by time. One day I will pass through Customs
and be admitted to my homeland. Whether that be by death or by
Christ's return for His church, I don't know—but I do know that a
certain future awaits where I will breathe the native air I have so longed
for. Until that great day comes, of course, I live as an expatriate in this
world system.

This means, of course, that I must be different from this world. Just as I stuck out in Rwanda, I should stick out here as well. This country (world) doesn't traffic in the same currency as my home. That which is valuable in my country has little worth here. The virtues and customs of my home are laughed at as odd or are accused of being rude in this place. The speech and topics of discussion are different. I live here now, but I won't live here always. This world isn't my home. I hold a passport to heaven!

To show the supernatural conditions in which we are to live, read carefully the following Scripture verses. As you read, ask yourself, "Can I do this in my own strength? Can I, by sheer force of will, live this way? Or do I need the continual help of God the Holy Spirit?"

A new command I give you: Love one another. As I have loved you, so you must love one another (JOHN 13:34, NIV).

My command is this: Love each other as I have loved you (JOHN 15:12, NIV).

We demolish arguments and every pretension that sets itself up against the knowledge of God, and we take captive every thought to make it obedient to Christ (2 COR 10:5, NIV).

[A]lways giving thanks to God the Father for everything, in the name of our Lord Jesus Christ (EPH 5:20, NIV).

Do nothing out of selfish ambition or vain conceit, but in humility consider others better than yourselves. Each of you should look not only to your own interests, but also to the interests of others (PHIL 2:3–4, NIV).

Be joyful always; pray continually (1 THESS 5:16–17, NIV).

As a prisoner for the Lord, then, I urge you to live a life worthy of the calling you have received. Be completely humble and gentle; be patient, bearing with one another in love. Make every effort to keep the unity of the Spirit through the bond of peace (Eph 4:1–3, niv).

When we take these verses at face value, we come to two startling conclusions. We see that these commands are so completely beyond our own abilities that we have to admit it is impossible to obey them as written. At the same time, because these are commands given by God, He evidently expects us to act them out consistently in our everyday lives. How do we reconcile these two conclusions?

We must remember that God "knows how we are formed, he remembers that we are dust" (Ps 103:14, niv). Therefore, He has no expectations that we will be able to meet His divine requirements on our own. Instead, He has given us the indwelling Holy Spirit Who is able to empower us, moment by moment, to live up to even these (literally) superhuman standards. God is able and willing to "equip you with everything good for doing his will," and to "work in us what is pleasing to him" (Heb 13:12, niv).

The Christian's life is impossible from a human standpoint. To achieve it, we must exercise a moment-by-moment reliance on God the Holy Spirit. *We must walk by the Spirit!*

A Supernatural Enemy

As I write this, Halloween has just come and gone. As I watched the advertisements for the movies shown on TV, I realized that monster movies have largely given way to horror films, particularly those of a supernatural nature. I find this interesting because, in one respect at least, the world has nothing to fear from Satan. He doesn't pour out his hatred on the lost. He doesn't have to: they are part of the world system that he manipulates. Those who do not know Christ are dead in transgressions and sins. They walk "according to the ways of this world and of the ruler of the kingdom of the air, the spirit who is now at work in those who are disobedient" (Eph 2:1–2, niv). They haven't been "rescued . . . from the dominion of darkness and brought . . . into the kingdom of the Son" (Col 1:13, niv). Therefore, Satan has no particular quarrel with them. Oh, he still hates them for no other reason than that God loves them—Satan hates what God loves—but his energies are directed only minimally at the lost. The majority of his efforts are directed against God's redeemed people.

There are two great supernatural energizing forces at work in this world. Satan is the energizing force of those who are lost (Eph 2:2), whereas God the Holy Spirit is the energizing force of those who are saved (Phil 2:13). This doesn't mean that the lost cannot be called to repentance by the Holy Spirit or that the believer is immune to attacks by the devil. It simply means that all people dwell in one domain or the other. There is no middle ground.

The real reason Satan attacks the believer is because we partake of the divine nature (2 Pet 1:4). Satan's real enemy is God Himself.

Satan was created as "the model of perfection, full of wisdom and perfect in beauty" (Ezek 28:12, niv). But he became proud of his exalted position and said in his heart, "I will ascend to heaven; I will raise my throne above the stars of God; I will sit enthroned on the mount of assembly, on the utmost heights of the sacred mountain. I will ascend above the tops of the clouds; I will make myself like the Most High" (Isa 14:13–14, niv). Therefore, he was driven in disgrace from the Mount of God (Ezek 28:16).

Despite his expulsion, he has lost none of his beauty or power. He "masquerades as an angel of light" and "his servants masquerade as servants of righteousness" (2 Cor 11:14–15, niv). This shouldn't be surprising. As we've seen, the natural man is able to spout (and accept!) all sorts of spiritual Jabberwocky that is designed to appeal to the flesh.

Satan has his own ministers whose task is to spread a false gospel. They teach salvation by the reformation of our nature rather than the transformation that comes through Christ. They announce that we are naturally good from birth and only need proper instruction to live righteously, in direct contravention of what God has said: What we really need is a new birth wrought by the Spirit. It is in this one area that Satan attacks the lost. "The god of this age has blinded the minds of unbelievers, so that they cannot see the light of the gospel of the glory of Christ" (2 COR 4:4, NIV). This is why there are so many false religions throughout the world. This is why the gospel of Christ is constantly under attack by those allegedly within the church who will teach you whatever you want to hear as long as it doesn't involve the sacrificial atonement of Christ.

We have an interesting clue as to part of Satan's motivation for hating humankind. It appears that he thinks God has treated him unjustly. Therefore, genuine sinners (not like him) who have been declared righteous are an affront to him.

Remember the story of Job? Job was a wealthy man but, more importantly, was "blameless and upright, a man who fears God and shuns evil" (JOB 1:8, NIV). Satan challenges God to see if Job is as righteous as he appears. God permits Satan to take away all Job has, in a moment, including his children. Then God allows Satan to go one step further and break Job's health. He is covered with sores and is plagued by nightmares. He is shivering with fever and his teeth are falling out. His hands and legs shake so badly he can hardly stand. As anyone would do in such a condition, Job seeks an answer from God.

Before God answers him, Job's three friends weigh in on the reason for his suffering. Everybody knows that suffering is a result of sin. Hence, they try to get Job to confess his sinfulness even when he has done nothing wrong. But have you ever wondered where his three friends got their destructive message? The first "friend" to speak—Eliphaz— tells us:

> *"A word was secretly brought to me, my ears caught a whisper of it. Amid disquieting dreams in the night, when deep sleep falls*

on men, fear and trembling seized me and made all my bones
shake. A spirit glided past my face, and the hair on my body
stood on end. It stopped, but I could not tell what it was. A form
stood before my eyes, and I heard a hushed voice: 'Can a mor-
tal be more righteous than God? Can a man be more pure than
his Maker? If God places no trust in his servants, if he charges
his angels with error, how much more those who live in houses
of clay, whose foundations are in the dust, who are crushed more
readily than a moth!'" (JOB 4:12–19, NIV).

I think it's pretty safe to say that Eliphaz's whispering visitor was an evil spirit, most likely Satan himself. What other spirit would cause the physical effects listed? Don't forget that he is the evil one so interested in Job in the first place. So what was Satan's complaint? "God didn't trust me. He charged me with error. If He is willing to accuse me, the greatest of His creation, how can man claim to be righteous, especially when I could crush him like a moth?" Can you hear the venom in this voice? Satan's offended sense of justice is the root of his hatred, the same hatred that both drives and consumes him.

Well, to answer Satan's question, we aren't more righteous than he is. The difference is that God has given us the righteousness He demands, so we can appear before His throne completely righteous in spite of what we have done. Oh, and by the way, Satan did have the power to crush Job like a moth—but then again he didn't. God was protecting Job and setting hedges about him so that Satan could go only so far.

If this is Satan's attitude toward Job, we can infer that it is his attitude toward all who are declared righteous by God, something that Satan will never experience. This is why a genuine spiritual battle is occurring around us all the time.

Finally, be strong in the Lord and in his mighty power. Put on
the full armor of God so that you can take your stand against
the devil's schemes. For our struggle is not against flesh and

blood, but against the rulers, against the authorities, against the powers of this dark world and against the spiritual forces of evil in the heavenly realms. Therefore put on the full armor of God, so that when the day of evil comes, you may be able to stand your ground, and after you have done everything, to stand. Stand firm then, with the belt of truth buckled around your waist, with the breastplate of righteousness in place, and with your feet fitted with the readiness that comes from the gospel of peace. In addition to all this, take up the shield of faith, with which you can extinguish all the flaming arrows of the evil one. Take the helmet of salvation and the sword of the Spirit, which is the word of God. And pray in the Spirit on all occasions with all kinds of prayers and requests. With this in mind, be alert and always keep on praying for all the saints (EPH 6:10–18, NIV).*

Notice that the devil is scheming against us. He uses the fallen angels at his disposal to wage his war against God's people. In fact, the war is so vicious that Scripture doesn't tell us "*if* the day of evil comes," but rather "*when* the day of evil comes." It is only a matter of time. However, we are to "stand against the devil's schemes . . . stand our ground . . . having done everything to stand . . . Stand firm then!" Seeing the word *stand* four times in this passage is instructive because it gives us a picture of Satan's battle plan. His attack appears to be designed to cause us to run away in fear. Satan's use of fear is also attested by Peter: "Be self-controlled and alert. Your enemy the devil prowls around like a roaring lion looking for someone to devour" (1 PET 5:8, NIV).

Maybe this is a bit counterintuitive to you. Wouldn't stealth be the natural tool and best friend of a lion stalking his prey? Think of a housecat's stalking stance, with ears back, fur sleek, and head low, tail twitching. Yet that's not the picture here at all. Instead, the devil is roaring for all to hear, as lions sometimes roar when stalking prey to instill panic in the animal being stalked. Terror causes the animal either to freeze or to react without thinking. Instead of using their natural defenses, they just bolt. Either option turns the prey into lunch. In the same way, Satan roars to instill terror in the hearts of believers. Fear is his main weapon.

Flaming arrows were used for one purpose in ancient warfare: to start a fire within the city walls. In addition to creating random destruction, this acted as a diversion, drawing men to fight the fire inside the city instead of fighting the enemy at the walls. Again we have the idea of deserting our post, of running away from where we should be. While the armor of God is multifaceted, the shield of faith is the means by which we extinguish the arrows. So, by whatever means attack comes, fear seems to be the weapon that is used to mount a direct assault on the faith of the believer.

At this point, someone might say, "I thought all we had to do is resist the devil and he would flee from us" (JAMES 4:7)? Those who take this point of view are reading this verse out of context and are, quite frankly, naive. Satan is a created being superior to all other created beings. "Even the archangel Michael, when he was disputing with the devil about the body of Moses, did not dare to bring a slanderous accusation against him, but said, 'The Lord rebuke you!'" (JUDE 9, NIV). So, how foolish is it to think that we can force the devil to run away merely by a sustained display of human willpower? That's ludicrous!

True, we are to resist the devil, but first we are to submit ourselves to God (JAMES 4:7, NIV)! Only when we have come near to God (JAMES 4:8), in moment-by-moment reliance upon His strength, can we expect the devil to flee. When we have submitted ourselves to God, the devil flees because "the one who is in you is greater than the one who is in the world" (1 John 4:4, niv). That's the only reason Satan runs away. Only the power of God can defeat the devil.

Before Satan, we are as easily crushed as a moth. Yet when we walk by the Spirit—when we submit ourselves to Him in moment-by-moment reliance on His power—we can stand our ground and Satan must flee.

A Substandard Nature

You don't have to be a Christian for very long to realize your limitations. Whether it be limitations regarding service or the ongoing struggle against sin, the believer soon learns that he is inadequate in himself to produce a righteous life. The "wanting to" is there, but the ability is not. This isn't a new problem, of course. The Apostle Paul spoke of his own struggle against sin in the same way:

> For that which I am doing, I do not understand; for I am not practicing what I would like to do, but I am doing the very thing I hate. But if I do the very thing I do not wish to do, I agree with the Law, confessing that it is good. So now, no longer am I the one doing it, but sin which indwells me. For I know that nothing good dwells in me, that is, in my flesh; for the wishing is present in me, but the doing of the good is not. For the good that I wish, I do not do; but I practice the very evil that I do not wish. But if I am doing the very thing I do not wish, I am no longer the one doing it, but sin which dwells in me (Rom 7:15–20, nasb).

It's crucial to understand what Paul is and is *not* saying here. When he says that he is no longer the one doing it, but sin living in him, he isn't trying to pass the buck or evade the responsibility for his own actions. Instead, he's saying, "Look, if it were just a matter of snapping my fingers, making up my mind, clicking my heels three times and saying 'there's no place like home,' then I'd just do it and be done with the problem of sin. But it's not that easy! There's something inside of me that keeps pushing me, prodding me, goading me to sin. So I don't do the things I want, and I end up doing the things I hate!"

If you've ever tried to live righteously, then you know exactly what Paul is talking about. If you don't know what Paul is talking about, then I suggest that you've never really put forth any effort to live as God requires.

It is this problem that walking in the Spirit addresses. Walking in (and by) the Spirit is what gives us the power to resist sin. We are powerless in the flesh; a conscious dependence upon the Spirit for power is what defeats sin in the believer's life.

This doesn't mean that God the Holy Spirit suddenly takes over my personality and I become a mindless robot! No, the Spirit works through our personalities, our thoughts, and the giftedness He has given to provide power that wasn't there before. It isn't that He replaces our faculties; rather, He empowers them! When we walk by the Spirit, we no longer have to choose sin! We are set free with power from above to live the righteous life we desire to live.

When we walk in the flesh—like the carnal man—the deeds of the flesh are obvious: "immorality, impurity, sensuality, idolatry, sorcery, enmities, strife, jealousy, outbursts of anger, disputes, dissensions, factions, envying, drunkenness, carousing, and things like these" (GAL 5:19–21, NASB). If this type of behavior is the natural result of walking in the flesh, what can curtail such wretchedness? Only the power of God expressed through the indwelling Holy Spirit!

But I say, walk by the Spirit, and you will not carry out the desire of the flesh (GAL 5:16, NASB).

The "if, then" statement in this verse is clear in the English. *If* we walk by the Spirit, *then* we will not carry out the desire of the flesh.

What is not clear is the force of this statement. The original language of this verse uses the strongest possible way to say "no,"* to show the utter impossibility of walking by the Spirit and carrying out the desire of the flesh at the same time.

Conclusion

What we need, therefore, to defeat the flesh, is the power of the Spirit, moment by moment. It is not by accident that we are told to "walk" by the Spirit, for we need His enabling continuously if we are to live righteously.

We need to walk by the Spirit if we are to be led into the good works God has prepared ahead of time for us to do. We must walk by the Spirit if we are to take our stand against the devil and his schemes. We must walk by the Spirit if we are to have any hope of living the supernatural life God demands.

We must recognize that in and of ourselves, we are powerless. Knowing this, God in His mercy has given us all the enablement we need, if we just consciously depend upon Him for our strength. Walking by the Spirit is essential to being filled with the Spirit. Being filled with the Spirit is the path to maturity.

---

*The strongest way to say no is to use οὐ μὴ with a subjunctive verb. In this case, the original uses οὐ μὴ τελέσητε, which is the second plural aorist active subjunctive of τελέω, "to cause to accomplish."

Discussion Questions

In each of chapters 14–20, we will be revisiting your answer to the question: "How do you get there?" Please look back at your answer to that question and examine it in light of this chapter.

1. In chapter 18, we looked at "grieve not the Spirit," and in chapter 19 at its companion, "quench not the Spirit." This chapter discusses the positive command to "walk by the Spirit" or "walk in the Spirit." As you read through this discussion, did the Holy Spirit bring anything to your mind? Is there some act of service to which he is leading you?

2. There are three reasons listed why we must walk by the Spirit. What are these reasons? How do you see them acted out in your own life?

3. What did you learn in this chapter about knowing God's will? In chapter 9, "Believing the Impossible," there were four points about knowing God's will which you copied out and tucked into your Bible. Is there anything from this chapter you would like to add to this card, to guide you in the future?

4. Has this chapter brought any questions to mind, or any thoughts you would like to discuss with the group?

5. Is there any issue you would like prayed for, or accountability in, over the course of this week?

6. Please note any other group members' answer hat you would like to follow up on this week, either by praying fo em or by making an encouraging contact.

Living in Canaan Part Six

Steve went on vacation shortly after his last conversation with Christine, so it was two weeks before she saw him again.

"So? Read anything interesting lately?" he inquired.

"If you're referring to the mistake that Ben made on the inventory—"

"Mistake!" Steve grabbed the top of the cubicle walls with both hands.

"Shhhh!" Christine said emphatically. "Don't make a scene. It's almost noon, let's talk about it over lunch."

As they sat down at the table, Steve kept shaking his head. "You can't possibly be gullible enough to believe that was a mistake."

Her words came out slowly. "Well, it might have been or it might not have been. I can't see into his heart and neither can you."

"Oh, brother," Steve groaned, rolling his eyes. He turned sideways in his seat and crossed his legs, supporting his weight with his right arm. Drumming the table with his fingers, he began shaking his head once again. "I knew I should've taken care of this myself."

He turned again to face her, his arms on the table, his hands folded in front of him. "What's wrong with you anyway? If it were any other woman, I'd just assume you're afraid of the confrontation, but—"

"Steve Carnes, you stop that right now!" Christine pointed her right index finger at his nose like an arrow. "There's a very good reason why I didn't do what I know you wanted me to do."

Steve began to push himself away from the table. "That's all right," he said wearily. "I'll take care of this myself."

"You're too late, Steve," Christine warned.

Steve looked at her sideways and spoke slowly. "What do you mean I'm too late?"

"I took the reports to Ben and asked him about them."

"You did *what*?" Steve gasped, now almost speechless.

"I took the reports to Ben to ask him about the discrepancy. He said it was a simple mistake and that he would correct it. He actually thanked me for bringing it to his attention."

"Oh, I'll bet he did," said Steve, throwing both hands in the air. "You know, of course, that he would have lost that new promotion over a 'mistake' of that magnitude. Probably would've lost his job as well." His tense body now slumped as if a great weariness had suddenly come upon him.

"I don't get you," said Steve, shaking his head stiffly. "Have you forgotten that Ben lied about you and swindled you out of what should have been your job? Have you noticed how he loves to humiliate you? Do you remember all this?"

"I remember," she said. Then, with a slight chuckle, added, "How could I forget?"

"Well, I know I haven't been a Christian nearly as long as you have, but I'm not completely ignorant, you know. I went home and looked up what you quoted when this all started. PSALM 37, right?"

"Yeah, that's right," replied Christine, genuinely surprised and somewhat delighted. "I've spent a lot of time in that psalm. That and PSALM 73. They go together. You can remember them because you can just change the numbers—"

"Yeah, yeah, I saw that. Look, I can see why you'd spend your time there. When you're hurting, promises from God are a good thing."

"Thank you, Martha Stewart," she laughed.

"Whatever," he grinned back. "Anyway, I read both psalms. You know what it says in PSALM 73?" he asked as he pulled a folded piece of paper out of his pocket.

"No, tell me," she said playfully and leaned in closer. This was the first time they'd been able to speak as brother and sister for a while and she realized how much she missed it.

"Liar." He grinned. "Anyway, verses 18 and 19: 'Surely you place them on slippery ground; you cast them down to ruin,'" he read. "'How suddenly are they destroyed, completely swept away by terrors!'"

"Okay," Christine said, still grinning, "I'm waiting for you to get to the part where I fouled things up."

"Don't you get it?" he asked, his eyes wide. "God just plopped him down at your feet, waiting to be destroyed, and you didn't do it." He slapped the piece of paper down on the table, confident he had proven his point.

"Steve," Christine said gently, "look at verse 18 again and tell me who is the subject of the sentence."

"Didn't know this would turn into an English test," he grumbled. "'You' . . . God is the subject."

"Right," she continued. "So who is the one who casts down the wicked? Is it me? Or is it God's responsibility to do it?"

"Well," Steve hedged, not willing to give up, "why couldn't God use you as His servant to do His will? Yeah, why not?" he challenged. "After all, if you don't do something, Ben will just keep pulling this stuff on other people. Rumor has it—" Here Christine rolled her eyes. "Rumor has it," Steve plowed on, "that he's already doing it to someone else. And I heard that he got his last job this same way. This guy's sick and needs to be stopped. I don't understand why you, of all people, can't see that and do the right thing."

"I'll tell you why, if you'll listen." she said seriously. "I was tempted to do what you wanted me to do. Actually, I was extremely tempted— but I couldn't. And if you'll really listen, I'll explain why."

"Okay, I'll listen," Steve promised.

Christine pulled her Bible from her purse and opened it to ROMANS 12. She pushed it across the table to Steve and said, "Start reading at verse 17." He read:

Do not repay anyone evil for evil. Be careful to do what is right
in the eyes of everybody. If it is possible, as far as it depends on

you, live at peace with everyone. Do not take revenge, my friends,
but leave room for God's wrath, for it is written: "It is mine to
avenge; I will repay," says the Lord. On the contrary: "If your
enemy is hungry, feed him; if he is thirsty, give him something
to drink. In doing this, you will heap burning coals on his head."
Do not be overcome by evil, but overcome evil with good.

"Steve," Christine said gently, "I can't take revenge, no matter how badly I want to. That type of attitude just isn't pleasing to God, for a number of reasons. First of all, I'm commanded not to avenge myself. That's enough in and of itself. But second, if I take revenge, then I'm taking away what God has reserved for Himself. I have to leave room for God's wrath. He says it's His right to avenge, and I have to trust that He'll do exactly that.

"Oh, I've reconciled myself to the fact that I might not see it when it happens," she said softly, looking down, "but I'm sure it will. God is a good God and He doesn't take it lightly when people mess with His children."

Looking up again, she said, "If Ben is hungry, I'm to feed him. If he's thirsty, I'm to give him something to drink. Under no circumstances am I to repay anyone evil for evil. I mean, it's right there in black and white—just read it. So no matter what, I'm to do good by him. Not because he deserves it, but because I'm most like God when I do. God loved me when I was a sinner in rebellion against Him, and He saved me anyway. It wasn't that long ago that God did the same for you, Steve."

Steve nodded slowly. "That's true," he admitted.

"So if God could love me, being what I am, I should love Ben, he being what he is." It might have been the way she said that last phrase, but both of them suddenly burst out laughing. Steve quit laughing before she did. He got up from the table and turned to walk away and then stopped. He looked back at Christine, his eyebrows pulled together, his eyes in a squint. He kept that look on his face as he shoved his hands in his pockets and shuffled away.

Do not repay anyone evil for evil. Be careful to do what is right in the eyes of everybody.

If it is possible, as far as it depends on you, live at peace with everyone. . . .

Do not be overcome by evil, but overcome evil with good.

ROMANS 17:17–18, 21, NIV

THE CAUCUS-RACE

What I was going to say," said the Dodo in an offended tone, "was, that the best thing to get us dry would be a Caucus-race."

"What IS a Caucus-race?" said Alice; not that she wanted much to know, but the Dodo had paused as if it thought that SOMEBODY ought to speak, and no one else seemed inclined to say anything.

"Why," said the Dodo, "the best way to explain it is to do it." (And, as you might like to try the thing yourself, some winter day, I will tell you how the Dodo managed it.)

First it marked out a racecourse, in a sort of circle, ("the exact shape doesn't matter," it said), and then all the party were placed along the course, here and there. There was no "One, two, three, and away," but they began running when they liked, and left off when they liked, so that it was not easy to know when the race was over. However, when they had been running half an hour or so, and were quite dry again, the Dodo suddenly called out "The race is over!" and they all crowded round it, panting, and asking, "But who has won?"

—*Wonderland*, ch. III, "A Caucus-Race and a Long Tale"

Chapter 21
The Best Way to Explain It Is to Do It

M ost of our discussion so far has been theological in nature. That is, we have taken a passage of Scripture and examined it to discover the truths about spiritual growth and maturity that we need to grow. This final chapter adds a few practical suggestions and insights as to how to live such a life.

- By its nature, being filled with the Spirit is the believer's moment-by-moment experience. Therefore, it is impossible to limit the spiritual life to morning devotions, or time in church, or any other specific format or ritual. In fact, any set of rules we "must" follow to be spiritual should immediately be tossed out the window! Nevertheless, it *is* a good idea to spend time every day alone with the Lord to review your life and your relationship with Him. We should examine our hearts to see if any sin is unconfessed, if we are indeed yielded to the Spirit, if we are consciously depending upon His power for our service and victory over sin. Note that the Bible makes no demands or commands as to the time or conditions of such self-examination. It is up to the individual to cultivate a dynamic relationship with the Spirit of God. We all have unique personalities, and we are dealing with a person when we interact with God. Personal relationships thrive best when rigid sets of rules are discarded.

We should also remember that spirituality is not an idealized future state, but a reality to be enjoyed in the present. The vital question is: Am I being filled with the Spirit now? This question should be on our minds constantly if we are to walk by the Spirit. The answer to that question shouldn't depend on a certain special feeling or a miraculous manifestation. Instead, it should come from the sure knowledge that our sins are confessed and that we have yielded to the Spirit. Let's face it, much of life consists of the ordinary. Most of our day is filled with the mundane: brushing teeth, putting on shoes, driving, eating, working, and so forth. It might be hard to imagine, but during these times we need to be filled with the Spirit. We are to have unbroken fellowship with God the Father through the Spirit regardless of the activities in which we are engaged. "Dear friends, if our hearts do not condemn us, we have confidence before God" (1 JOHN 3:21, NIV). This confidence must be present moment by moment as we walk through this life.

I've found that people like to speak of "absolute" devotion, "complete" surrender, "total" submission. We've seen that there are well-defined conditions that allow us to be filled with the Spirit so that He is accomplishing in and through us all that He desires. That being said, from God's standpoint, all our devotion is limited, all our surrender incomplete, all our submission partial. Even though His enablement is perfect, our response to it is human and therefore subject to improvement. This is part of the growth process. We won't arrive at sinless perfection in this life—not because God fails to provide the strength, but because we only partially appropriate the strength He provides. Freedom from sin is conceivable, but only to the extent we make it possible.

- We should remember that we are material beings inhabiting physical bodies. The union of the material and immaterial should be thought of as a compound, not a mixture. If I pour the contents of two salt and pepper shakers out on the table, given enough time and a razor blade, I could separate the two ingredients back into their proper containers. That's because the salt and pepper pile is only a mixture. What I could not do is separate the sodium from the chlorine in the salt. They are bound together in a compound. If I separate these two elements—if I break the bond between them—I no longer have salt. In the same way, the material and immaterial are bound together in our bodies. If we break that bond, death occurs.

  The fact that we are a compound has broad implications for our spiritual life. Have you noticed that you're more susceptible to temptation when you're sick than when you're well? That's because the material and immaterial interact. You never take your body somewhere that your spirit doesn't follow. Because the material and immaterial parts of us interact, we should never mistake physical fatigue as a sign of spiritual weakness. Sometimes what we need more than prayer is sleep. Self-examination is important, but occasionally we would be better served with a dose of fresh air during a relaxing walk.

- The spiritual life is not passive. Yes, it is true that we serve only through the enabling of God the Holy Spirit. But that doesn't mean we sit back and do nothing. Instead, the spiritual life is an enlarged, vital life, in which our natural abilities and spiritual giftedness are used to the fullest. It is common for someone to be physically exhausted after an intense time of service. My Sunday afternoon nap is almost an ordinance of the church! After the morning services, I'm so tired I don't even eat. I just go home and crawl into bed to rest for the evening service. And I'm not alone! Nearly every pastor I know takes a nap after preaching on Sunday. The Spirit uses us to our fullest potential, enabling us as our faith allows. However, it can be (and usually is) exhausting.

There is one vital distinction: It is one thing to be exhausted by the work, it is another to be weary of it. The former is what happens when we give ourselves fully to the work of the Lord through the power of the Spirit. The latter is what happens when we try to go it alone using our own strength.

- Similarly, the spiritual life is full of temptations. In this regard the spiritual man is the same as any other person. "No temptation has seized you except what is common to man" (1 COR 10:13, NIV). That's because we still have the three traditional enemies of the believer hounding our footsteps: the world, the flesh, and the devil. Yet, we have the promise of God that He will provide what is necessary to resist. "And God is faithful; he will not let you be tempted beyond what you can bear. But when you are tempted, he will also provide a way out so that you can stand up under it" (1 COR 10:13, NIV). Hence, we recognize that there is always the possibility of sin, but never the necessity of sin.

- True spirituality is genuine. That means if we are doing something or saying something just to appear "spiritual," then at that precise moment we *aren't* spiritual. If you are merely repeating pious-sounding phrases when you have no experience with the reality those words describe, you're simply a liar. Likewise, we shouldn't try to imitate someone else's personality, mannerisms, figures of speech, and so forth. I remember when I taught homiletics (preaching), it was sometimes comical to speculate what famous preacher the student was trying to mimic! I had to pound away at the fact that God has called *you*, not the person you are when you imitate someone else.

If you have a sense of humor, use it to the glory of God. If you don't (and let's face it, a lot of us don't), then stop trying to manufacture what you haven't been given. Instead, be humble enough to recognize that God called *you*! The goal is to be transformed into His image, not the image of a person you admire. God has called you, all of you, to serve Him. The whole person is involved in spirituality. Therefore, if you are naturally extroverted, bring that character trait under the control of God the Holy Spirit. If you are by nature more introverted, stop trying to be someone you're not. Instead, let God transform you by the renewing of your mind so your whole person may serve Him.

- Remember also that you are dealing with the most kindhearted Father in all the universe. He knows our thoughts and hearts before we speak, so it is always appropriate to speak the truth to Him. The greatest joy that can be known is knowing Him. The joy of heaven will be our interaction with the person of God Himself. We can come before Him with heartfelt thanksgiving for our victories as well as contrition for our defeats. Confession of our sin always works to cleanse us and restore us to fellowship. Unlike our human fathers, we never have to wait to see what kind of mood God is in to decide whether to approach Him. His mood toward us was permanently set at the cross.

For this reason, we can share with Him our deepest fears, greatest hopes, darkest shames, sadness and joy, doubts as well as thanksgiving. God knows what's on our hearts already, so why not tell the truth? This is not to say that we may come before the Father and accuse Him of being what He is not: unfair, unjust, cruel, or uncaring. We can tell Him honestly that we are confused at those times when we don't understand. Always, the Spirit is there to provide comfort and strength in our sorrow. We are His family. Though we are often disobedient, foolish, and immature, He is endlessly patient as we continually seek Him.

- Finally, we should not attempt to increase our faith by our own feeble manipulations. Instead, we should be obedient to the Spirit's leading, and He will put us in situations where He shows us His glory and goodness so our faith will be increased. The Spirit desires to work through us as individuals, so you may remain you and still be filled with power from on high. This power is available right now if you will but turn from your sin, say yes to the Spirit, and consciously depend upon His power as you walk.

It is because we have both the privilege and the power to serve Him in the present that the Apostle Paul could write:

For this reason I kneel before the Father, from whom his whole family in heaven and on earth derives its name. I pray that out of his glorious riches he may strengthen you with power through his Spirit in your inner being, so that Christ may dwell in your hearts through faith. And I pray that you, being rooted and established in love, may have power, together with all the saints, to grasp how wide and long and high and deep is the love of Christ, and to know this love that surpasses knowledge—that you may be filled to the measure of all the fullness of God.

Now to him who is able to do immeasurably more than all we ask or imagine, according to his power that is at work within us, to him be glory in the church and in Christ Jesus throughout all generations, for ever and ever! Amen (EPH 3:14–21, NIV).

This is my prayer for you as well.

Discussion Questions

1. This chapter closes out our study with an emphasis on the practical side of spiritual growth. As was mentioned, it is important that each person have time with God, yet the routine, length, and so on, of those sessions will be different based on each person's make-up. Are you currently practicing time alone with God? If not, would you commit to doing so, in whatever way is most natural to you? If you are doing so, do you feel what you are doing is what is best suited to your own nature and schedule? Or are you following someone else's predefined rules for what constitutes "spirituality"? Make sure this time is not only happening in your life, but also that it is a true time of fellowship with the Lord, and not just a routine rule-following item on your "to do" list.

2. Are there physical issues that may be affecting your spiritual walk? Do you need to make any changes regarding sleep, eating, exercise, or scheduling?

3. An interesting point was made about our temptation to compare ourselves with, and try to imitate, other believers. Do you find yourself doing this? If so, do you understand why this is counterproductive to the spiritual life and ministry God has for you?

4. Has this chapter brought any questions to mind, or any thoughts you would like to discuss with the group?

5. Is there any issue you would like prayed for, or accountability in, over the course of this week?

6. Please note any other group members' answers that you would like to follow up on this week, either by praying for them or by making an encouraging contact.

7. Choose one person from this study with whom you would like to stay in contact—preferably someone you didn't know personally before beginning this book/study group. Write his or her name here, as well as suggestions for how you would like to maintain this relationship and be a blessing to this person.

n the morning the news broke, Christine couldn't help but notice the spring in Steve's step and the huge grin on his face as he hurried to her desk. "You were right, you were right, you were right," he chanted quickly. "How many times do I have to say it? You were right!" At this he threw his head back and let loose a huge laugh. Steve had always had a great sense of humor, but Christine had never seen him like this. He was positively giddy.

"Um . . . once is enough, I think," said Christine, totally confused.

"Hmmm, it looks as if someone hasn't seen the memo!" he crowed. "Feast your eyes on this!" He shoved a piece of paper toward her. "Then look at this," he said, waving that morning's paper.

She read the memo, but she couldn't believe her eyes. Ben Ackerman had been fired. The memo was vague, but the fact that he no longer worked for the company was clear enough. Then in the newspaper, already open to the correct page, she read the headline, "Local

Businessman Charged with Embezzlement." As she quickly scanned the article, she caught words like "FBI," "scandal," and "prison."

"Is this great news or what?" Steve laughed. "Oh, Christine, you were right, God cast him down suddenly. Ben 'feet-on-slippery-places' Ackerman is toast. Yes!!" He punched the air several times.

When he finally really looked at Christine, he saw that she was wiping some tears from her eyes. "That's okay," Steve said in a calming, yet puzzled, voice, "lots of girls cry when they're happy . . . "

"This isn't happiness, Steve. Oh, I feel vindicated and what has happened is just, but I'm not happy."

"Now what?" Steve exclaimed, shoving his hands in his pockets and wrinkling his forehead.

"Did you know that he's got a wife and two kids?" Christine asked.

"No . . . no, I didn't." Steve looked down and shuffled his feet. "I guess it's tough luck for them." Then, looking up suddenly, he argued, "But she must have known what he was like when she married him, so I have a hard time—"

"She should've known? Like I should've known when I married Tim?" Christine asked pointedly.

"That's not what I meant."

"But that is what you said."

Steve let out a long breath through his nose and didn't reply.

"I've anticipated this moment, Steve, because I firmly believed that God would be my avenger. And because I knew that sooner or later this day was coming, and that God might allow me to see it, I've thought about what the godly response would be. I want to be like God, Steve. So I want to feel as He feels right now. After praying about it, I posted this verse on the wall." She pulled down a note card and handed it to him.

> *Do not gloat when your enemy falls; when he stumbles, do not let your heart rejoice, or the LORD will see and disapprove and turn his wrath away from him* (PROV 24:17–18, NIV).

"Christine, I don't get you." Shaking his head, Steve just walked away.

"Few people do," she said quietly to herself. Turning back to her desk, she was reaching for a client folder when she glanced at another reminder she had pinned to the wall.

But I tell you who hear me: Love your enemies, do good to those who hate you, bless those who curse you, pray for those who mistreat you (LUKE 6:27–28, NIV).

Christine paused, letting the words sink in. Bowing her head, she offered a quick prayer that Ben would repent and be saved, along with his entire house. She asked that God would provide for Ben's family and that somehow He would give them the grace to stay together. Then, almost automatically, she prayed the prayer she had prayed every day since her divorce:

"Turn your ear to me, come quickly to my rescue; be my rock of refuge, a strong fortress to save me. Since you are my rock and my fortress . . ." she paused as tears filled her eyes. *"Since you are my rock and my fortress . . ."* Christine stopped again. She swallowed the large lump in her throat as she wiped the tears from her cheeks with the palm of her hand. "Thank you, oh great God, for being my rock and my fortress," she whispered. Then she began again, silently now: *"Since you are my rock and my fortress, for the sake of Your name lead and guide me."**

---

*PSALM 31:2–3, NIV.

Christine straightened in her chair and blew her nose. Taking in a long, deep breath, she blew it out quickly. "Wait till I tell the girls at Bible study what God has done," she thought. She sat perfectly still for a few moments until a slight smile crossed her lips. Then, picking up the folder she had reached for, she went back to work.

The spiritual man makes judgments about all things, but he himself is not subject to any man's judgment: "For who has known the mind of the Lord that he may instruct him?" But we have the mind of Christ (1 COR 2:15–16, NIV).

THE WHITE RABBIT AS HERALD

Glossary

belief (saving faith): The combination of the intellect and the will so that the sinner desires the cleansing from sin offered by God.

Christian service: A manifestation of the Spirit through the individual believer, in which the believer accomplishes the good works that God has prepared in advance for him to do, utilizing the gifts that He has given.

deep things of God: Those spiritually discerned truths that make us act differently from the world.

filling of the Spirit: Our spiritual state when the Holy Spirit is accomplishing in and through us all that He desires.

God's love: God's yearning for and delight in the well-being of those he loves. This love is so completely self-forgetful that God is willing to express it even if it involves self-sacrifice.

grieving the Holy Spirit: Causing God the Holy Spirit to feel grief because of the believer's sins. The believer cannot be filled with the Spirit as long as the Holy Spirit is grieved.

justification: The judicial act of God whereby He declares the believing sinner righteous.

perspicuity of Scripture: The concept that the Bible is sufficiently clear and complete, in context, to express the message that God desires to communicate.

propitiation: The satisfaction of God's wrath by means of a sacrifice.

quenching the Spirit: Saying no to the Spirit's leading. The believer cannot be filled with the Spirit while in this condition.

Sabbath-rest: A state of permanent spiritual maturity.

spiritual maturity: The quality of those who, through the power of the Holy Spirit, both understand God's Word well enough and have consistently put its truths into practice long enough that they are capable of distinguishing good from evil in practical circumstances and are competent in teaching others to do the same.

walking in the Spirit: An unbroken reliance upon God the Holy Spirit to empower us to accomplish what He desires in us.

Endnotes

Chapter 2

1. Friedrich Böringer, *Die Kirche Christi und ihre Zeugen,* quoted in *The Fathers of the Church,* "In Place of a Preface," combined ed. of *The Fathers of the Greek Church* and *The Fathers of the Latin Church* (1842; repr. Peabody, MA: Hendrickson, 1998), at viii.

Chapter 6

1. William F. Bauer, "ψυχικός" in *A Greek–English Lexicon of the New Testament and Other Early Christian Literature,* trans. William F. Arndt and F. Wilber Gingrich, 3d ed., rev. & edit. Frederick William Danker (Chicago: University of Chicago Press, 2000) [hereinafter BDAG], s.v.

2. J. P. Louw and Eugene Albert Nida, *Greek-English Lexicon of the New Testament: Based on Semantic Domains* (2d ed., 2 vols.) (New York: United Bible Societies, 1989) [hereinafter Louw & Nida].

Chapter 8

1. BDAG, s.v. νωθρός.

2. BDAG, s.v. ἄπειρος, § 31.51.

3. BDAG, s.v. γυμνάζω.

Chapter 10

1. BDAG, s.v. ἄπειρος.

Chapter 12

1. The story of Death Valley presented here was taken primarily from Cecilia Rasmussen, "How Death Valley Got Its Apt Name," *Los Angeles Times,* April 23, 2000.

2. Daniel B. Wallace, *Greek Grammar Beyond the Basics: An Exegetical Syntax of the New Testament* (Grand Rapids, MI: Zondervan, 1996), 689–701.

Chapter 14

1. Justin Kruger and David Dunning, "Unskilled and Unaware of It: How Difficulties in Recognizing One's Own Incompetence Lead to Inflated Self-Assessments," *Journal of Personality and Social Psychology, 77*(6): 1121–1134 (1999).

2. Ibid., 1121.

3. BDAG, s.v. κατάριμα.

Chapter 15

1. Vittorio Gallese, "Intentional Attunement. The Mirror Neuron System and Its Role in Interpersonal Relations"; accessed October 27, 2008, at http://www.interdisciplines.org/mirror/papers/1, 1121–1134.

3. Louw & Nida, § 88.96.

4. *Myths about Alcohol;* accessed October 29, 2008, at http://www.19thcircuit court.state.il.us/bkshelf/resource/alcohol_myth.htm

Chapter 16

1. Simon Louvish, *Mae West: It Ain't No Sin* (New York: St. Martin's Press, 2005), at 82–83.

2. Ibid., 91.

Chapter 17

1. Louw & Nida, § 75.5.4.

2. BDAG, s.v. κατάρτισμός.

Chapter 18

1. Charles C. Ryrie, *So Great Salvation: What It Means to Believe in Jesus Christ* (United States: Victor Books, 1989), 45.

2. Ibid.

3. Bill Bright, *Have You Heard of the Four Spiritual Laws?* (Bright Media Foundation and Campus Crusade for Christ, 2007), 2.

4. BDAG, s.v. ὁμολογέω.

Chapter 19

1. Louw & Nida, § 68.52.
2. BDAG, s.v. σβέννυμι.
3. BDAG, s.v. προφητεία.
4. BDAG, s.v. συσχηματίζω.
5. BDAG, s.v. μεταμορφόω.
6. BDAG, s.v. ἐυεργέω.
7. Louw & Nida, § 13.9.

Scripture Index

Note: Entries in **boldface** indicate a substantive or extended discussion of the Scripture passage cited.

flesh
control by, 128
desires of, 141, 294, 305–6
as enemy, 173, 295, 321
forgetting, 249
opposition to Spirit by, 146, 247–48
reliance on, 94–95, 96, 244
by carnal man, 81–84, 103, 105–6, 193
fleshly behavior, 106, 194–95, 305
saying no to, 78, 207, 247
walking in, 305
weakness of, 217–18
forgiveness, 85, 129, 250
judicial, 272
parental, 272
of sins, 261
free will, 286
fruit of the Spirit, 55, 141, 294
confession and, 272
qualities produced as, 203, 228
peace as, 142, 145, 298

gender neutrality, 14
gentleness, 54, 55, 145, 297
of God, 237
gifts, 240–41, 246
exercise of, 239, 245–46, 249, 320–21, 322
faith in, 240–41
godliness as, 231
for good works, 237–38
grace, 239, 249, 279
pastors as, 238, 239, 245
rest as, 142
righteousness as, 267–69
glorification, 80, 137, 139
glory, giving to God, 10, 205, 324
goals, 29, 41, 218
God. *See also* Holy Spirit; Jesus Christ
abiding in, 244

becoming like, 201. *See also* godliness
character of, 162–65, 181, 228
love as attribute, 220
nonhuman, 241
control by, 10
deep things of. *See* deep things of God
direction by, 280, 288
enemy of, 299
faithfulness of, 87, 110, 162, 165, 271, 321
fellowship with. *See* fellowship
the Father, 136–38
gentleness of, 237
holiness of, 220, 230–31
image of, 95, 171, 250, 260
kindness of, 225, 322
knowledge of, 95, 229, 297, 322
love of, 162–63, 220–25, 253, 299
name of, 205
nature of, 246–47
omnipotence of, 220
omnipresence of, 145–46
patience of, 224, 323
people of, 160
plans of, 164, 235
pleasing, 79–80, 85, 86, 96, 129
ability for, 272, 284
character qualities for, 228–34
decision making and, 121
enablement by Spirit, 210, 272
necessity of faith for, 109
by offering living sacrifice, 280, 281–84
by service/works, 239
preoccupation with, 249
presence of, 230
promises of, 139, 155–56, 160–61, 204, 229
conditional, 289
fulfilled, 176
to Israelites, 172
misrepresentation of, 264–65

God, promises of *(continued)*
    Sabbath-rest, 173–75
    salvation, 259–60
  protection by, 86–87
  provision for needs, 108, 109–10
  purposes of, 136–37
  response to, 247
  resting by, 148, 175
  satisfying, 80
  singing and, 171
  the Son, 138–39. *See also* Jesus
    Christ
  the Spirit, 139. *See also* Holy Spirit
  strength from, 301–2
  submission to, 257, 303, 319
  things of. *See* deep things of God
  thoughts of, 104, 230
  turning away from, 157–58
  will of
    acting independent of, 108,
      236–37
    commitment to doing, 287
    doing, 236–37
    for individual, 108
    knowing, 241, 287–90
    obedience to, 84, 108, 281, 290
    prayer in accordance with, 252
    reliance on, 95
    surrender to, 286–87
    testing, 203, 236, 279, 280, 284,
      288
    understanding, 23
  work of, 229
    in individual, 41, 145
  wrath of, 225, 260, 265
  yielding to, 203, 210, 284, 289
godliness, 129, 209, 249
  faith for, 281
  as gift, 231
  Spirit's production of, 228–34
goodness, 55, 136–37, 236, 300
  Spirit's production of, 248
gospel, 174, 264
  false, 264–65, 299–300

grace, 157, 165, 225
  gifts, 239, 249, 279
graciousness, 162
gratitude, 171, 247. *See also*
  thankfulness
growth, 82, 175
  Christian, 10–11
  lack of, 90–91, 106
  in righteousness, 214
  spiritual. *See* spiritual growth

habits, 166
hearts, hardening. *See* rebellion
heaven, 295–97
Hebrews, Book of
  audience for, 133–36
  warnings about rebellion/sin in,
    154–62
holiness, 85, 220, 225, 230–31
  discipline for, 273
  of Law, 215, 217
  of living sacrifices, 284
holy, 230
Holy Spirit
  acceptance of, 66
  access to, 105, 237, 250
  allowing control by, 208, 257, 280
  conviction of sin by, 266, 272
  departing from believer, 257, 278
  dependence on, xiii, 286
    conscious, 294, 305, 323
    dependence on power of, 294,
      318
    reliance on, 82, 92, 295, 298, 303
  enabling/empowerment by, xii,
    xiii, 245–46, 295, 319
    continuous, 306
    for knowledge attainment, 58
    to please God, 210, 272
    for resisting sin, 305–6
    for righteousness, 219
    for service, 235–41, 249
    for supernatural life, 297–98
    for walking by Spirit, 294, 298

of will, 286, 287
of works, 319
filling with. *See* filled with the
Spirit
fruit of. *See* fruit of the Spirit
grieving, 209, 257–58, 269, 274,
279
continuous, 273
indwelling by, 71, 81–82, 146, 208,
298
continuous, 257, 278
for participation in divine
nature, 229–30
as interpreter, 289
leading by, 247–49, 288–89, 295
obedience to, 323
refusal of, 278, 280
into truth, 68
love and, 219–20, 222
manifestation of, 239, 241
man without. *See* natural man
ministries of, 219, 225, 228–53
enabling service, 235–41, 249
encouraging praise and
thanksgiving, 246–47
interceding, 251–52, 289
leading. *See* leading by, this
heading
producing godliness, 228–34
teaching, 241–46, 287
testifying to salvation, 230,
249–51
opposition to flesh by, 146, 247–48
as perfect translator, 205, 242
power of, 217, 306
quenching, 209, 278–87
relationship with, 56, 203–4,
244–45, 288
communion with, 257
fellowship with, 239, 274, 286
resistance to, 278, 282
revelation through, 37, 57, 104–5
righteousness through, 219
sealing by, 139, 258, 274

sensitivity to, 95, 158
sharing, 230, 239
speaking by, 135, 250
speaking for Son, 204, 241–42
spiritual growth and, 72, 82
spiritual maturity and, 72, 306,
319
strength from, 323
transformation by, 286
understanding through, 58–59,
60, 105, 242
virtue cultivation and, 229
walking by. *See* walking by (in)
Spirit
yielding to, 249, 280, 318
humanity, 56, 320
humility, 297, 322
humor, 322
Hunt, Jefferson, 152–53

idolatry, 164, 165
if, 158–59
image of God, 95, 171, 250, 260
immaterial, 36–37, 320
immaturity, 56, 133, 323
inaction, 40
incompetence, 192–94
ineffectiveness, 232–33
infants, 124, 127. *See also* children
information, necessary, 40
inhibition, 207
instruction, biblical, 13
intellect, 67, 68, 244
intercession, 138, 251–52, 289
interpersonal relationships, 87
Ironside, H. A., 136–37
Isaiah, 181
Israelites, 155–56, 165, 173
God's promises to, 172

Jabberwocky, spiritual, 64–72
Jesus Christ, 102
conformance to image of, 137. *See
also* Christlikeness

Law, 155
  ceremonial aspects of, 219
  dying to, 261
  effects of, 214–16
  freedom from, 247, 249, 295
  holiness of, 215, 217
  innate, 67
  life and death by, 216–17
  living by, 196, 214–16
    under covenant of, 30
  moral requirements of, 219
  natural laws, 71
  nature of, 214
  Old Testament, 259
learning, 146
  refusal of, 166
  rest and, 142–43, 144, 147
  slowness of, 91–92
Liddell, Alice, 2
life
  righteous, 305
  Spirit-filled, 319
  spiritual, 318, 320–21
  supernatural, 295–97, 298, 306
location, determining, 39
Lord's Prayer, 84
lost. *See* unbelievers
lots, casting of, 287
love, 55, 145
  commandments re, 70, 140–41,
    219, 259, 297
  experiencing, 220, 251, 323
  God-produced, 219–20, 222
  God's, 162–63, 220–25, 253, 299
    unending, 223–24
  human, 219, 220, 221–22
  knowledge of, 224
  walking in, 84
  of worldly things, 223, 224

maps, 28, 34–42
  as correct representations, 38–39,
    43
  fixed destinations on, 40–41, 43

  God-provided, 30
  interpretation of, 39–40, 42, 43
  need for, 29
  purpose of, 40, 43
  reading, 22–23
  route choices, 40–41
  trusting, 152
  truthfulness of, 34, 38–39, 43
  wrong roads on, 41–42, 43
material, 36–37, 65, 320
material plane, 69, 82, 320
  salvation and, 265
maturity, spiritual. *See* spiritual
  maturity
mercy, 271
Michael (archangel), 303
mind of Christ, 58, 104, 106, 204
  knowing, 59
  knowledge from, 289
  Spirit-filling to have, 236, 288
minds, renewing, 284, 285–86, 322
ministry, 240–41
  of Spirit. *See* Holy Spirit
mirroring, 200–201
mixtures, 320
morality, legislating, 216
moral principles, 67
Moses, 156, 164, 165–66
motivation, 71
  for good works, 237
  of spiritual man, 106–7
murder, 282–83
music, 170–72, 246
mysticism, 12

natural laws, 71
natural man, 56, 60, 64–72
  ability to accept spiritual truths,
    65–69, 72, 85, 105, 244
  basis of judgments, 106
  conclusions about things of God,
    69, 71
  love of God and, 222–23
  material things and, 71

by not moving to maturity, 28
persistence of, 55–56, 304–5
possibility of, 321
power of, 96
prolonged, 93, 128, 161, 273
punishment for, 161, 271
remedy for, 259, 271
removal of, 259
resisting, 295, 305–6, 321
Sabbath-rest and, 147
self-will and, 84
slavery to, 201
temporal judgment of, 161
unknown, 210, 258–59
singing, 170–72, 246
sinlessness, 128, 148, 270, 271, 286, 319
sin nature, 68
sinners, 223, 300
sleep, 320
soils, parable of, 233–34
Solomon, 127
spiritual consciousness, 65
spiritual growth, 71–72, 78, 318. See also spiritual maturity
ability for, 194–95
God's desire for, 23
need for, 248–49
practical aspects of, 318–24
progress of, 202
backward movement in, 92, 95
lack of, 80–81
stopping, 94–95
relying on Spirit for, 72, 82
time needed for, 79
spirituality, 66, 249, 288
genuine, 321–22
rules for, 318
spiritual man, 57, 60, 201
ability to receive God's truth, 103
carnal man distinguished, 196
judgment ability, 106, 245
motivation of, 106–7
opposition to, 107

spiritual maturity, 12, 231, 318. See also journey, spiritual
attaining, 28, 29, 178–79, 239
growing into, 175
individual paths to, 41
striving for, 179–80
babies in Christ, 77, 78, 106
commands re, 28, 29, 41
commitment to, 95
defined, 124–29, 147
as destination, 132
Holy Spirit and, 72, 306, 319. See also filled with the Spirit
judgments of right and wrong, 128–29
knowledge and, 126, 202–3
maintaining, 147–48
of natural man, 71–72
permanent, 179
possibility of, 28–29
practice for, 97–98
principles of, 23, 41
spiritual truths, 37–38, 318
ability to understand, 65–66
ability to receive, 77, 103
acceptance of, 105–6, 244, 262, 266
by natural man, 65–69, 72, 85, 105, 244
access to, 81–82, 85, 92
application of, 84, 263
assumptions re, 110
contrary to flesh, 82
difficulty of, 77, 82
milk/meat distinction, 126
discernment of, 58, 69, 92
experience of, 65, 103
heart reality of, 250–51
love, 70
perception of as foolishness, 67–68
rejection of, 94–95
responding to, 171
retaining, 96

walking, 29–30
 action required for, 143–44
 direction of, 132–33
 by faith, 85–87
 in flesh, 305
 with God, 201
 in the light, 270
walking by (in) Spirit, 84, 141, 143,
  148, 210
 need for, 306
 power from Spirit for, 294, 298
 power to resist sin, 305–6
 prayer and, 252
 as reliance on God's power, 304
 as requirement for being filled
  with Spirit, 196, 209, 294
 walking in the Spirit defined, 295
warfare. *See* conflict
weakness, 239, 252, 320
wealth, 234
Wiersbe, Warren W., 12
wilderness, 154
will (human), 84, 286, 287
 action according to, 236–37
 belief and, 263, 266, 267
 lack of, 267
wisdom, 58
 access to, 72
 fleshly, 106
 God's, 231

one's own, 144
 worldly, 69, 84
word of Christ, 171
word of God. *See* Bible
words, meanings of, 174
words, spiritual, 58–59, 105, 125
work, 71. *See also* effort
works, 203, 214
 accomplishing through Spirit, 319
 enduring, 290
 God's, 41, 145, 229
 God's plan for, 235, 239, 241, 281
 good, 69, 237–39, 241
 individual calling to, 288, 322
 motivation for, 237
 preparing people for, 237–39, 245
 salvation and, 263–64
 without faith, 233
world, 173, 295, 321
 conforming to pattern of, 280,
  284–85, 286
 destruction of, 244
 difference from, 297
 energizing forces in, 299
 forgetting, 249
worldviews, 54
World War I, 248
worship, Christian, 170, 246, 284

yielding. *See* God; Holy Spirit

For more information on growing in Christ,
please visit
www.becomingmature.org.

To contact Bruce Baker with questions
or to schedule a speaking engagement,
e-mail him at
brucebaker@becomingmature.org
or call Grace Acres Press at
888-700-GRACE (4722).

If you are interested in ordering
quantities of this book, please call
Grace Acres Press for a quantity discount.

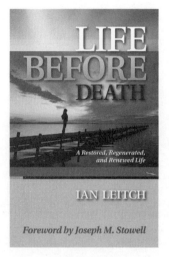